IN IT FOR THE LONG RUN

IN IT FOR THE LONG RUN

Breaking records and getting FKT

DAMIAN HALL

Vertebrate Publishing, Sheffield
www.v-publishing.co.uk

First published in 2021 by Vertebrate Publishing.

 Vertebrate Publishing
Omega Court, 352 Cemetery Road, Sheffield S11 8FT, United Kingdom.
www.v-publishing.co.uk

Copyright © Damian Hall 2021.

Front cover Helvellyn at dawn, summer 2020. © *inov-8.com/James Appleton*.
Author photo © *inov-8.com/Dave MacFarlane*.
Other photography © *Damian Hall unless otherwise credited*.

Damian Hall has asserted his rights under the Copyright, Designs and Patents Act 1988 to be identified as author of this work.

This book is a work of non-fiction. The author has stated to the publishers that, except in such minor respects not affecting the substantial accuracy of the work, the contents of the book are true.

A CIP catalogue record for this book is available from the British Library.

ISBN: 978-1-83981-043-5 (Paperback)
ISBN: 978-1-83981-044-2 (Ebook)
ISBN: 978-1-83981-057-2 (Audiobook)

10 9 8 7 6 5 4 3 2 1

All rights reserved. No part of this work covered by the copyright herein may be reproduced or used in any form or by any means – graphic, electronic, or mechanised, including photocopying, recording, taping or information storage and retrieval systems – without the written permission of the publisher.

Every effort has been made to obtain the necessary permissions with reference to copyright material, both illustrative and quoted. We apologise for any omissions in this respect and will be pleased to make the appropriate acknowledgements in any future edition.

Cover design by Jane Beagley, Vertebrate Publishing.
Production by Cameron Bonser, Vertebrate Publishing.
www.v-publishing.co.uk

Vertebrate Publishing is committed to printing on paper from sustainable sources.
This book has been accounted for as Carbon Negative by Our Carbon.

Printed and bound in the UK by TJ Books Limited, Padstow, Cornwall.

For Barbara Hall and Mark Townsend.
Thank you.

CONTENTS

1. Challenging times 1
2. Before running 17
3. Becoming a runner 29
4. Early experiments in ultrarunning 41
5. The Spine Race and other mishaps 53
6. Three big ones and an FKT 65
7. Fear and loathing on the South West Coast Path 79
8. Turning 'pro' 92
9. High on Charlie 106
10. Underdog and under bog 119
11. Crew to be kind 132
12. Blowing hot and cold 147
13. Getting in a(nother) Paddy 161
14. Skywalker or Solo? Nope, a bear of very little brain 177
15. The waiting game 187
16. #PWFKTea 199
17. Edale 211
18. The aftermath 222
19. Yeah but why? 228
20. Acknowledgements 245

1

CHALLENGING TIMES

'His legs swelled prodigiously.'

I've never wanted anything so badly. Nothing in the whole world is more appealing right now than the simple but elusive pleasure of ceasing forward motion – ceasing all motion – and crumpling to the ground, to lie in that seductively soft and invitingly squishy, that irresistibly luxurious, bog.

Oh to allow my leaden eyelids to close, to be vertical and limp in that peaty swamp. As I shuffle pathetically through the dark, I gaze longingly at the dirty, wet ground, willing it to hoover me up. Even just for a fleeting moment. Oh, please let me sleep. Beautiful, lovely, not-being-awake sleep.

It's about 4 a.m. and I've been on my feet for two days and one and a half nights and have run 180 miles. I'm trying to break a record for running 261 miles on the Pennine Way. Everything was brill. But now everything is less brill.

My legs are disobedient lumps of mahogany. My feet abandoned me in the last bog. My backside growls at me (not like that – well, actually, like that too). My ... I'm too tired to list my other ailments. There's a heavy monster on my shoulders, pressing me ever downwards. The powerful urge to flick the switch to off is overriding everything. Something we do every day without thinking has been banned, and has therefore become so despairingly appealing. I'll never neglect you again, sleep! I've always loved you! Honestly, I've always thought you were wittier and more attractive than boring old, criminally overrated wakefulness.

But a very little part of my very little mind knows that if I snooze, I may well lose. Plus Nicky Spinks said I can't.

Who knew running 261 miles would be a little bit difficult?

* * *

I was obsessed with football (in particular Arsenal Football Club). I was obsessed with the Heroic Age of Polar Exploration (in particular Captain Robert Falcon Scott). I was obsessed with 1990s Aussie popstress Natalie Imbruglia (I can't go into that for legal reasons). And I'm obsessed with running. In particular, long distances in lumpy places – bimbles, if you will.

Only one of those obsessions has led me to routinely rub Vaseline all over my bathing-suit area (yes, *all* over), repeatedly bonk in woods in the middle of the night (significantly less pleasurable than it may sound to the lay-ear), and eat alarming amounts of custard for breakfast.

But I truly feel sorry for people who've never done those things. I also feel sorry for people who've never face-planted into a bog or had a power sob, for people who have a full set of civilised-looking toenails. I feel sorry for people who don't have alarms stored for 5 a.m. and 4 a.m., for people who can't use the words 'disappointed' or 'happy' without placing the brilliantly versatile adjective 'super' in front. I feel sorry for people who don't know the difference between a DNF, a DNS and the MdS (is this getting TDS?), or what FKT stands for. I feel sorry for people who don't run.

This is my horribly self-indulgent story about my often misguided but ultimately life-changing midlife-crisis adventures in ultramarathon running, where I went from completing a first marathon dressed as a toilet to a Great Britain international trail runner (at forty) in four years. And semi-accidentally broke a few records too.

This book is about the glorious if occasionally hurty joy of running long distances in lumpy places (and bogs), and the attraction of doing so outside of organised events. Running challenges, speed records and fastest known times (FKTs) may look like they offer the same thing, but can actually offer something very different. But why do so many people repeatedly bash themselves up doing impossible-sounding endurance challenges? It must be more than masochism, social media humblebrags and the chance to knock back double rations of Tunnock's bars. *Mustn't it?*

'Ultramarathon' is an American word accredited to ultrarunning pioneer Ted Corbitt in 1957, to describe footraces longer than the classic marathon distance of 26.2 miles. Technically an ultra can be 26.3 miles (though the shortest are usually 50k), all the way up to the Sri Chinmoy Self-Transcendence 3,100-Mile Race (the distance isn't even the main insanity; runners go repeatedly around the same block in New York). A few are timed events, such as twenty-four-hour races where you see how many miles you can run around a track. A few are on roads (yuk). Some are in deserts, in jungles, in the Arctic. But the very best ones, I've found, are around 100 miles and they take place in mountains (aka lumpy places). But this book should come with a warning, because this stuff is seriously addictive. I was warned too! But I didn't listen.

It's a niche sport, but lots of people do this stuff, and have been doing it for a very long time. Ultra-distance challenges are inherently testing, but they aren't as difficult as they sound (you can hike lots, eat lots and chat to lots of like-minded loons). And despite – no, partly *because of* – the distances involved, it seems to make people inexplicably happy. But the best news is that you don't necessarily need to sign up for an event. You can pick a place and time, grab a mate and have a DIY adventure. And that's primarily what these things are: safe adventures. And they can be life-changingly meaningful.

* * *

When you next overhear someone in a pub say 'We're just not designed to run marathons', feel free to tell them that they couldn't be more wrong. Also feel free to ignore them and just sit there smugly in the knowledge that you know the opposite is true. (That's probably what I'd do.)

You see, running literally made us who we are today. It made us human. Only eating, sleeping and indulging in consensual team push-ups are more quintessential human activities than running.

Around seven million years ago our ape ancestors started coming down from the trees and turning into bipeds. But why did they give up speed, upper-body power and greater safety in the trees, in exchange for what on the surface looked like becoming slow and wimpy? Also, why do we have such little hair compared to other primates? In the whole history of vertebrates (good name for a book publisher, that), we're the only running biped that's tail-less. We have ninety-five per cent of the same DNA as chimps. Yet noticeably we have an Achilles tendon and they don't. And a comparatively huge gluteus maximus (even if physios are forever decrying their weakness). Our feet are arched, while chimps' are flat. Chimps don't have a nuchal ligament, which helps hold the head up high. Humans possess an extraordinary number of eccrine glands – between two and five million – that can produce up to twelve litres of sweat a day.

Even if you haven't read the *Fever Pitch* of running, Christopher McDougall's *Born to Run*, you've likely guessed where this is going. All these idiosyncratic parts of our contemporary anatomy evolved to our advantage and that advantage allows us to run a long way.

The ability to run long distances to obtain food, via persistence hunting antelopes on the African savannah, enabled us to thrive as a species, to outlast the Neanderthals and other creatures with bigger claws and fangs, argue American biologist Dennis Bramble and anthropologist Daniel Lieberman. Antelopes were faster, but after a while they needed to cool down, so they slowed or stopped. We weren't as fast, but because of world-class temperature regulation, we could keep going, following an antelope for hours. Finally the inadequate sweater (sounds like something you get for Christmas) would overheat, we would catch up and tuck in our serviettes ...

We're the world's best sweaters. It's our secret weapon. (Explain that to any non-runners in your household who complain about the honk of your freshly discarded running kit. Actually, don't bother. It doesn't get you off the hook.) Travelling on two limbs instead of four helps optimise oxygen supply. Over time, we lost almost all of our fur, to sweat even more effectively. The new supply of protein enabled our brains to expand, until they were seven times larger than any other mammal's. We evolved as a species, to be able to run. And running helped us evolve as a species.

Until the evil chair (beware the chair) got invented. Then things went mostly downhill.

Originally all humans would have been runners. It wasn't a hobby our ancestors picked up in their mid-thirties then started getting on everyone else's nerves going on about how amazing it is. It was how we got food, transportation and a survival aid. Ten thousand years ago, though, agriculture blossomed and there was less need to run for our supper. Running instead became the act of the messenger (a prestigious job in many cultures), the soldier, the sportsperson and the, er, king.

Rameses II (1303–1213 BC), pharaoh of Ancient Egypt, had to run alone in front of huge crowds before his coronation to prove himself worthy of the throne, then repeat the feat thirty years later (and every few years after that) to clarify he was still 'fit' for the job. But that was nothing compared to fellow Egyptian king Shulgi. A hymn from the time alludes to him running between holy feasts in Nippur and Ur and back again, an estimated 200 miles in twenty-seven hours. Which seems a little too fast to be believable (if it's not on Strava ...), but it might just be the original fastest known time (FKT).

Running was central to Greek mythology, with gods Atalanta and Achilles both heralded for their athletic prowess. The Greeks of course gave us the Olympics, and one ancient race (although not ultra-distance) had full armour and large shields as mandatory kit, so heavy they could barely run. So in that respect very much a precursor for the Spine Race.

The early foot races clearly weren't testing enough for some. Ageus of Argos won the 4.6-kilometre Olympic Dolichos race in 328 BC and afterwards ran sixty miles home to tell his folks. In a display of shonky one-upmanship, the likes of which we didn't see again till 2020 in the Pennines, Drymos of Epidauros also ran home after a win, notching up some eighty miles.

According to Edward S. Sears's excellent *Running Through the Ages*, Spartan runner Anystis and Alexander the Great's courier (or messenger, a full-time runner) Philonides, ran from Sicyon to Elis together in a day, some 148 miles.

The first great FKT controversy came from an ultramarathon. A mixture of myth, poetry and history tell how Athenian messenger Pheidippides hot-footed it 140 miles from Athens to Sparta before the Battle of Marathon to ask for help. Over time, this version has been muddled with another story about a messenger running twenty-five miles from Athens to Marathon before possibly falling down dead (lack of electrolytes, surely), which inspired the birth of the marathon at the Modern Olympics in 1896. Edward S. Sears labels the Sparta version 'historically sound' (and it inspired the Spartathlon ultramarathon of the same route), adding that if the Olympics had paid attention to history rather than poetry, a 140-mile ultramarathon would have been included.

People have been running long distances ever since we came down from the trees. From Inca messengers up in the Andes to Chinese ultramarathon-running soldiers and Scotland's Highland Games (which date to the eleventh century and likely witnessed the birth of hill/fell running as we know it), everyone was at it. Organised events were probably a rarity rather than the norm.

Fast-forward to the late-seventeenth century and pedestrianism was a wondrously crackpot pastime of heroic lunacy and magnificent skulduggery. Modern ultramarathon running (and race walking) was born from running and walking contests that made front-page news. Professional 'peds' would run, walk or use a combination of the two (much like today's ultra 'runners') to attempt absurd feats (and end up with absurd feet) in organised contests. These might be outlandish individual wagers to travel on foot from, say, Paris to Moscow. Industrialisation brought leisure time and disposable income, and huge crowds gathered to watch, placed huge bets and helped turn these eccentric sportspeople into celebrities. Pedestrianism was both the first professional sport and the original international spectator sport.

Long before The Proclaimers sang about walking 500 miles and 500 more, fellow Scot Robert Barclay Allardyce (of the same Barclays who would build a fossil-fuel-supporting banking empire) did just that. In the summer of 1809 some 10,000 spectators gathered on Newmarket Heath to see if the 'Celebrated Pedestrian' could walk 1,000 miles in 1,000 hours, ticking off at least one an hour for forty-two days and nights. Total betting reached £40 million in today's money, including a wager by the Prince of Wales.

Barclay's sage strategy was to walk a mile at the end of each hour, then another one straight after, on loops of a half-mile course, allowing himself maximum rest before his next outing. Predictably the twenty-nine-year-old's pace decreased, from fifteen-minute miles to twenty-one-minute miles, and his weight dropped from eighty-five kilograms to seventy kilograms. As the days passed, Barclay become so lethargic supporters stuck needles in him to try and keep him alert, and fired pistols by his ears (which is exactly what I could have done with in the Pennines in July 2020). 'His legs swelled prodigiously,' reported a spectator. But remarkably, Barclay finished and won his bet (the equivalent of nearly £800,000 today), while his achievement spawned a competitive walking craze in Britain and later the US.

After losing a bet about who would win the 1860 US election, Edward Payson Weston's forfeit was to walk 478 miles from Boston to Washington DC, in time for the new president's inauguration. Twenty-one-year-old Weston, described as a man 'unencumbered with self-doubt', set off on his odyssey that would demand almost fifty miles per day for ten days. He was immediately hauled over by the police, who wanted to discuss the small matter of some debts he owed. But he sweet-talked his way out of a cell and was doing very well, till he became topographically embarrassed (to be fair, signage and maps were nothing like today) near Philadelphia and went twelve miles the wrong way, arriving in Washington four hours late for Abraham Lincoln's inauguration. However, the Wily Wobbler (as Weston would later be nicknamed due to his wobbly gait) did get to meet the new president, who, tickled by the tale, offered to pay his train fare home.

Weston realised walking for wagers could be a full-time living. He spent eight years touring Europe, controversially chewing coca leaves (the first known instance of doping?), and attempted to walk 2,000 miles around the shires of England within 1,000 hours – which he only narrowly missed. At the age of seventy, he speed-walked from San Francisco to New York, some 3,900 miles, in just over 100 days.

Weston lectured audiences on the great health benefits of exercise, warning that these new-fangled automobiles were making people lazy.

In a cruel twist, he was injured by a New York City taxicab in 1927 and never walked again.

The first notable achievement of Norway's Mensen Ernst's twenty-five-year pedestrian career was in 1819 when he ran seventy-two miles from London to Portsmouth in nine hours. It was just a warm-up. Ernst's reputation mushroomed with a thirteen-day, 1,500-mile journey from Paris to Moscow in 1832. The following year he travelled 1,577 miles from Munich to Nauplion, carrying letters from the Bavarian king to his son Otto, King of Greece. Ernst claimed to have been robbed of his money and maps, arrested as a spy and imprisoned for two days, but still managed to complete his ultra-distance challenge in twenty-four days. Next he travelled from Constantinople to Calcutta and back. This time he was reportedly shot at, robbed, and bitten by a snake, as he covered the 5,000-mile round trip in fifty-nine days, averaging a very impressive eighty-five miles a day.

Wait! Eighty-five miles a day? And what was that earlier? The distance from Paris to Moscow, as the crow flies, is 1,500 miles, so that's ... 107 miles a day. Not impossible. But very, very unlikely.

Norwegian author Bredo Berntsen found numerous flaws in claims made about Ernst in his biography *Des Stauermannes Mensen Ernst*. But some of it probably happened. And his claims weren't that unlike some of the ones we still hear today.

Sadly, the evolution of the bicycle from a penny farthing around the end of the nineteenth century led to the end of the pedestrianism era, as six-day bike races replaced six-day ped matches as a favoured spectator sport. 'The races went from three or four miles an hour, to ten or fifteen,' says Matthew Algeo, author of *Pedestrianism: When Watching People Walk Was America's Favorite Spectator Sport*. 'And the crashes were much more spectacular.' How could the Wily Wobbler compete with that? But the pedestrian spirit, the idea of attempting a ludicrously long self-powered challenge, outside of an organised event, most definitely endures (pun intended).

At least as far back as the 1860s, 'adventurous individuals, and sometimes groups, [were] testing themselves in the Lake District fells and achieving ever more impressive "walking rounds", writes fell-running historian Steve Chilton in *The Round*. An 1864 round (i.e. circuit) by Rev. J.M. Elliot of Cambridge included nine of the highest summits in eight and a half hours, the genesis of the twenty-four-hour concept (how many summits can be reached in that timescale). The criteria were established in 1904 and the Lake District's 24-Hour Fell Record is still going strong, with Kim Collison stretching the record to seventy-eight in 2020. There were and still are many other rounds too, but the twenty-four-hour version had the most appeal. It's the genesis of the Bob Graham Round and Britain's thriving long-distance off-road running culture.

In 1871 hiking brothers John and Robert Naylor completed the first recorded JOGLE (John o'Groats to Land's End: top to bottom of Britain), averaging twenty-five miles a day over nine weeks and 1,372 miles. There's always been natural crossover between walking and running. They're part of the same movement pattern, and both pedestrianism and contemporary race-walking authorities have struggled at times to define the difference. For the distance runner, a hike can be a deliberate preservation tactic, sometimes weariness or laziness, sometimes it's just too steep. Walking records have organically turned into running records. (And later when I'm humblebragging about running 100 miles, remember that I usually hiked a good chunk of it – the steeper the 'running' challenge, the more time spent not running.)

The first recorded twenty-four-hour traverse of the Welsh 3,000s (then thirteen, now fourteen, peaks above 3,000 feet) dates to 1919 or 1920, by members of the redoubtable Rucksack Club and the legendary Eustace Thomas. Other 'excursions' around that time included Derwent Watershed (37.5 miles in eleven hours and thirty-nine minutes) and Colne to Doveholes (fifty-one miles in seventeen hours and fifty-seven minutes, 'including wait for meals at various pubs of about two hours!', record old Rucksack Club journals). And in 1922, when Thomas was over fifty, he broke the Lake District 24-Hour Fell Record by covering 66.5 miles with 25,000 feet of ascent in twenty-two hours.

Thomas's time wasn't bettered until 1932. Keswick hotelier and mountain guide Bob Graham didn't look like a natural athlete. He was short and stocky, but also teetotal and vegetarian, with excellent knowledge of Lakeland fells. The story goes that in 1932, to celebrate his forty-second birthday by extending the 24-Hour Fell Record, he ran and hiked a 140-mile circuit of forty-two fells in twenty-three hours and thirty-nine minutes, eating fruit pastilles and boiled eggs. And people didn't believe him.

He did do it. But he was in fact forty-three, it wasn't his birthday and the round is nearer sixty-six miles, with 27,000 feet of ascent (Everest is 29,032 feet). The rest is true, even if the contemporary BG route is closer to a 1960 run by Alan Heaton, with four substitute summits after Graham's were deemed insufficient. In preparation, Graham is said to have walked each fell barefoot, to toughen up his skin and save his 'gym shoes' (this was before inov-8 or the barefoot running craze). On the big day he fuelled on bread and butter, strong tea, milk and fruit (nutrition hasn't advanced as much as Big Sports Nutrition would like us to think). He walked the uphills and ran the downhills 'with extraordinary speed', wearing shorts, 'tennis shoes' and a 'pyjama jacket' (again, judging by recent designs, neither has Big Sportswear). I like to think Bob really was wearing his Thomas the Tank Engine pyjamas.

There are reams of rounds, long-distance trails and established challenges for hikers and runners all over the UK. Naturally, some carry more weight than others. JOGLE/LEJOG is at least ten days of fighting smelly cars on dirty roads, which makes the record all the more impressive. The National Three Peaks Challenge (summiting the highest peaks in Scotland, Wales and England inside twenty-four hours) is something of a noisy fundraising jamboree, an entry point for outdoor challenges. It has rarely attracted top-level athletes, probably because you spend more time in a car than on a hill, though fell-running deity Joss Naylor did it in 1971.

The Bob Graham is many times tougher than the tri-country drive. It's the holy grail of Britain's running challenges, with around 2,500 completions by the end of 2020, and likely as many again unsuccessful attempts. The challenge is well known in wider running circles too. London Marathon creator, Olympian and Roger-Bannister-pacer Chris

Brasher attempted it thrice, all unsuccessfully. Ultragods Scott Jurek and Kilian Jornet have both completed a Bob. 'Quite possibly one of the most difficult courses I've done in my life,' said US star Jurek after his BG, which he accomplished with just sixteen minutes to spare in 2014. 'But so beautiful.' The Bob is the Big One.

A picture has sometimes been painted where non-race records/FKTs have only recently sprung out of the racing scene. But as you can see, if anything it's the other way around. The canon of UK long-distance running records is the JOGLE/LEJOG; the Big Three 24-hour rounds: the Bob Graham plus the Paddy Buckley and Charlie Ramsay Rounds (the Welsh and Scottish equivalents); the Lake District 24-Hour Fell Record, the two Munros records (the complete round of 282 and the 24-hour record); and the Wainwrights (a 325-mile, 214-peak challenge in the Lakes). Oh yeah, and the 261-mile Pennine Way, our oldest National Trail. It's open to debate. But to me they're the ones that matter. Though there are lots more. And if you don't like the look of any of them, you can just create your own.

Much as we like to think all runners are unwaveringly wholesome folk who'd sooner take up triathlon than tell a fib, this stuff does need some kind of policing. So are these Guinness World Records? The short answer is no – but they are records. The longer answer is that individual fell runners have rarely bothered getting their records verified by Guinness, though Fell Runners Association (FRA) long-distance-records custodian and serial fell-record-breaker himself Martin Stone used to submit some. It's a load of fussy paperwork, which is hardly foolproof, can take months to ratify and seems archaic now we have things like Strava. Plus the Bob Graham Club (BGC) and FRA are scene arbiters, making Guinness seem irrelevant to the average fell-botherer.

The BGC have a clear set of rules and verification criteria on their website, which include another person confirming they witnessed you reach each peak (hence why they don't publicly acknowledge solo attempts or records). Charlie Ramsay and Paddy Buckley maintain completion lists for their respective rounds (the rules do differ slightly and the Paddy has no website, other than the generic if useful *gofar.org.uk*).

For government-funded National Trails such as the Pennine Way and the South West Coast Path, each route's association is usually happy to play the de facto historian, but might struggle if they have to be the judge.

Record claims for LEJOG/JOGLE do tend to covet Guinness, though, as there's no other obvious arbitration body. So it is all a bit hotchpotch. And then there's that American phrase ...

In the early 2000s, US ultrarunners Buzz Burrell and Pete Bakwin found themselves frustrated trying to find the fastest times for trails they were attempting to set speed records on. 'It was hard to figure out what the record actually was,' Pete says in Ally Beaven's quite-good-in-places *Broken*. 'Even when we got in touch with the person who probably held the record, he couldn't give us a straight answer. I didn't like the vagueness, and set up a simple website to record these types of speed records on trails, and to record the stories surrounding them.

'The phrase *fastest known time* was something I heard around. Buzz was using it back in the 1990s, as were a few other people. It seemed a natural fit because we didn't necessarily know what the *actual* fastest time was, only what we were able to find out about.' The FKT initialism gained traction in the US, then spread across the Atlantic. Even if you won't find anyone running a Bob Graham FKT (more anon).

Buzz and Pete co-founded *fastestknowntime.com*, which has increasingly become the authority on such things, both a database and rulebook for off-road running records and occasional arbiter of disputed claims, even if it's led to some Americanisation of British terms and rules, the most basic being: record your run on a GPS device.

'It's obviously a bit easier to set FKTs in the US,' says GB ultrarunner, coach and impudent controversialist Robbie Britton. 'Because in the UK we're got all these wonderful athletes from the seventies and eighties who set these great standards. But equally there's been a lot of improvements in the form of sports nutrition, training theory, kit and so on that might help the most recent generations. Take the Pennine Way: it's basically a tarmac path compared to when Mike Cudahy was first to run it under three days, right?'

There were no GPS watches or Strava when Mensen Ernst and

Pheidippides were making outlandish claims. There were in April 2016, though, when Shropshire man Mark Vaz claimed a new LEJOG record of seven days, eighteen hours and forty-five minutes, knocking a stunning thirty-one hours off the previous best. An incredible achievement (even if he didn't use a tracker). According to his social media posts, Vaz must have run the 156 miles from Edinburgh to Inverness in twenty-four hours and twenty minutes. Not technically impossible. But very, very improbable. And after a very short rest, he would have had to follow that up with a 119-mile run to John o'Groats in just under twenty hours. Again not impossible, but absolutely remarkable, especially coming at the end of multiple days of 100 miles and from an athlete we'd never heard of.

'For me it's simply unbelievable,' wrote respected ultrarunner Gary Kiernan on website *Run247.com*. 'If ratified, [the new record] would rival some of the greatest feats of human endurance ever seen. To say this is an unbelievable feat is something of an understatement ... He is a middle of the pack social runner. Some of the best have come close to the world record but never beaten it. For him to do it is inconceivable.'

'It would have been close to beating the greatest runner ever, Yiannis Kouros, and that is not happening anytime soon. It just undermines the sport that we love,' Rob Young told the *Shropshire Star*. The *Marathon Man* author was looking to run across the US and break a record of his own (ahem).

After being hassled online, Vaz finally owned up to his skulduggery in a defiant, semi-coherent Facebook post. It felt like a seminal moment for FKT scrutiny and community policing. People had certainly cheated before, but because of the high profile of the record and his fibbing being so brutally exposed in the Social Media Age, it was big news in the UK ultrarunning community. The start of a new era for records/FKTs. And the creation of a limited-use new verb: to Vaz it.

In most cases, both pre- and post-Vaz, the running community has a decent idea whether an individual runner is capable of a claim they make. People don't just buy a pair of daps and break the Pennine Way record. But the Vaz moment felt like the end of an era of innocence. There used to be a lot more trust in the world. Maybe it was misplaced?

During Dan Lawson's two attempts at the JOGLE/LEJOG record, the previous best, set by Andi Rivett in 2002, came under scrutiny. 'It is, alone, his only world class performance in a career of pretty average ultrarunning,' reported *fastrunning.com* (a site, it should be noted, co-founded by Dan's good friend Robbie Britton; though I agree Rivett's run looks dodge). Though the 2002 record had been verified by Guinness, on very little proof, lots about it doesn't add up. Dan is world class at this stuff, European 24-Hour Champion, and he couldn't get close on two attempts. 'How can someone with no pedigree beat a record by eleven per cent at their first attempt and then retire back into obscurity?' asked *fastrunning.com*. Guinness have been petitioned to annul Rivett's 'record'.

When I first heard Rob Young's record attempt to run across America being questioned, I felt for him. I'd just finished running the South West Coast Path over eleven days and empathised with the horror of working yourself into the ground only to be fearful you might not be believed. Facebook was abuzz with rumours his tracker had been recording his support vehicle's progress (as he rested in it), rather than his. I was able to chat to Rob on the phone in New York for a magazine story, just after he stopped, apparently due to injury. Rob has a tragic backstory and a youthful enthusiasm it's hard not to fall for. Unlike Vaz, he was known as a solid ultrarunner. He had good answers to my questions, but verbally squirmed after each of the three times I asked that he share his GPS data to prove his innocence. Two independent academics later adjudged he had cheated. It felt really quite sad.

In July 2020, in an event that threatened to break our very small corner of the internet, Sabrina Verjee was ahead of Paul Tierney's record for the Wainwrights Round for four days. Until she developed a knee problem and struggled to descend the fells. She continued, but with physical assistance from supporters. Some happily helped her move downhill, but some wouldn't, on ethical grounds. Eventually her pace fell irretrievably behind the men's record, but impressively she still reached Moot Hall, six days, seventeen hours and fifty-one minutes after she started out, ostensibly as the first woman to complete the Wainwrights.

There was a good deal of media excitement and a new record was widely reported. Sabrina went on ITV talking about her run, saying of previous Wainwright record holder and fell omni-deity Joss Naylor, 'I think he was impressed that I beat his time.' However, senior fell-running figures explained that they didn't feel it appropriate for her to claim a record because of the significant physical assistance she benefitted from. Behind-the-scenes discussions continued and three days after arriving at Moot Hall, Sabrina unclaimed the record in a Facebook post that started, 'It's not a record' (her quotation marks), adding that she 'completed the Wainwrights round to my own satisfaction'.

'She completed the Wainwrights,' says Martin Stone. 'But not in a style that could be considered for a record.' In September 2020, Mel Steventon became the first woman to complete the Wainwrights in a continuous journey without physical assistance, in thirteen days and twelve hours. The Bob Graham Club, which archives Wainwright Round completions, lists Mel's run, but not Sabrina's. 'I have a lot of respect for Sabrina,' says Nicky Spinks. 'I think it's a shame the events happened as they did.'

'I never tried to conceal that I was being physically assisted,' Sabrina told me. 'I was not in a race and there were no written rules. I told media I wasn't claiming a record, but they didn't report that. My motivations are different to some people's. I've never been motivated to "take a record", really. For some, the record is the be all and end all, but for me it's a token gesture of recognition.'

In the October 2020 issue of *The Fellrunner*, an influential magazine that goes out to 8,000-plus FRA members, Martin clarified the guidelines: 'To be clear, record attempts by individuals should be without physical support provided by pacers while the contender is moving, unless the contender intends to retire.'

The sport of long-distance mountain/fell/hill/bog running, or ultra-distance FKTs if you insist, has no international governing body or universally agreed rules, though you could argue that a certain code of ethics is widely understood. But that Wild West feel is part of the appeal. It's an adventure. It'll make you happy, I promise.

As of January 2021, 7,600 global FKTs had been registered on *fastestknowntime.com*. There are many reasons why personal challenges/records/FKTs have mushroomed in popularity (not just because a virus stole our races in 2020), which is what this book's trying to explore.

Before we go on, another word from Martin. 'Call me an old fart,' he wrote in *The Fellrunner*, 'but I really dislike the [initialism] FKT with a vengeance. What happened to the good old mountain running record? I accept that FKT is quite a descriptive way of describing something you're not 100 per cent sure is correct or true, but if an achievement is clearly a record, then let's call it a record – not yet another term that we've adopted from the States. We have our own heritage, history, way of doing things and describing them. Brits have been chasing records in the mountains for more than 150 years. FKTs have only been around for maybe twenty years. End of rant!'

Perhaps this is British running's version of Britpop?

Indeed there was a horribly pregnant pause after I first used the word in conversation with Nicky Spinks ... Most fell runners interviewed in this book don't like the initialism.

So should FKTs get FKTed? The problem is, some runner-writers rather enjoy using juvenile puns.

2

BEFORE RUNNING

'We're not going to the cinema, Damian.'

As a kid, I often had those dreams. The ones where you're standing at the school bus stop when the horrifying realisation dawns that you have no clothes on the lower half of your body. And the queue of schoolchildren turns gleefully your way ...

I also often dreamt I could fly. I preferred those dreams.

As a toddler, I was always wandering off. When I was a little older I was always wandering off, getting muddy and climbing trees. I was a dreamy, sensitive and naive kid, I think. But happy. Even if I point-blank refused to consume anything resembling a vegetable and pretty much only ate macaroni cheese smothered in tomato ketchup. I thought squirrels were brilliant. Still do.

Financially, things weren't as easy as my middle-class lilt implies: we lived in a council house and sometimes other people's houses, I had free school uniform and at one point my dad took on a paper round. But, as the cliché goes, I was rich in other ways. Almost all my childhood memories are outdoor ones.

Having rejected much of mainstream popular culture, including television (a terrible secret which added to my sense of insecurity – though naturally I've since eschewed it too), my parents aren't sporty. But we'd often go hillwalking and all holidays were in tents, in Devon, Wales, Scotland. Rather than *Grange Hill* – which terrified me when I finally saw it – my imagination was filled with Robin Hood, The Lord of the Rings and King Arthur. Tellingly, perhaps, impossibly heroic quests of endurance would see a gallant knight travelling barefoot for three years through mountains and marshes to slay a dragon using only a magic twig and win the heart of a beautiful princess who lived in a lake. In photos it's rare I don't have a sheath knife and I'd play at being a fantastical action hero for hours – with other kids or on my own.

I was mostly very happy. But on reflection I had a kind of chronic outsider syndrome. For one reason or another, we moved around England a fair bit up till I was about twelve: Gloucestershire, Oxfordshire, Devon, Dorset, London, Buckinghamshire, Gloucestershire again. I would always join school late and was the new kid in class three times. This made me anxiously keen to fit in, and I was strongly drawn to groups and teams. I can't have been a complete shrinking violet, because I remember boasting I was the fastest runner at my Buckinghamshire primary school. It was a very small school.

My dad has never called himself a runner, but he would sometimes 'go for a jog' and at sports day he won the fathers' race. I remember him completing the National Three Peaks Challenge (climbing all the highest peaks in England, Scotland and Wales within twenty-four hours).

I was okay academically. But we moved when I was nine, to Stroud and Wynstones, a Rudolf Steiner School. It was an abrupt change and wearing a white polo-neck and buckled shoes probably didn't help me socially. Neither did the couple of times I fainted. There were strange new subjects: music, German, watercolour painting and a weird dancing thing called Eurythmy. I was behind everyone else, so I went from being told I was good at things, to being told I wasn't.

I realised you could gain esteem more easily by cheeking teachers than by doing your homework. My parents got letters and phone calls about my behaviour and would later describe the issue as a personality clash with the teacher, who when I left opportunistically told the class he'd expelled me. To be fair, he was really encouraging with my drama and English. And I bet I was a right little git.

We moved to the small Cotswold town of Nailsworth and three football-obsessed brothers lived down the road: Fraser, Ross and Jamie

Hillhouse. If I was going to hang out with them, I needed to be into football too. Every day we punted a ball about in fields till we were unrecognisably muddy. I loved being accepted in a little gang, like Robin Hood.

At my new, large comprehensive school, Archway, I saw sport, rather than cheeking the teacher (though I sometimes did that too), as my route to social acceptance. Every break-time I played football. The problem was, having started later than most, I was bobbins.

I was subbed off at half-time in my first ever football match. Selected in goal, I can still recall the paralysing fear as the opposition striker bore down on me, the ball in the net before I could un-paralyse myself. That happened three times. The manager did the smart thing and hooked me. That set the tone for my early sporting life.

For Whiteshill Under 12s I was a substitute all season. I sometimes got five or ten minutes to run about a bit at the end, if the result wasn't at stake. I was usually a substitute for Archway too, an ineffective midfielder/attacker, a less skilful Alexander Hleb. Early in my 'football career', my parents asked if they should come and watch. I felt too embarrassed, so they never did.

But I kept at it. Over time I improved (five-a-side helped) and years later even scored two goals for the school team. I still remember them clearly now, even if one was a two-yard tap-in. 1994 saw the highlight of my football career. Long before they were taken over by eco-energy magnate Dale Vince and certified as the world's first carbon-neutral football club by the United Nations, Forest Green Rovers, in effectively the seventh division, started a youth team.

I went along, but was out of my depth, finding it terrifying playing with the first team in training: semi-professional men against us skinny teens. I actively didn't want the ball and unsurprisingly wasn't selected for the squad. But late in the season, injuries took a toll and the manager called me up for two games. One was an 8–0 home defeat to Swindon Town (who were YTS apprentices, unlike us plucky amateurs) in which I came on as sub at left wing and slid around in the mud a lot without touching the ball. The other game was away in the Midlands somewhere and we lost 3–1, although I did provide the hockey assist (the pass that led to the assist) for our consolation strike. Heady times.

One training session we did the Beep Test, a phrase that strikes fear into most sportspeople. You run approximately twenty-metre intervals, turning quickly to run back the other way, all in time to a tyrannical beep, which gets gradually faster. If you don't cover the ground before the beep, you're out. It got increasingly painful as more players dropped out, until just three were left: a first-team player who was also a postman, my mate Danny Moore and me. As soon as the first-teamer dropped out, they stopped the test. I was fitter than the semi-professional players; I just couldn't kick a ball very well. (Danny is now a very successful triathlon coach in Sydney and coached fellow Wiltshire ultrarunner Anna-Marie Watson to a fourth-place finish at UTMB in 2017.)

Until I rediscovered running, those were the highlights of my sporting career. The added idiocy of sticking so doggedly to football when I was pants, was that I was good at hockey. I played centre half – the most energetic, playmaking position – for the school, was vice-captain and even scored a delicious hat-trick against hockey-mad Wynstones. But hockey wasn't cool.

Archway loved football and rugby; all other sports were afterthoughts. Occasionally the PE teacher would surprise us (it had to be a surprise or the forged-letter industry would go into overdrive) by sending us on a cross-country run. On my first organised run, aged twelve, it was raining and muddy and there were a couple of stout hills, yet I seemed to find it easier than most people. I loved the sense of working hard, feet pounding into mud, feeling damp but strong, rain mixed with sweat on my tongue.

Out of 200-plus kids, I was sixth or seventh. I remember that feeling. I was used to feeling below average at sport – at everything, really. I remember my teacher, Mr Smith (father of the Editors' lead singer; I would also be taught history by the stepfather of The Verve's lead singer – doubly fitting if you know the band's hit songs) seeking me out to say well done. I loved the honesty and simplicity of the effort. There was no hiding, no ball to mis-control or teammate to shout at you.

We lived at the top of a hill, so visiting friends inevitably involved a hilly run, cycle or walk, and I guess I was always fit. I'd do paper rounds too, cycling up and down, and often walk 1.5 miles to and from the school bus stop (with my trousers on). But running without a ball seemed boring.

One afternoon in the sixth form I spied a notice announcing an inter-schools cross-country meet at Archway that night. 'May as well,' I thought. I remember Marling, the rival neighbouring grammar school, had a tall kid who was really good, called Alex double-barrelled something. He seemed oddly slow when I caught him near the end and won. I don't really know how, other than most kids my age were more into cider and cigarettes.

I was disappointed to learn that the race was the final in a series of three. However, the best-placed runners would progress to the next stage to decide selection for country level. From my one race I was second overall in the region and was awarded a small, round, black plaque in school assembly. I've still got it. I awaited my selection letter with excitement. Finally, here was something I might be good at it. It never came. I made more effort to learn about the cross-country calendar for the following year.

A year later, in front of the class, my form tutor Helen Roper promised me a Jaffa cake if I won the cross-country meet at Archway. And sure enough, she was there at the finish line dangling it at mouth height. At the next race I was only half-listening to the briefing about a complicated route and lazily assumed I'd just ask a marshal if I was leading. Which is exactly what happened. The race official was a boy on detention who hadn't been listening either. 'Is it that way?' I spluttered. 'Dunno,' he said. So I took a turning into the woods. And everyone else followed. By the time it dawned on me we hadn't seen a marshal or a marker for a good while, we were running on a busy A road. I gambled on turning left, which thankfully, some miles later – certainly more miles than the race was meant to be – brought us back to the school, albeit from the wrong direction. Like something from a Carry On film, the teachers, supporters and race officials all had their backs to us as we approached.

Not long before the third race, my first real girlfriend, Emma, dumped me. But we were still chatting on the phone regularly (you were always meant to 'still be friends' after a teenage separation). She had intimated she might come along and watch the race, in her home town of Cirencester. Nothing motivates a broken-hearted sixteen-year-old like the thought that he might win back an estranged sweetheart. After my win, I remember scanning the school field for a glimpse of her, futilely.

Winning three out of three, I thought I would gain selection for the county trials this time. And felt equally confident I would turn the invite down. An angry teacher phoned me on a Sunday evening. I calmly pointed out the letter had said we should reply 'if we were interested in being selected'. As I wasn't, I hadn't. I didn't race again for twenty years.

I still can't fully explain my keenness to reject my hard-earnt place. I'd finally found something I was okay at – and yet I didn't pursue it. To be clear, I showed only a hint of generic promise, purely from being regularly active rather than any genetic talent, as my unspectacular marathon personal best (2:38) would later prove. But I was winning local races and yet somehow it didn't interest me much. Instead I doggedly did something (football) I wasn't very good at (though I enjoyed it nonetheless).

There was little support or encouragement for running. I hadn't heard of the concept of a running club. I had no idea how, when or where to train or race. But maybe I would have shunned it anyway. Solo sports weren't cool. I prioritised being accepted by my peers, even if it took me away from what I was good at.

I enjoyed Army Cadets too, where rising through the ranks to Colour Sergeant and earning badges and awards felt effortless. I loved long yomps in the Forest of Dean and charging round in woods at night getting muddy. I was fairly serious about joining the army for a while, but got annoyed that adult cadet instructors kept telling me I needed a haircut – which made me do the opposite.

There were a few incidents of petty crime in my teens. I was caught scrogging (stealing apples we had no plans to eat), and liked to rile farmers by cutting down their wire fences, building dens in their hay bales or firing my air rifle at their barns. As well as smoking dope, I dealt drugs very briefly at university (though I found the idea of making money from my friends so awkward that I didn't make any). I was even involved in a break-in at a cricket club and I should have been caught drink driving, but somehow passed a 3 a.m. breath test. I'm deeply ashamed of the latter two episodes.

Yep, I thought I was quite the Colin Smith of *The Loneliness of the Long Distance Runner* fame. With a loving, middle-class bohemian upbringing, it's hard to see where those incidents came from. Unless of course, along with football, it was a clichéd rebellion against just that? Or simple attention-seeking? Or maybe I was just a normal teenager? I still find it difficult to keep my driving licence clean and my wife says authority tends to bring out my 'inner fourteen-year-old'. But in person I hate the stress of confrontation and am usually conflict-averse.

Maybe I was still angry at the world for Emma dumping me, which she did twice, but from the age of sixteen till the end of university, I smoked dope most days. When I get into something, I really get into it. Football, tea, The Smiths, travelling, the euphoric melancholy of The National (which I've listened to almost every day for a decade), banana and nut butter on toast for breakfast (Meridian crunchy cashew, since you ask). And later, running. I see something similar in my nine-year-old daughter, who recently got into The Beatles. She doesn't just know every song on every album, but the Fab Four's birthdays and eye colours too. She's also incredibly stubborn.

Smoking dope – shock horror – only made me more lazy academically and my A level results were hilariously bad. I took two and only passed one, English, with a grade N (for 'Nearly') for Media Studies, ironically the area where I would spend much of my working life. I laughed it off at the time. But there was a deep sense of failure. My parents were amazing about it, saying 'If this is one of the worst times of your life, you'll have had a pretty good life.'

While most of my peer group went off to university, I did two more A levels and got a place at the University of Derby a year later. This time, I wasn't the new kid in class. I belonged as much as anyone. The social scene was intoxicating, literally and metaphorically. The A level failure had given me the kick up the backside I needed and I worked relatively hard at times, partly because in Sociology you don't actually have to do very much – plus you can study football fandom. I was so into the sociology of football fandom that I did a Master's degree too, and seriously considered a PhD.

But the idea of being a football journalist appealed more and, having written for the university magazine and an Arsenal fanzine, I started sending stories and ideas to publications. I wasn't very good. But I kept at it. I remember the magical feeling of seeing my first paid writing in December 1999 in my local Derby petrol station. Soon I was in London working as a football journalist for *FourFourTwo*'s (the UK's bestselling football magazine's) new website. My obsession had paid off.

I like writing, because it gives you a second chance. In social situations, once you've spoken, the words have gone, perhaps before they were ready, causing offence or misunderstanding. With writing, you get a second and third chance to go over the words and get closer to what you really mean. Not that that always turns out well, as you can see from this lousy book.

My job changed a bit, I lost some enthusiasm and when I split from my girlfriend and some good friends went travelling to Australia, I followed them, via South America. Travelling felt like university again: lots of young people hanging out with money to spend, hedonism in the air and adventures to be had. I loved it and kept it up on and off for most of the noughties.

Living in London had deprived me of nature. On an overnight bus from Buenos Aires to Mendoza, halfway down the Andes, I woke to see giant, snow-topped triangles leering over me like giants. I couldn't take my eyes off them. I desperately wanted to be in amongst those mountains.

I was alone halfway down Argentina with about twelve words of Spanish (I discovered the words for 'years' and 'anus' are very similar). I followed three Israelis from my hostel on to an overnight bus south to Patagonia. They spoke Spanish and wore baggy trousers with lots of zips on. I wore ripped jeans, old-school Puma daps, a brown fake-leather jacket and my day pack was a record bag. In El Chaltén, we all signed up for a guided glacier hike. As I tried to attach crampons to my Pumas in a tent in the middle of a snowy wood came the comment 'We're not going to the cinema, Damian.' My jacket didn't even do up. There followed a cold few hours trudging through cloud and snow before the guide turned us back. I was pleased, because I couldn't feel my hands. But sad too, because I loved being out in that extreme environment, the edginess, the vulnerability, the sense of impending drama.

I did a four-day hike in the World-Heritage-listed Torres del Paine National Park in Chile. There was something about being out in these gloriously lumpy places that made me feel happy and free. It just felt so much more me than partying and city living.

Reading Jon Krakauer's *Into Thin Air*, the gateway drug of mountaineering books, kick-started a fascination with mountaineering. Then I chanced upon *Into the Wild* by the same author. In it Krakauer explores the life and death of idealistic young American Chris McCandless, who expires in the Alaskan wilderness. But the book is really about the irresistible call of the wild and it had a big effect on me. I wanted to do wilderness pilgrimages like 'Alexander Supertramp'. Albeit ideally without dying.

I was compiling a library of Everest disaster books, alongside other mountaineering classics by the likes of Chris Bonington and Maurice Herzog. That evolved into a fascination with Captain Robert Falcon Scott and the Heroic Age of Polar Exploration. Even though dogs, ponies, skis and (arguably) tractors were all available to him on his quest to pioneer a way to the South Pole, Scott preferred the purist concept of man hauling (i.e. men dragging 200-kilogram sledges across the snow). His tragic stubbornness was both a strength and a weakness, and his four-month, 1,800-mile Antarctic saga in unseasonably bad weather ended fatally, less than a half marathon from help. It's still the greatest known endurance accomplishment of all time. (*Endurance*, semi-coincidentally, was Sir Ernest Shackleton's ship for his most famous southbound epic from 1914–1917, and carried twenty-seven men and one cat.)

I cried as I read Scott's diaries, soaked in Edwardian restraint and pathos: 'We took risks, we knew we took them; things have come out against us, and therefore we have no cause for complaint, but bow to the will of Providence, determined still to do our best to the last ... Had we lived, I should have had a tale to tell of the hardihood, endurance, and courage of my companions which would have stirred the heart of every Englishman.'

My favourite scene from all the Star Wars films is Luke Skywalker wandering lost and barely alive in the epic snows of Hoth in *The Empire Strikes Back*. It's a bit like Scott. And a lot like the Spine Race.

I've always been really inspired by endurance: continuing when things get really difficult, when not continuing is much more appealing. Scott is a hero to me. Yes, in hindsight not every decision he made in a place almost no one else had ever been before was the best one. But he kept going, in impossible conditions, despite so much working against him.

The irony is that now I have a more rounded view of what a hero is, I can see I had one right in front of me: my mum. She worked incredibly hard teaching young adults with complex needs including autism and disabilities, and producing stirring Shakespearean plays. She is devoted to her three children, patient and forgiving beyond reason, making sacrifices to keep the family together. She fought off serious bowel cancer with a dignity that protected me from the worst fears, though they were very real. She once quit a job in solidarity with another worker and only ever answers enquiries about a long-term health issue with 'Oh, not bad, thanks.' Luke Skywalker, in contrast, repeatedly attacked his chronically asthmatic father.

Anyway, there's not a great deal of cold adventuring or mountaineering to be done in Australia, but there's some world-class trekking: around World-Heritage-listed Fraser Island; through Tasmania's gothic landscapes on the six-day Overland Track; in the oily Blue Mountains and other national parks next to Sydney, where I lived for six years. I loved the feeling of setting off on a multi-day micro-adventure. There's something about chasing a horizon, reaching a summit ... You knew it'd be tiring, you'd get blisters, sore shoulders, feel hungry (because you'd forgotten the can opener). But those minor sufferings always seemed to coincide with feeling very happy. It was also about simplicity – you just had to eat, drink and keep moving forward. My wardrobe reversed. Now I was wearing baggy trousers with zips on.

I worked on a travel magazine for scandalous wages but amazing perks, including several trips to New Zealand. They have proper mountains in the Land of the Long White Cloud, and designated Great Walks (like our National Trails, but better). I remember feeling chuffed with hiking the sixty-kilometre Kepler Track over three days, with a requisite soaking, blisters and back chafes, but a huge sense of contentment; only to learn some people ran it in one go, on the Kepler Challenge. I was dumbfounded. But a little bit intrigued too. It was the first time the concept of ultramarathons piqued my consciousness.

I did as much tramping in New Zealand as I could: the Rees-Dart trek over six days, the three-day Tongariro Northern Circuit and the two-day Ball Pass Crossing in Aoraki/Mount Cook National Park. On the latter I arrogantly removed my crampons too early and took a slide on some ice, getting intimate with some rocks and bloodying myself up quite a bit. I could have died, like Alexander Supertramp. But I felt so alive (partly because I was close to not being). It was a moment of life-changing, found-God-like intensity. I also got lost in mist on top of a mountain for a couple of panicky hours, er, searching for a *Fellowship of the Ring* filming location. But let's keep that to ourselves.

I left Sydney with my girlfriend, Amy, in 2006 and travelled for eleven months through Latin America. I would run sometimes to keep fit, we trekked and I climbed some mountains. Fantasying about Joe Simpson's near-fatal adventure in *Touching The Void*, I summited Tocllaraju (6,034 metres/19,797 feet), also in northern Peru. Albeit with a guide. Although it was spectacular, there was a disappointing amount of just hanging around.

Live Ecuadorian volcano Chimborazo (6,263 metres/20,548 feet), the highest point on Earth because of the equatorial bulge, was more of an adventure. Temperatures of -10 °C hurt my hands, the altitude hurt my head, and the relentless steepness in the soft snow filled my legs with lactate. My group finally made both summits in the midday heat, one of which I semi-collapsed on. The descent pushed me into new areas of endurance. As laptop-sized rocks, released from the softening snow, whizzed past us, I was falling asleep on my feet and stuffing snow in my mouth to rehydrate. I begged '*Uno momento, por favor!*', but the mountain was unsafe. We had to keep going. I was sure some of my friends were having a picnic on a nearby mound and felt annoyed they hadn't invited me. A first hallucination. It was the hardest physical thing I'd done.

Only two of the six guided groups made the summit that day and when I finally stumbled back into the refugio thirteen hours after I'd left it, I was buzzing with a sweet sense of exhaustion mixed with euphoria. It was the same feeling I would later get from ultra-distance challenges, a profound high, better than any drugs I'd tried, or even the buzz from scrogging apples. It was like some new physiological and metaphysical threshold had been breached. I wanted more. Amy says when I was reunited with her I acted 'very weirdly', ate a burger and promptly fell asleep.

Latin America was amazing, but back in the UK I was still searching for something, perhaps to do with physical adventure. Partly with that idea in mind and partly to rediscover my country of birth, I trekked Alfred Wainwright's Coast to Coast route, 180 miles from one side of England to the other, wild camping. I loved the sense of independence, self-reliance and empowerment as I tramped up and down fells in the Lake District, spying eagles and stags. According to my guidebook the trek took most walkers upwards of twelve days. I was determined to do it in ten.

It got a bit hurty, doing twelve-hour days, totally unnecessarily. Towards the end some pub lunches ended in a shot of whisky to dull foot pain. But it's easy to forget all that in the midst of the North York Moors swishing in a mesmerising sea of purple. I went through every emotion: pain, despair, gratitude (strangers shared food and offered lifts), euphoria, and deep satisfaction. In some ways it had been a better adventure than anything I'd done abroad. I hadn't run a step – the idea was still alien to me – but it was my first personal best on a recognised route.

There was something else too. In the Yorkshire Dales, near the tiny village of Keld, I saw a wooden waymarker pointing north to more moody landscapes. Something about that direction, those atmospheric if forbidding moors, the slightly less-well-trodden path stayed in my mind, nagging me. The waymarker said 'Pennine Way' ...

3
BECOMING A RUNNER

'It's unlikely anyone will get from Edale to Kirk Yetholm as fast as Mike Hartley.'

I would discover the Pennine Way properly in 2011. The same year I also discovered the two most life-changing things I've ever chanced upon: distance running and parenthood.

I would be introduced to a bewildering new world of sleep deprivation, teary tantrums and lemon drizzle cake being a perfectly legitimate breakfast option. Parenting, on the other hand, has been a comparative doddle. I use that quip in my semi-reluctant public-speaking engagements. It doesn't get much of a laugh there either.

We were living back in the UK, in Bath. I was thirty-five, feeling a bit unfit and unhealthy after proofreading a book late into several nights had got in the way of good lifestyle habits. 'I know, I'll do that half marathon everyone in Bath is always banging on about,' I thought and signed up, oblivious to how life-changing it would be. Or to the fact I was about to become a classic midlife-crisis cliché.

I knew nothing about kit, training or nutrition, but my brother-in-law James had run the Bristol Half so he was my Yoda. 'Eat a lot of pasta the night before,' he said. He'd run his in 1:48, which gave me something to aim for. I was playing five-a-side football regularly and might run once a week to keep fit for it. So I extended a couple of runs to around ninety minutes, which felt epic. My legs hurt, my head was dizzy. I liked it.

On the big day I was surprised and thrilled by the infectious atmosphere: bands playing 'Chariots of Fire', crowds cheering and offerings of treats, even if my clumsy effort to collect a jelly baby from a cardboard plate saw them catapulted across the street. Once I wriggled free of the throng, I ran and ran, felt generally amazing and beat James's time, clocking 1:40. I felt I could have run further and perhaps faster, and the finish-line euphoria felt like a new drug. I was hooked. I signed up again as soon as entries opened for the following year. And for the 2012 Brighton Marathon. But first I had a date with the Pennine Way ...

I'd set myself up as a freelance outdoor journalist and when *Country Walking* editor Jonathan Manning was asked by Aurum Press if he could suggest someone to write a new official guide for the Pennine Way, he put my name forward, among others. Somehow I earnt the commission.

The Pennine Way is 268 miles (431 kilometres) of trail with 38,000 feet of elevation, mostly along the top of the Pennines, the backbone of England. They're not mountains, rather rugged hills and sometimes waterlogged (i.e. boggy) upland plateaus. The legendary path leads from Edale in Derbyshire's rugged Peak District, through the glorious Yorkshire Dales and along the stirring Hadrian's Wall to the scandalously underrated Cheviots and Kirk Yetholm just over the border in Scotland. 'The Pennine Way is the original, the classic, the daddy,' I would write (just before I too became a daddy). 'It's the oldest, roughest and toughest of them all.'

I knew I would love the Pennine Way before I'd properly set foot on it. Reading about the Mass Trespass on the Peak District's Kinder Scout in 1932, a wonderful piece of civil disobedience which led to changes in law that freed up land for us common folk to roam on (even if we still have no right of access to ninety-two per cent of England), affected me at the time. It feels salient again in 2021, when civil disobedience may be the only course of action (à la Extinction Rebellion) to force politicians unburdened by ethics to make the changes urgently needed to avoid our impending climate and ecological emergency.

Journalist, First World War conscientious objector and later secretary of the Ramblers Association Tom Stephenson was part of the Mass Trespass. In 1935 two American girls wrote to the *Daily Herald* newspaper asking for advice on a walking holiday in England. Was there anything here like the Appalachian Trail in the US, they wondered? The short answer was a regrettable no. Stephenson recognised that the remote wilds of the 'lonely entrancing' Pennines were an excellent place for a long-distance trail and wrote in the same newspaper: 'Wanted – a long green trail' and called for 'A Pennine Way from the Peak to the Cheviots'.

Secretly, he hoped to use the path as an excuse to open up the moors, much of which was out of bounds to walkers, reserved for rich Etonians and other toffs to needlessly kill grouse. Both of Stephenson's wishes would happen, but he would fight for another thirty years for the Pennine Way to exist. Now there is a hero.

Not everyone loves the bleakness of the Pennine Way, including *Daily Mail*-reading misogynist and guidebook author Alfred Wainwright, who wrote 'You won't come across me anywhere along the Pennine Way' at the end of his 1968 guidebook, *Pennine Way Companion*. 'I've had enough of it.' Which made me like it all the more. Wainwright would later call Mike Cudahy a 'bloody fool' for running the trail over three days.

I set off from Edale in April 2011, just after my first half marathon, intending to fit in half of the fabled footpath before the birth of our first child in May. After nearly a decade abroad, it felt so British. Sure, I didn't love every step of it; Blenkinsopp's charm is esoteric and hard, reservoir-side trails made my feet sore. But those peaty, heathery moorland plateaus, curious groughs and mythical bogs stirred me. 'The route tiptoes through landscapes that inspired great writers, such as the Brontës, William Wordsworth and Charles Kingsley,' I wrote in my guide. 'It's a history lesson on northern England, a fascinating geological field trip, a tour of cosy pubs, welcoming cafes and of numerous charming villages you've probably never heard of but may never want to leave. But most of all it's a walk through life-affirming natural beauty.

'On a personal note, the Way proved to me that, despite Britain's pandemic [oops, not sure I'd use that word now] of cars, tarmac and things that beep, you can still escape all that and in northern England find wild, remote and plain beautiful places, offering a giddy sense of liberation.'

I got home in time to see our first child born. Which was, in case any disproportionate gushing about running here is misleading, The Best moment of my life, equalled only when her brother arrived two years later. Presumably it's the same for most parents, but never before or since have I felt a stronger sense of purpose: I will do whatever it takes to look after this soft little bundle.

I went back to walk the rest of the Pennine Way that summer and despite my knee buckling under my twenty-kilogram pack (perhaps that one-kilogram tripod wasn't really necessary?) on the steep descent to Dufton, my strong feelings for the trail were only enhanced.

I don't think I've ever felt satisfied with anything I've written. There's always something I would tweak, or more likely delete. My Pennine Way guide is the work I'm proudest of. With what I can see now as a signature level of obsession, I had bought and read every Pennine Way and Pennines book I could find. From Wainwright to Mike Hartley, from *Last of the Summer Wine* to that tree that stars in a Kevin Costner film, I immersed myself in its stories. When you go all in, you care. And what you produce has more meaning.

Talking of Hartley, I wrote: 'Some complete the Pennine Way in twelve days, others in twelve years. It's unlikely anyone will get from Edale to Kirk Yetholm as fast as Mike Hartley. In July 1989, the fell runner ran the 268 miles in a Herculean two days, seventeen hours, twenty minutes and fifteen seconds. He halted only twice, including to knock back fish and chips in Alston. On average, however, most one-go walkers take a massively more sensible sixteen to nineteen days.'

I wouldn't have called myself a runner when I wrote that in 2011. But a seed had been dropped into fertile ground. Several more seeds were planted in the first half of 2012. *Outdoor Fitness* magazine was launched by Jonathan Manning. It was full of kit and training advice, but above all, brilliantly photographed, irresistible and inspiring outdoor adventures. I was suddenly learning about fell/hill/mountain/trail running and something called ultramarathons. I wanted to do those things! And the best way to be able to do those things was to do them as a journalist. So I bombarded him with story ideas.

At the invitation of Salomon community manager Matt Ward,

Jonathan sent me to a Snowdonia training camp for the French brand's fell runners, including stars Tom Owens, Ricky Lightfoot, Angela Mudge and Rob Samuel. I hadn't heard of any of them. Fell running wasn't a term used in Wiltshire, where I now lived. I was hearing about mind-blowing races that went to the top of Snowdon, Ben Nevis, even on the Everest Base Camp trek route. My horizons hadn't just been broadened, they'd been stretched beyond recognition. I wanted to run up and down mountains too. 'Once you try trail running, you don't go back,' said Tom. Four years later I would be in the same Great Britain trail-running team as him.

I was intrigued by how passionate they all were about running in hills and green places. They told me it was better for them, made them stronger, fitter and less prone to injury than running on road or track. And better mentally too. Someone aptly called it 'soul running'. As a hiker, there was still a nagging sense of guilt that running was rushing. 'But you see,' said Rob Samuel, 'when you run, you go twice as far and see twice as much.' That simple argument made running seem existentially okay to me. Since swapping hiking boots for X-Talons, I've seen so much more, had my emotions (not to mention more sensitive areas) rubbed rawer, experienced things more intensively, made more memories and just got out more.

As I quizzed Matt Ward, both for the piece and my own earnest interest, he recommended a book called *Feet in the Clouds*. I ordered it straightaway and devoured it when it arrived. Although fell races themselves still seemed to belong to this northern culture I knew nothing about, it felt irresistibly appealing. And I heard about the original British 'FKT' too, the Bob Graham Round. Not for the first time, I was an outsider keenly wanting to belong.

For the 2012 Brighton Marathon, I had a charity place for WaterAid and needed to raise £1,000. I doubted my mates would sponsor me unless I did something a bit wacky, so when I was offered the choice of costumes between a tap and a toilet, there was only one option. If I did get the runs, it'd at least be appropriate. Though I hoped people wouldn't take the piss, that the event wouldn't wipe me out or drain me too much.

The big day brought glorious sunshine. I guzzled down a couple of bowlfuls of porridge and banana, three cups of tea, a Snickers, a gel, a bottle of Lucozade, donned my toilet outfit, and set off to the start, bloated and burpy. I fancied a sub-3:30 was possible and started out strongly, loving the interactions with crowds. The first few shouts of 'You look a bit flushed, mate!' were entertaining, though the novelty went down the U-bend later when I seriously needed the toilet and there were none, other than the fake one I carried. By mile fifteen I'd snuck ahead of the 3:15 pacer. I felt amazing. You can wing a half marathon if you're reasonably fit. Not a marathon.

My longest run ever was seventeen miles. At mile eighteen, a switch flicked to 'off'. Suddenly everything became much more difficult. I'd hit the fabled wall. Rarely has a metaphor felt more fitting. It feels like you've run smack-bang into a barrier made of bricks. All your air, all your strength, is gone. Your legs and arms feel wobbly, like they're not yours. Everything is saying stop.

The wall is understood as a combination of poor fuelling (I had two gels – not enough), inadequate pacing (I'd been tanking it) and inadequate endurance (like, duh!). In other feel-sorry-for-myself news, my feet and legs were sore, blisters throbbed. I grabbed some sweets from an aid station, but it was too late for a resurrection.

Someone shouted that I was the first fancy-dress runner, which gave me a boost. But a guy wearing merely a pair of fairy wings passed me – feck sake, does that really count as fancy dress?! As did the 3:15 pacer. I had to pause to stretch in the finishing straight, my calves fizzing with the threat of cramp. The crowds were amazing, creating a hurricane of positivity. They made me feel like a hero: Super Toilet-Man. Three hours and seventeen minutes after I started running, finally I could stop. I had a silver blanket around me, my ears hummed with white noise and a sensation of bittersweet relief flooded my body. I was a marathon runner. I was a runner. This felt like me.

Amy says my idea of fun isn't the same as most people's, and without realising it I was already doing ultra-distance challenges of sorts – just without running them. Being back in the UK after most of a decade abroad gave me a lust for domestic adventure. Trekking Coast to Coast and the Pennine Way had been life-affirming, but early parenthood doesn't sync with ten-day walks. Part motivated by work (though as the pay often didn't even cover the expenses, turning adventures into magazine stories afterwards was primarily a way to legitimise my absence), but more because I simply felt drawn to them, I was ticking off established outdoor challenges.

Usually with my childhood friend Tim 'Bevo', I attempted several established challenges, including the National Three Peaks (accomplished with just a few minutes to spare and something of a sprint finish – my first bit of running in big lumps), the Yorkshire Three Peaks, the Welsh 3,000s, a self-designed Dartmoor round and even some Cairngorms Munros. I loved racing up and down lumps to a deadline. The tyranny of the ticking clock is addictive and at each finish that same feeling of happy weariness washed over me. It felt both pointless and meaningful. Running challenges would have appealed to me instantly. I just didn't know they existed. Though on Ben Nevis in freezing-cold clag I remember seeing two women jogging past wearing vests and bumbags, chatting merrily away: the first time I saw fell runners.

My trekking and hillwalking experiences were excellent prep for trail ultramarathons (which can to an extent be power-hiking contests). These challenges were leading me organically and inevitably towards bigger outdoor adventures.

At the end of August I visited Chamonix for the first time. The trip wasn't connected to running but included another mini epiphany. I still considered myself an aspiring mountaineer and had been incredibly fortunate to be sent to climb Mont Blanc, the highest peak in Western Europe. Magazine assignments are rarely this good. I arrived full of excitement. As was the town. Almost everything was focused on adventure, from the shops selling eye-wateringly expensive kit, to the people wearing eye-wateringly expensive kit, to the huge peaks rocketing skywards on either side of the valley and paragliders circling overhead. Curiously, lots of thin people wearing the same green gilet were wandering around, slowly and stiffly, and loud Eurotrash was on loop.

I heard someone mention something called 'UTMB' …

With Tim, our guide from New Zealand's Adventure Consultants and another Kiwi client, I stayed in amazing Alpine huts with three-course meals and beer on tap, and worked on mountaineering skills. But due to a recent fatal avalanche or my fellow client's nervousness on technical terrain, we were unable to climb Mont Blanc. We had a much more moderate but still exhilarating climb up 4,248-metre Mont Blanc du Tacul and made it back down to Chamonix safely. Even if it didn't always feel like we would.

The Aiguille du Midi ridge is a knife-edge traverse. It has a 2,000-metre-plus drop to the left, all the way down to Chamonix, and on the right a steep slope leading sharply down to rocks and a messy, icy half-death. I've done numerous bungee jumps and skydives, but this was more hair-whitening. It would have been very nervy anyway, but when you're roped to someone much heavier and less confident, your chances of survival diminish. It was Type 3 fun (not fun at the time, or afterwards).

On the way home I debated whether I should do things like that now I was a father. It seemed too selfish. Ultrarunning offered the chance to have adventures with a greater chance of continuing to be around for my children afterwards. That moment nudged me away from mountaineering and towards the wonderfully ouchy fun of running long distances in lumpy places.

Though I'd done less than a handful of races, I became one of those annoying running evangelists. I read (cliché alert) *Born to Run*, *Ultramarathon Man* and every ultrarunning book I could find. My mountaineering and polar exploration library, which had been suffocating my football library, was being pushed off the shelves by running books. They were all I asked for for birthday and Christmas presents, and all I bought for other people (regardless of whether they were runners).

I had been playing football regularly since I was twelve (only interrupted by travelling). But I suddenly realised I didn't want to any more. I might pick up an injury that would stop me running. It was a strange and big moment, telling my five-a-side teammates I hadn't brought my kit because I had an 'injury', the slightest knee concern I would've happily previously played through. One obsession had superseded another.

The flexibility of running was a huge advantage to a new parent. You train whenever and wherever you can – all you need is your daps. Even if it was often before 7 a.m. or after 7 p.m., when my daughter was asleep, running felt wonderfully simple, and emancipating. Plus initially progress was fast, those early races all PBs.

The switch from a team sport to a solo sport felt significant. Gone instantly was that Sunday-league-football frustration of letting your team down with a missed penalty (something I had a knack for). Or playing a blinder that hadn't mattered because your keeper had punched the ball into the net. There was something more honest, potentially less frustrating about it being all on you.

You know where you stand in individual sport. With everything else in life, I don't know how good I am. Am I a good husband? In those sleep-deprived new parent days especially, it didn't seem like it. Am I a good father? I can do better, not least in the afternoon after a long run, when I might get unfairly snappy. Was I a good journalist? I always seemed to be stupidly busy, yet my bank account was empty. But when I run a race or a challenge, I get clear feedback. You are the fifteenth best. Or you are two minutes better than last time. The doubts and insecurities are gone.

When comedian Frankie Boyle was talking to a BBC podcast about his alcoholism, he said: 'I remember having my first drink at fifteen and just going, "Yes! Yippee! This is it!" … There's a feeling sometimes addicts get that this substance completes them. That's kind of what it was for me.'

That's exactly what it was like for me. Except instead of a substance it was running.

I am happiest when in my T-shirt, shorts and muddy daps. I don't feel as emotionally comfortable in other clothes. Sure, there's been some imposter syndrome at times, especially when attempting new distances. But every running and outdoor challenge has felt more natural to me than most work or social scenarios. I pretty much wear running clothes 24/7. It sounds a bit wanky, but I wonder if I simply feel more authentic, more me, in my running clothes.

Anyway, that's boring. But talking of kit, those annual winter-running magazine tips that invariably include getting your kit ready the night before? Nonsense. You're wasting good running time there. Sleep in it. I've learnt there are two types of runners: those who get up when the 5 a.m. alarm goes off, and those who press snooze. Guess which one wins races and breaks records?

I genuinely believed – and kind of still do – running could solve all the world's problems. If everyone went running, they'd be happy, less angry with each other. Until they got Achilles tendonitis, anyway. At social gatherings I'd struggle to hold a conversation about other people's interests or news. Work, eating and talking to people were just annoying, trivial things you did in between runs. Amy said I started talking about running like it was a drug. I was addicted.

It hasn't always been completely healthy. 'All you care about is running,' my son said to me once, which stung and made me evaluate whether I was letting running get in the way of being a good parent. (He's also complained that 'UTMB takes you soooo long, Daddy' – he's a harsh critic.) But I think I can be a good parent by showing how running showcases some life metaphors: persistence and hard work tend to pay off; the things that are the hardest to get are usually most worth getting; and, most important of all, low mood = eat food.

Getting a run in feels so vital that it's difficult to think of a scenario other than a family health emergency I would allow to supersede it. It's at times been a marriage-troubling hobby. Early on I was given a dilemma of meeting a good childhood friend I hadn't seen for a year, or joining two guys I hardly knew for a recce of a local race route. And with only very brief hesitation, I chose the latter. I'm still fine with that, to be honest. I really don't have a social life. I talk to my daps.

I've found huge mental benefits of running, documented in numerous studies. Whenever I've exchanged a different, er, point of view with Amy and gone for a run, I come back and apologise. Even if it wasn't my fault (which is always). That release of endorphins is undeniably meditative, feeds our biophilia, our innate desire to be in nature. All my best ideas come to me while running (even if they're usually about doing more running). Whenever I feel stressed I go for a run. And the problem shrinks. I see it now with my kids. If they've been squabbling or irritable, we get them outside in the green stuff and their moods are transformed in a flash. Every time. Suddenly they're full of life, talking, climbing, running. Happy.

And then there's the runner's high. It's real, it's addictively good, and if you've never experienced it you should put this book back where you stole it from right now and go run. For me it's something like flying: there's a transcendental lightness of being that's both physical and a state of mind; forward propulsion starts to feel automatic and effortless, and you start to lift up out of your body; your mind is floating, you feel a kind of serene, mild but unmistakable euphoria … and then I usually get attacked by a dog or brush against some stingers and the spell is broken. But till then it's amazing. Indeed it's no coincidence the Marathon Monks of Mount Hiei attempt to run 1,000 marathons in 1,000 days or Indian spiritual leader Sri Chinmoy is the creator of the world's longest ultramarathon. It is something like an orgasm. Not the really good bit, but the peaceful bit that follows. (Though if you feel that tired then you've, er, bonked.) Scientists have studied this, identifying a morphine-like release of endorphins. That has been disputed and it may even be as simple as increased blood flow just making everything work better. But I and millions of others know that if you run you feel happier.

Is there an ultrarunner's high? I think it's a bit different. The lows are lower, so the highs do feel higher. Especially at the finish line. How can you be hurting so badly but feeling so good? That makes no sense and yet also makes complete sense.

Getting home from a long run is the best. Tea and nut butter on toast taste a thousand times better. And you're chatty and happy, and all the non-runners in the house will tell you to shut up and stop being annoying. But they're not getting any Strava kudos, that's why they're grumpy. And then a weary peacefulness settles in and you feel great for the rest of the day. Till 4 p.m., when you bonk and start snapping at everyone.

When non-ultrarunners discover what you do it's a weird mix of ego and awkwardness. 'You run how far?!' I often start apologising, saying,

'Well, we hike a load of it, to be honest.' Then next time you see them they ask how your hiking is going. At children's parties you're always introduced to someone who once did a triathlon.

It's also an obvious antidote to the ills of modern life. Firstly there's the physical aspect. My physio Matt Holmes, strength and conditioning coach Kriss Hendy and technique guru Shane Benzie are united in their hatred of the chair and how it's made us weak (I got a standing desk just to make them shut up). But at least as much psychologically. Trail running puts you in the present moment, where Buddhists believe we get meditative healing. Rather than worrying about things I haven't done and things I need to do, I only think about the here and now. And that's peaceful and wears away some of the stress built up by work and technology. Plus you're away from a screen.

I feel sorry for non-runners. What do they think about? What do they do with all that time that we spend daydreaming about running?

Naturally I nagged Jonathan at *Outdoor Fitness* to let me write a story about my new-found passion. 'Sure,' he said. 'But not the Brighton Marathon. How about I send you on your first ultramarathon?'

Gulp. He'd called my bluff...

4
EARLY EXPERIMENTS IN ULTRARUNNING

'I can't stop thanking people and laughing weirdly.'

'I'm probably going to die, aren't I?' began the magazine write-up of my first ultramarathon, The Wall, in June 2012.

I gazed in awe at the seasoned ultrarunners on that start line at Carlisle Castle. They had weird knee-high sock things, weird straws coming out of their chest-carried water bottles, weird really tight shorts. They looked like aliens. But cool aliens. I wanted to be a cool alien too (apart from the shorts).

The Wall was sixty-nine miles over two days. While the idea of an absurdly long journey tapped into my treasured notions of heroic quests, I was equally fascinated and terrified – not least because the Brighton Marathon in April was by far my longest run and I'd rolled my ankle the week before on Crib Goch.

As part of the story commission I interviewed Gary Vallance for ultrarunning advice. 'The trick is to just go a little slower than your marathon pace,' he said, 'keep putting fuel in, and you find you can just keep going and going ... '

Gary warned ultras can become addictive, that he'd done about ten 100-milers. There's no way I'd ever want to do that. Why would anyone?

I'd heard I needed a walking strategy, so every fourth minute I slowed to a hike for sixty seconds. But everyone kept asking if I was okay, so I just ran. My first ever ultramarathon checkpoint was a moment of fantasy. It was like a children's birthday party without the balloons, hyperactive little people and tears (yet). There were sandwiches, pies, fruit, crisps, sweets, chocolate bars, fizzy pop, all free! I sat down and tucked in. I was already carrying more than ample snacks. But I stocked up further, leaving (reluctantly) some ten minutes later with a much heavier pack. I've always had a sweet tooth. This was the sport for me.

I was soon swapping life stories with fellow runners. Everyone was so friendly. It felt like a team event. The route was often tarmac, but the green hills were better eye candy than Brighton's shop fronts. I made the classic beginner's error of running the first proper downhill with wild exuberance, which came back to haunt my quads soon enough. I was overtaking folk as I arrived at camp thirty-two miles later.

I was in the top third of finishers, even if my legs and feet were in bits – a heavily strapped ankle had caused an issue behind my knee. 'I find it satisfying when runners scream,' said a masseuse, and I didn't disappoint her. I treated myself to an on-site pint with my new ultra pals before settling into my tent, my grunting and groaning giving the wrong impression to people under neighbouring canvas.

On day two, my legs felt predictably stiff and uncooperative at first. Just thirty-seven miles to go. Gulp. But my legs gradually loosened up on a hiked uphill. At a checkpoint two hours in, I learnt I was in the top twenty, which didn't help the oft-ignored sensible side of my brain. The devil on the other whispered that it was good to get miles under my belt while I was feeling okayish. Something in my head wasn't letting me merely complete the race, but demanding I do the best I possibly could.

I wouldn't say I'm particularly competitive, but Bevo and I have a one-vs-one penalty shoot-out competition that's been going on for twenty-two years (I'm winning 83–74). Amy loves to tell how in December 2014 I ran a ten-kilometre Santa race fundraiser, dressed as Father Christmas. I was winning near the end, but misheard/ignored a marshal and went off course. After a few minutes dashing back and forth like an angry red and white hornet I finally reached the finish line. I was not the first runner to do so. And I did not take that news, shall we say, in the spirit of the occasion. Apparently an angry Santa is quite an amusing sight. So yes, with certain sports and competitions, I do have a strong innate desire to win.

Anyway, fatigue breeds emotion and cheers from locals and staff would send my spirits soaring. Five hours in, socialising was an exchange of grunts. Faces were sterner, with people locked into personal worlds of pain and purpose. 'I find that, like Captain Scott's dogs in Antarctica,' I wrote in *Outdoor Fitness*, 'I need someone running in front of me or my motivation dwindles. My toes tell me they'll soon be joining my quads in writing a stern letter to their MP about all of this.'

I longed for checkpoints, not just for sustenance but for the banter and reassurance that I wasn't the only one suffering. At the last pitstop I ate an orange. It was *the best orange I've ever tasted*. Make that the best *thing* I'd ever tasted. I walked frequently, looking like a rejected Silly Walks sketch. I couldn't imagine anyone could run in my ruinous state. Then a woman jogged past as if on a carefree Sunday run.

After zigzagging through the edge of Newcastle, I reached the River Tyne, rounded a corner and ... that bridge was the finish! I realised that I was running quite fast (well, eight-minute miles). I felt reenergised, like I'd had a shot of something banned. I felt so annoyed to have this left in the tank that I went even faster.

'A stampede of wildebeests couldn't stop me getting to that bridge,' I wrote. 'When I reach clapping spectators I'm genuinely fighting back tears. I feel so grateful to them. I sprint across the bridge to the finishing line. After sixty-nine miles and thirteen hours, rather suddenly, it's all over. I'm buzzing with relief and euphoria, and a small, perverse amount of sadness that it's done. I've achieved something I thought was beyond me. I've graduated as an ultrarunner. Though I can sense I'll be a bit broken for a few days, it didn't kill me, and I never once thought "I'm never doing this again". In fact, I know I will.'

Although the Brighton Marathon had felt amazing to finish, running an ultramarathon was better: the sense of accomplishment, the superior scenery and camaraderie, all that cake. I wanted more. I was fascinated by that moment when I thought I had given my all, yet found I had much more to give. Who had decided to back off early, my body or my mind?

It fits with Professor Tim Noakes's central governor theory: that my brain was playing a trick on me, trying to make me stop, preserving energy in case there was a sabre-toothed tiger around the corner. Our mind is often trying to ensure that we have ample in reserve. But if we're always holding back, we'll never find out what's possible. Nine years later I'm still fascinated by the often deceitful relationship between mind and body during ultra-distance challenges.

* * *

In late 2012 I fell in with the wrong crowd. As I commuted from Box to Bath, I'd often spot a runner heading the same way. He looked different from other runners: serious, experienced, like he knew stuff. He wore kit with the initials OMM on it, and three-quarter-length tights. He looked like he did challenges that were long, muddy and involved big lumps. I wanted to know what he knew. As serendipity would have it, our village magazine carried an interview with the same man, Alex Copping, an academic at Bath University and an impressive ultrarunner. Ignoring the idea I would almost definitely seem like a stalker, I looked him up and emailed him.

Having recently moved to Box (we specialise in quintessential village names around here; The Shoe and Old Sodbury aren't far away) I was oblivious to its significance in ultrarunning history. The five-time Comrades winner Arthur Newton twice broke the 100-mile world record in the 1920s and 1930s. Both times he ran on the A4/Bath Road to London, starting in Box. The A4 is yards from my house. *It's your destiny, Luke.*

There must be something in the air here, because I had been toying with the idea of running the 102-mile Cotswold Way in one go under the usual guise of a magazine story. I asked Alex if he thought it was doable, not knowing he'd been involved in record attempts on the trail himself. He added me to the Bath Bats mailing list and became an enthusiastic mentor and training partner. I still run with Alex and his now-faster-than-us son Otto most weekends.

I started getting emails from Andy Mullett, aka Chief Bat, and it seemed I could just turn up for a night-time trail run. I was nervous about joining this mysterious, hardcore group, but their next run started at a pub just down the road so I didn't have a good enough excuse. I downed

EARLY EXPERIMENTS IN ULTRARUNNING

a bottle of Lucozade just before, sure that I'd be too slow for these rugged night runners. After being warmly welcomed, we went for an enjoyable six miles in the dark (hence the Bats moniker) and I chatted to Paul King (now a highly regarded endurance coach) about local races. The evening was rounded off in jovial style with ale and chips.

On my second Bats outing I got talking to Allan Cox, who asked 'Are you a distance runner?' with a special reverence on the word distance. I said a hesitant yes. I wasn't sure what he meant exactly. But I wanted to be one.

I quickly felt accepted by the group. I had very luckily stumbled on the running version of The Avengers. Members included GB marathoner Holly Rush, GB trail runner Lizzie Wraith, some very fast local runners (James Donald, Matthew Maynard), sports dietician Renee McGregor, future record-breaking ultra-distance cyclist Ian Walker and elite triathletes, plus a guy called Tim Laney, who I heard mentioned in venerable tones. Not that there is any membership as such. The night-loving rapscallions remain determinedly unofficial and informal.

In pubs and trails around Bath, the Bats filled my impressionable little head with big ideas. Allan regaled me about Ultra-Trail du Mont-Blanc (UTMB) and the incredible finish-line experience where your family could join you for the run-in. When I asked Tim Laney for recommendations he said 'Hardrock is fun!' Tim has placed fourth at the notoriously gruelling 100-mile race, has completed Leadville 100, has done Britain's Big Three 24-hour fell-running rounds, was in the first team at UTMB's super-hurty PTL race and was even an extra in *Chariots of Fire* in that famous beach scene.

The Bats gave short shrift to hugely intimidating distances and challenges and made everything sound possible, even if 'Type 2 fun' was a popular phrase (meaning it's not fun at the time, but it is afterwards). Twenty-four-hour fell-running rounds and 100-mile races were something to be laughed about. Lizzie Wraith, a softly spoken woman with steely eyes, not only won Lakeland 100 but broke the course record. And placed third at Lavaredo Ultra-Trail, a very competitive seventy-five-mile race in the Italian Dolomites. That made an impression on me too.

There was talk of something called the Dan Booth Round, scheduled for just before Christmas. Dan was a popular Bat who'd passed away recently and used to train for fell-running rounds with a twenty-four-mile circuit of the trig points on Bath's surroundings hills. Like any unconventional, night-time meet-up, it was irresistible. The route was a mixture of hilly countryside and quiet Bath streets. Some trigs were on hilltops, others hidden in bushes or stingers; one was even on private land (which didn't unduly concern anyone). The run had a thrilling undercurrent of unorthodoxy, a frisson of *Fight Club*. It's not what normal runners, let alone normal people, do. I was shattered by the end. But we were treated to a fine meal and drinks at Bat Iwein's house. These were my kind of people.

The more I ran, the better I seemed to be at it. In early 2013 I was running most days (usually about an hour), with something a bit longer (usually only two hours) at the weekend when my daughter had her midday nap, and I sometimes cycle-commuted to Bath (a twelve-mile round trip). My Bath Half PB was whittled down to 1:20 and I became accustomed to finishing in the top ten in local races like the Slaughterford 9, the Dursley Dozen and Relish Running 10ks. I loved racing and definitely trained to race, rather than the other way around.

My ill-paid career in journalism helped get me free entries to races I often wouldn't have afforded otherwise and I was able to class doing what I loved as 'work'. The trouble is that magazine editors want jeopardy in their stories, so once you've written about running sixty-nine miles, the next challenge needs to be bigger. Running the Cotswold Way was still an ambition and I learnt there was an inaugural race on the route, Cotswold Way Century, that September. The idea of running 100 miles was intimidating, but I knew people who'd done that now, which made it seem possible. Journalism also got me easy access to experts and that's how I accidentally got myself a coach and a technique coach.

Ultrarunning was booming and new races were springing up all the time. I'd been invited to a press launch for Race to the Stones, a 100k along the Ridgeway National Trail, where I met a self-styled performance coach who asked me 'Do you know how to train for ultras?' with a slightly condescending tone. I didn't. But I really wanted to know. Before I got home, I'd hatched a plan where this coach would train me for Race to the Stones, Cotswold Way Century and my first sub-three-hour marathon. I couldn't afford to pay him, but he was happy with magazine coverage.

After meeting in a gym for a 'VO2 max test' (to ascertain my maximum rate of oxygen consumption) on a treadmill, he gave me a training plan and away I went, buzzing with motivation. Although something troubled me. I've always been fairly lean, so was surprised when be recommended I lose two kilograms – 'just give up beer and bread,' he said, a little obnoxiously. He gave me a list of banned substances, including pasta, rice, nuts, muesli and in fact almost all carbohydrates. Though crunchy nut cornflakes were apparently a good breakfast option. I quizzed him on a couple of items and his answers were vague and unconvincing.

Nevertheless, he was an ultrarunning coach (albeit without qualifications) and I wanted to be an ultrarunner, so I swapped sandwiches for salads at lunchtimes and became a little too conscious of what I was eating. He put the idea in my head that skinny meant fast. A rumbling tummy became a pleasing sensation. Going to the toilet was a win. I'd be lighter after. I'd rarely weighed myself before, but was now doing so twice a day. Jumpers got baggy. I forced a new hole in my belt. My wedding ring got loose. Friends commented that I'd lost weight. They meant it in alarm, but I took it as a compliment.

His advice was irresponsible and dangerous: run a load more and eat a load less. That way lies chronic fatigue/Relative Energy Deficiency in Sport (RED-S), injury and eating disorders. When he gave me another training plan and suggested I lose two kilograms more, it just felt instinctively wrong and I didn't.

My hunch was confirmed some months later when a magazine sent me for all sorts of fancy tests and measurements at the futuristic GlaxoSmithKline Human Performance Lab in Brentford, used by Premier League clubs and the Brownlee brothers. As well as a VO2 max of 64.7 millilitres per kilogram per minute (decent for an amateur athlete but distinctly average for an elite runner – Kilian Jornet's is apparently 89.5), my body-fat percentage was 6.5. 'I wouldn't go any leaner,' I was urged.

'Too lean means a reduced immune system and a struggle to recover from hard training.' I don't like how thin I look in the photos accompanying the story.

It was on another magazine story commission that I first met the smiley chatterbox who would have a much healthier impact on my running, technique coach and movement specialist Shane Benzie. I assumed I ran well enough. How complicated could it be?

'Runners will happily spend £150 on a pair of shoes, but won't spend money learning how to run well,' he said. 'Run a load of miles with bad technique and you'll just get injured. But learn to run with natural technique and we utilise the elasticity and tensegrity of our fascial system – free energy – rather than stressing our muscles unnecessarily and wearing them out too soon. In an ultra we want our body to last as long as possible.' Okay, he had my attention ...

We ran and Shane videoed us. He was diplomatic about my, er, 'form', but has since described it as 'an accident waiting to happen'. A photo from that run is horrifying: over-striding, heel-striking, lazy arms, head rolling forward, slow cadence. I couldn't have got running more wrong. Shane explained how to run like Mo Farah and I went home buzzing with excitement. I was also fascinated by his claim that children automatically run with great technique. We unlearn this by spending so much of our waking time sitting down and getting weak.

Shane would admit I'm one of his slowest learners. My body just wants to be as efficient as possible (i.e. lazy) and my mind (again, lazy) lets it. But he tries to get ultrarunners to really run, rather than the classic ultra shuffle, little more than an energised walk. He encourages me to 'load the bow', aim for a tripod landing, increasing my vertical oscillation and stride length, to get more – free! – elastic energy. His ideas definitely developed me as a runner. I love everything about running. He is only interested in one aspect: how to do it. I've never met anyone so obsessed with one thing.

We've been in touch ever since, had numerous one-on-one workshops (I've needed them), and now that I'm a coach too we've put on day workshops together. I consider him a friend. Even if catching up with him is a nightmare as he's usually in Kenya or Mongolia, studying movement in runners or indigenous tribes. He's the Indiana Jones of running and hugely in demand, coaching almost every ultrarunner who's won a race in the UK and co-authoring *The Lost Art of Running*. It's heart-warming to see someone so passionate about something turn it into such a big success.

* * *

The inaugural Race to the Stones 100k, my second ultra, was scorchio, at 30°C-plus. I ran through yellow oilseed rape fields, undulating chalky downs and cool beech woodlands. At the halfway checkpoint I learnt I was in the top ten, and also that it's difficult to run with a bowl full of boiling hot soup. I got dehydrated, had stingy wee and accidentally skipped a bit of the course, jumping up a placing (and owning up).

'Miraculously, despite having run ninety kilometres, more than ever before, I arrive at the final checkpoint feeling good,' I write in a now-defunct magazine. 'The sky is golden, a utopian summer haze blanketing the lowlands. I dash through the dramatic ancient earthworks of Barbury Castle, down to a broad chalky path. The last section goes on forever and I fear I've fired off all my ammunition too soon. But finally I'm running towards a big inflatable arch with the world's most wonderful word on it: finish. I collapse into a chair and get sprayed with beautiful water as I share handshakes and maniacal laughter with fellow runners. It's taken me eleven hours, four minutes and forty-seven seconds. I'm rather astonished to learn I've finished sixth. Holy feck and smeck. I'm exhausted. But ecstatic.'

Okay, again not the most competitive ultra in the world or even this end of the country. But I had both loved the experience and got another sign that this stuff might suit me. And if 100k was possible, 100 miles might be too …

In training I averaged fifty miles a week. I can't remember if it was in the plan or my own idea, but my preparation peaked with a forty-mile run (not something I'd recommend to coaching clients now, as the fatigue and injury risk are likely to outweigh the benefits). Wearing calf guards, a hydration vest and disturbingly bright clothes, I got curious looks from commuters as I caught a post-work train to Dursley, forty miles from Box. Then I ran home, mostly along the Cotswold Way; getting a bit lost, a bit sore and a lot hangry.

The week before my first 100-miler was a nervy time. I speed-read Bryon Powell's *Relentless Forward Progress*. And panic-bought enough nosh for a children's party. Was running 100 miles even possible for me? Would I be 'changed forever', like Dean Karnazes wrote in *Ultramarathon Man*? Would bits of me fall off? (No.) Would I age dramatically? (Yes.)

'I was guessing it might hurt,' I wrote in *Men's Fitness*. 'But then so do most things worth doing.'

Tourists looked on bemused as a multicoloured river of compression-clad runners flowed down Chipping Campden high street. I was at the front, with a small group which included Nick Weston, Simon Baker and Rob Forbes, enjoying the scenery, chatting, scoffing KitKats. I could see for miles along the sun-kissed Cotswold Edge and waves of euphoria washed over me.

At around thirty miles, though, tiredness kicked in. I dropped back, it got dark and there were lots of woods, which felt a bit *Blair Witch*. I tripped on a tree root and went head over heels. Near Stroud, about halfway, I bumped into Nick and Simon again and we ran across the valley together through giant cornfields and up through beech woods. As we passed three miles from my parents' house, I boasted how I knew the area especially well. Then found myself caught in a bramble thicket.

We were a team. There was a group of four runners ahead and it wasn't said directly but we wanted to catch them. We took it in turns to lead, flying over hilltops, through quiet villages and dark woods, like wolves chasing fresh scent. We saw headlamps down the hill in front of us, and gave chase. We caught them in the woods. They (including Rob and future GB athlete Sarah Morwood) looked tired as we cut through their middle, exchanging perfunctory pleasantries. It felt callous, but they'd become our prey. I sizzled with adrenaline. We surprised some cows in a field, who started some kind of circular stampede, accidentally aiding our escape from the group behind. Then we were the hunted.

With a marathon to go, blisters were forming on the soles of my feet. My hips and ITBs hurt. Thick fog and route confusion were never far away. Two friends of Simon's turned up at ridiculous o'clock to cheer him on. I was grumpy with them, for no reason other than I was pathetically tired. I felt raw and vulnerable, but grateful to Simon and Nick for letting me run with them through the night. There was the unspoken question: were we friends or foes? I liked being part of a gang. But I didn't want to hold anyone back. In the dewy morning, with about twelve miles to go, Simon politely said he planned to push on at the next aid station. Splitting up felt emotional.

I was a zombie, shuffling unthinkingly ahead, feeling sorry for myself. But I remembered the classic ultrarunning pick-me-up: it never always gets worse. Within five kilometres of the finish, like a dying hero in a film, I told Nick to push on and grab second place. He'd been carrying me for a while, too polite to say. He'd kept me running sections I'd otherwise have hiked. But Alex and Otto Copping turned up to pace me in, which gave me a boost.

'It's 9.20 a.m. on a Sunday morning and Bath tourists look at me in bafflement and probably disgust as I run towards the abbey, the finish,' I wrote. '[I'm] dirty, sweaty and probably only semi-recognisable to my wife and two-year-old daughter in a small clapping crowd. I feel drunk with relief and happiness, massively elated. I can't stop thanking people and laughing weirdly. I don't know how I don't cry.' It had taken me twenty-one hours and twenty-nine minutes and I'd placed third.

I'd run 100 miles! The next day, looking at finish photos online – especially the four who finished after us, arm in arm – the waterworks flowed. Fewer than half the people who started CW100 finished. Running 100 miles had been ouchy. But it felt so good. Had it changed me? You could say that.

I felt like I'd experienced everything on that run: doubt (can I do it?), nerves (will I wee myself?), fear (I will, won't I?), happiness (running is brill), companionship (will you be my friend?), gratitude (thanks for being my friend), confusion (are you actually my friend?), desperation (please be my friend), discomfort (everything hurts now), something very primal (wait, am I a wolf now?), struggle (I don't care, I want to stop), weariness (I want to stop and sleep), resurrection (Oh wow, I suddenly feel amazeballs!), frustration (but there's still twenty miles to go!), euphoria (I'm going to finish this!), satisfaction (I have finished this!) and a deep sense of peace afterwards (this way for a hug, everyone!).

No one sums it up better than US ultrarunning legend Ann Trason, who said running 100 miles is like living a lifetime in one day.

I wanted more. And I was about to get it. I had a place at 2014's 268-mile Spine Race.

5

THE SPINE RACE AND OTHER MISHAPS

'I didn't know where I was, what I was doing.'

I had a magazine commission to run a sub-three-hour marathon two weeks after my first 100-mile run. 2013's inaugural Bournemouth Marathon started well enough, with natural exuberance and sugary drinks pushing me along at the requisite six-and-a-half-minute-mile pace. With an hour gone I was still on target, but the struggle was getting real. On a secluded stretch I spied a fellow runner caught short and watering the plants. He apologised, needlessly, and we laughed it off. But as we ran together I realised it was the inappropriately named Jez Bragg, the UK's top ultrarunner. He'd won UTMB and recently set a record for a hugely inspiring fifty-three-day run down the length of New Zealand.

I was star-struck and behaved like the obsessive fan in *I'm Alan Partridge*, peppering him with questions. But after he ducked off to the toilet again, this time in more formal facilities, I let him run in peace.

'I'm going to beat Jez Bragg!' I said to myself in disbelief. I didn't, of course. At about twenty-two miles, Jez (who, an obsessive fan would know, also came to ultramarathons from a hiking background and clocked the same debut marathon time as me) sauntered past, wishing me luck, but further denting motivation.

Talking of incentives, I wouldn't get paid for the story if I didn't run a sub-three-hour marathon. That's perhaps why I haven't DNFed an ultramarathon yet. Most of my early challenges and races were magazine stories, where sometimes a photographer also might not get paid if we didn't achieve what we'd proposed. So I got it done. It's not the money. I hate letting people down.

Running 261 miles takes some motivation too. (Incidentally, the Pennine Way is officially 268 miles, but that includes some optional detours, which the Spine Race doesn't take, though Mike Hartley included the 2.5-mile out and back to the Cheviot summit. So both the Spine and Mike's record are closer to 261.)

When I first heard of the Spine Race, which calls itself 'Britain's most brutal race', a single-stage format (so the clock is always ticking) along the Pennine Way in January, it sounded like utter insanity, and totally compelling. 'It's almost perfect in its cruelty,' said race co-founder Scott Gilmour. With my emotional and professional investment in the legendary trail and a new but intense curiosity about distance running and how far it was possible to go, the idea didn't just catch my attention but grabbed it in its jaws and wouldn't let go.

I remembered occasional Twitter updates from the first race in 2012: so and so had arrived at the checkpoint in Hawes. I'd go to work, come home, eat dinner and just before bed learn so and so had arrived in Alston. The next day Bellingham. It went on and on for up to seven days. All that time in darkness and biblical weather. All that suffering. Would anyone make it to Kirk Yetholm? From eleven intrepid starters that first year, just three got to the finish.

The second year saw the start list jump to thirty. Again, I followed the tweets with my imagination aflame. What were those people going through? Was it anything like Luke Skywalker lost on Hoth or Scott struggling in the Antarctic? This time fourteen people made it to the finish.

I pored avidly over Spiners' blogs till I knew their stories by heart. There were tales of frozen water bottles, trench foot, hallucinations … 'I didn't know where I was, what I was doing,' David Lee wrote of his desperate sleep deprivation. 'I didn't know I was taking part in this event.' There was something about the next-level voluntary torture, playing a game of survival, that fascinated me. It seemed both totally unnecessary and yet heroic. It was so compelling as a follower. What must it be like as a runner? Could *I* possibly hack it?

Sign up for the things that scare you, right?

My training plan suggested back-to-back-to-back forty-mile runs, which I know now is pretty idiotic. But I did it, just about, via some 4 a.m. alarms. I was invited out for Christmas drinks by some colleagues at Future Publishing. It was agonising to say no thanks, but the running was more important. Fatigue, I thought, validated the idea I was training well. Like the Grinch, the Spine kind of ruined Christmas. I was too fearful of the challenge ahead, too obsessed with kit and training to relax with family.

After two experimental years, the third Spine Race in 2014 mushroomed to a start list of seventy-five. Online tracking was introduced, primarily for safety. But it was excellent marketing too and friends would later tell me they spent long hours watching my dot, or 'Daddy's wiggly line' as my two-year-old daughter called it (and it did get very wiggly).

Competitors are allowed seven days to travel the Pennine Way. There are five main checkpoints, roughly every twenty-four hours, providing hot meals, medical support and a place to sleep (sometimes on a wooden floor), though athletes must otherwise be self-sufficient, carrying a huge mandatory kit upwards of five kilograms. You're allowed a resupply or drop bag that's ferried on ahead of you. In Edale the night before the race the other contestants looked calm but the briefing was mostly about how to avoid dying.

We set off on a cloudy morning but with sunshine forecast – at least Charlie Sproson thought so: my future friend is still the only person to start the Spine Race in shorts. We ran across snow and 'treacherous icy flagstones, through energy-sapping mud and over fields that had morphed into lakes during one of the wettest Januarys on record,' Nick Mead would write on the *Guardian*'s website. Conditions were causing broken trekking poles, hips and wrists, with Mark Hines, author of several books on ultramarathons, an early DNF. I ran all of the first day with Nick, who had his brother supporting him in a camper van (as was allowed at the time).

I got less than three hours' sleep in my tent on a f-f-f-freezing Ickornshaw Moor. At lunchtime I bought a large slab of lemon drizzle cake in Malham, possibly the best decision I made in the race.

The weather deteriorated – 'Absolutely horrendous conditions', tweeted Scott Gilmour – and the rocky Pen-y-ghent became an icy scramble in the dark. I was topographically confused when Mark 'Bez' Berry and David Carr, who I'd shared my cake with earlier, caught up with me. They were great company, but I was holding them up. However, the two saints insisted on sticking with me. They either thought I wasn't safe on my own or hoped I had more cake. There were hours of stinging rain and aggressive wind, sore feet on icy rocks, deep weariness and, when we finally got to Hawes at 11 p.m., tears.

Eight grown men openly cried at the checkpoint that night (no women did, it was pointed out to me later). The village hall looked like a disaster zone, with bags, kit and traumatised faces everywhere. 'You fucking well will finish this race!' said the Spine's Mother Superior, Nici Griffin, which was what I needed. Well, that, dry socks, a gallon of tea and some sleep.

I tried to grab some on a wooden floor, but didn't get much. I heard Nici on the phone. 'Does anyone speak any Spanish?' she yelled. It was 2013 race-winner Eugeni Roselló Solé calling in a DNF from the Tan Hill Inn with hypothermia. The previous year he'd finished with footballs of ice attached to his shoes. Charlie would DNF here; Nick had DNFed at Pen-y-ghent. In my emotional and fatigued state, these bits of news felt catastrophic.

I left as daylight broke, inside the top ten. I felt shellshocked; it was every bit as hard as I had fantasised. The afternoon sun splashed across the moors and I got my mojo back after a big bag of chips from the lonely Tan Hill Inn. I caught glimpses of Andy Mouncey behind and though company felt inviting, I wasn't just thinking about completing now. I was starting to cautiously think about competing. So I didn't let him catch up.

I left the Middleton-in-Teesdale checkpoint, just over halfway, at about 3 a.m., under magical falling snowflakes. I was surprised to realise I felt inexplicably amazing. Sure, I had generic complaints and discomforts and kinesiology tape all over my feet. But hunched up in my waterproof I felt bizarrely happy. I was having an adventure. I was surviving.

The sky lightened as I hit Hick Cup Nick, a huge glaciated canyon and one of the greatest views in England. On the way down to Dufton, I felt an almost alarming level of happiness and surreal euphoria. These were extinguished by the bastard named Cross Fell. The highest and officially coldest place in England outside the Lake District was plastered in snow and the path kept vanishing. In Greg's Hut I was plied with noodles, chocolate and good cheer by Spine legends John Bamber and Paul Shorrock. I was learning that it's the amazing staff and volunteers who give this event such a special atmosphere.

I left checkpoint four, near Alston (176 miles in), at 1 a.m. Till then I had physical fatigue; from there I was mentally fatigued too. I had no idea what day it was and charging my phone seemed really complicated. I thought I saw ultra celebs Mimi Anderson (also a DNF) and Mark Hines there. But I was losing trust in what my eyes were telling me.

That weird and delicious euphoria returned just in time for the tortuous ups and downs of Hadrian's Wall. When a lady approached across a field, offering tea and a bacon roll, I thought I must be hallucinating. The amazing woman fed every Spiner that year and has done so every year since, despite being nothing officially to do with the race. Locals gave me unsolicited food and drink at other times too. There's something about people striving to do extraordinary/ridiculous things that attracts others. Perhaps it's the same reason Romans went to the Colosseum to witness gladiators having their arm munched on by a lion. But perhaps there are still lots of kind people in the world.

Towards the end of the penultimate day, unbelievably I was gaining on third place. Instead of sleeping at the final checkpoint in Bellingham, after a plate of pasta and a couple of teas, I decided to give chase. At first, I flew. But then a lethargy bomb went off. Sleep deprivation conspired with a huge calorie deficit to whack me over the head with a giant mallet. I tried a power nap three times. But it was too cold and a little voice in my head suggested I might never wake up again. So I trudged pitifully onwards, staggering like Skywalker on Hoth, fighting against the force.

Up on the Cheviots, I saw huge red Chinese lanterns being set off from a nearby hilltop and began to follow them. But when I checked my GPS, I was way off route. Embarrassing enough when thousands may be watching your dot online, but even more so if you've written a guidebook for the very trail you're not on. I trudged round in confused boggy circles till grey daylight finally arrived. Ahead of me, rocks turned into people and weird serpentine shapes, only to disappear again (I hadn't yet twigged that the lanterns had never existed). I felt like I hadn't seen another human for days.

In an emergency hut I stopped for a brew, and woke with my head sliding down the wall towards the flames of my gas cooker. I had no water anyway. A combination of ibuprofen and paracetamol wasn't preventing my knee from hurting. Or my shins. Or hips. I was a wreck; I cried and cried out loud. It was a lovely day. But the fatigue, the emotional rawness, the desperation for it to be over, were almost overwhelming.

On the afternoon of day six, when I finally reached the road near Kirk Yetholm, a local runner joined me, saying 'I wanted to see what people who do the Spine look like.' (Neil Rutherford would later become a Spiner too.) After kissing the wall of the Border Hotel and getting a medal from Mark Hines, I was bought a pint of orange and lemonade (alcohol didn't seem wise) and a cake.

It felt like I had some kind of traumatic stress. It had been a real adventure (albeit with a tangible safety net) that had put me through the emotional shredder, tested me, frightened me, humbled me, reduced me to tears, but ultimately made me feel alive. Exactly what I wanted. The sense of satisfaction was huge.

That year thirty of the seventy-five starters finished the race. 'After 127 hours and 11 minutes, with a lot of luck and many moments of generous help from others, I finished the 2014 Spine Race, in a very surprising fourth place,' I wrote on the *Telegraph* website. 'I struggle, even weeks later, to describe just how good that feeling is. And why, exactly, I'm desperate to do it all again.'

'[The Spine] isn't just a foot race,' I wrote on the *Guardian*'s running blog. 'For some, it's an obsession. I struggle to contain and explain the effect the Spine has on me. It's a combination of three of my greatest passions: the Pennine Way, distance running and getting unrecognisably muddy. Almost all of us need more adventure, more wildness, more exercise, more bogs in our lives. And there are few better ways of getting all than the brilliant Spine Race.

'Above all, it's that immense sense of freedom, powerful sense of mission, glorious feeling of being in wild, rugged and remote places with like-minded people, high on endorphins and too many caffeine gels and wonderful, rare simplicity of days that I'll enjoy. Swapping screens and bleeping technology for moody moorlands, enigmatic rock formations and melodramatic skies, for a whole magnificent week.'

I couldn't run for several weeks afterwards, as the tendons around the front of my ankles and shins were angry. I went down a T-shirt size, from medium to small. I had disgusting night sweats, jumping out of bed in the middle of the night to sort out my kit in a panic. My big toe has been weird ever since and rebels against the idea of having a toenail. When any race or challenge gets hurty, I simply ask, 'Is it as hard as that first Spine Race? Nope? Well, crack on then, you whinging wussbag!'

Something about it seemed to suit me. The race psychologist (I've never done another race that has a psychologist on the staff) Dr Fiona Beddoes-Jones thought the key skill for those who did well was their adaptability. She also thought my sense of humour had helped. Which would be a first.

I also felt the challenge had tapped more into my experience as a trekker than as a runner. The simple things, really: getting calories in (even if I didn't always get it right), staying warm (staying dry is a pipe dream), foot care (I only had one small blister), putting up with stuff (chafing in the bath-suit area) and just generally looking after yourself. Hill experience was much more valuable than knowing what my VO_2 max was. When the Spine bubble burst and post-adventure blues hit hard, the only cure was to sign up again.

* * *

Maybe my second full season of ultrarunning was always going to be a difficult second album. But nothing else in 2014 went as hoped. I had my first disappointing race and attempted my first running challenge, also unsuccessful. Our second child, a son, was born in April. Which was unspeakably amazing, but inevitably affected my training. I'm not blaming him exactly. But I guess I sort of am.

The nohtaraM nodnoL (see what they did there?) was one of my favourite ever runs, though. Organised via a Facebook group, around forty runners met near Big Ben at 4 a.m. on the morning of the London Marathon, to run the route backwards. A brilliant combination of anarchy and fun, finished at the race's 'start' not long before the slightly more popular version kicked off.

Around then I read about Steve Way in the *Guardian*, who went from a sixteen-stone, twenty-a-day smoker to running the marathon for England at the Commonwealth Games and breaking the GB 100k road record, both at the age of forty. At thirty-eight that felt inspiring. A close friend also died unexpectedly after being hit by a car while walking on a pavement. Life is short.

Lakeland 50 is a popular fifty-mile race in the Lake District. Despite the uneven playing field of an unmarked course, the race doubled as a rare, official trial for the GB Trail Team, which attracted the country's top ultrarunners. The men's line-up included GB ultrarunners Marcus Scotney, Kim Collison and Lee Kemp, plus Danny Kendall (known for his impressive exploits at Marathon des Sables) and Stuart Mills (known for winning Lakeland 100 twice and his long but compelling blogs). After fourth place at the Spine and third at my first 100-miler, how would I do against the UK's best?

I really hadn't trained much. I remember a rare twenty-mile bimble being so tiring I stumbled into a pub mid-run, desperate for a pint of lemonade. But I'd grown in confidence and there was a small idiotic part of me saying, 'You did well at the Spine and that was 260 miles – how hard can a good result at just fifty miles be?' Very hard, it turns out. Comparing a 260-mile race with a fifty-mile race is like comparing being repeatedly run over by a ten-tonne truck at two miles per hour to being attacked by a madman with a chainsaw. They both hurt a lot. But in very different ways.

At the start I cockily told my good friend, fellow Bath Bat and then-Lakeland-100-record-holder Lizzie Wraith my training hadn't been great but I planned to 'go out hard and hold on'. I should have paid more attention to her raised eyebrows. Both the weather and early pace (six-and-a-quarter-minute miles) at the front were scorching. I idiotically kept Scotney and Kendall in my sights for three miles. Then I bonked. Hard. I walked for a bit in embarrassment, while more sensible runners shot past, including my Bats mates Lizzie and Matt Maynard, who would place second and eighth.

I recovered to place fifteenth. Hardly a disaster, but I was nearly two hours behind the winner Collison. It was a blow to my ego and a useful reminder of how wonderfully humbling ultramarathons can be. After my first disappointing race experience, my thoughts turned for the first time to attempting an established ultra-distance challenge.

The Bats were always telling stories about mirthsome mishaps on 'the Bob' and these stand-alone challenges seemed to have a special aura. I briefly considered a Ramsay Round, but it seemed too daunting. Instead, I fixed my sights on the South Wales Traverse. The seventy-three-mile, thirty-one-summit, 18,000-foot-vert challenge in the Brecon Beacons is the southern Britain equivalent to the Bob Graham, according to Wikipedia and most folk around here, anyway. Alex Copping joined me in surprisingly cold August clag at the start, a small lay-by on a remote road, at 4.20 a.m.

My first undoing was navigation. Map reading has never been my forte – I'm too impetuous and enjoy getting topographically confused to the extent it's often wilful. I didn't know the Beacons at all and the terrain soon had me despairing. Paths and trods were intermittent or non-existent, while rocks, tussocks and bogs all mocked me. It was fell running (i.e. there's no path) and I wasn't a fell runner. One minute you're leaping over a stream or bog that looks like it could swallow you whole, the next scrambling over rocks, or tumbling down a grassy slope so steep you wouldn't dare sledge it. This isn't running in the conventional sense.

It's something much more fun (even if you don't always agree at the time).

As I reached the Storey Arms activity centre at midday, the first twenty-four miles had taken eight hours. I was still on course for a twenty-three-hour finish, but every stage had been slower than scheduled, and I had to prance about for Jon, the photographer (who'd also been volunteered as road crew), for a magazine story.

This was my first experience of running to a schedule. You're a slave to a cruel master. Yes, you helped create that master. But you did it in the comfort of your warm, well-lit home, without any real knowledge of what the terrain is really like and when you were listening to the *Top Gun* soundtrack (legally valid mitigating circumstances). You start to hate the schedule. You're always underperforming; it's permanently unimpressed.

It was 8 p.m. when I left Llangynidr, with Jon warning of a superbog on Waun Fach which once needed two men to rescue him. I needed to make up sixty minutes to finish under twenty-four hours. Dwindling sunlight found me on a wonderful long ridge in the Black Mountains. Under a pinky-yellow sky and above a plateau, I tottered along a clear trail, with waves of peaks either side, all exclusively mine. I felt free, happy and alive. And then it all went wrong (again).

Darkness isn't conducive to good navigation or fast running, and on the dreaded Waun Fach my head torch battery dwindled to almost nothing, colluding with fog to make visibility pathetic. It was boggy, tussocky, a labyrinth of deep channels (there's a good path up there now). My feet found air and I face-planted into a bog, taking the map with me. At least I had a GPS. Phew! Then that died.

I was alone in the dark, lost in a mountaintop superbog, with almost no light. I wasn't really enjoying it any more.

I was worried about my torch dying completely before I could locate my crew in Mynydd Du Forest, so I wasn't especially diligent about reaching the summit of Pen Twyn Mawr. Which is my way of saying, I knew I probably hadn't. But I didn't care. More bush-whacking and a disagreement with a thicket of tall stingers, which on my sore legs felt like shards of glass, were the last straw. I was going to quit. Jon and Alex would be pleased, I reasoned. We could all go home. Besides, I was out of batteries, so it wouldn't be safe, would it, to carry on?

It was about 11 p.m. when I finally reached my crew. I didn't directly say I was quitting. But I suggested 'some alternatives' to continuing, such as not continuing right now and instead getting some kip somewhere, then finishing it off in the morning (so we would still have a magazine story of sorts). Or perhaps next week? Next year, then?

Their response was both disappointing (at the time) and perfect (in retrospect). Instead of calling me a big Jessie, as Alex should have, he asked what the weather was like on the tops. 'Really good now, a big moon, almost no wind.' How were my legs? 'Pretty good.' What did I want to eat? 'An apple and a sausage roll would be amazing ... Oh wow, thanks.' I needed batteries? Here you go. Drat. I had no excuses.

My mojo returned briefly. But somewhere after 1 a.m. it buggered off again. Gels failed to defibrillate me and I was hiking flat sections. I realised I might have gone around Lord Hereford's Knob (which didn't register the juvenile titter it normally would) rather than over it. But I didn't care. It seemed an age till I reached snoozing Alex and Jon at the Gospel Pass after 2 a.m. With some eight miles to go, I'd assumed sub-twenty-four hours wasn't possible, but I might as well finish. Alex joined me for the last leg in the mist, but I could barely keep up. I tried desperately to stay in sight of the two luminous stripes on his leggings. After a while I asked, 'Alex, what time is it?'

'3.20 a.m.'

'We've got an hour!'

Holy cowpat, Batman! There was still hope.

I felt as fresh as an out-of-date yoghurt. But in a situation that would give me déjà vu six years later, we were in a race against the clock, in the dark, on the Offa's Dyke National Trail.

With less than three kilometres to go, we were searching despairingly for the crucial turning to take us off the ridge and down to Llanthony's twelfth-century ruined abbey. We found one. But the GPS said we weren't there yet. Should we play it safe or gamble? We gambled (obvs). We hammered it downhill, a knee-juddering descent of several hundred metres, spying the lights of the abbey below. There were going to be just minutes in it. 'There it is!' yelled Alex, waking half of Llanthony. The giant arches of the abbey loomed welcomingly out of the dark. As I finally tagged the ancient wall, Alex said, 'We've got twelve minutes to spare'.

Amid the drama of the dash for glory I'd forgotten about the two missing peaks. It was only when analysing my gpx file a few weeks later that my errors became clear. Because the editor was explicit that stories had to have a successful outcome, the magazine write-up did, dishonestly, imply I'd completed the challenge. Which I'm ashamed of, but I didn't think anyone was harmed by it (other than my reputation, by admitting this). I didn't seek to register a completion anywhere and in October 2020 I finally went back to do it properly.

I returned to Cotswold Way Century in September 2014 with eyes on a win. But again, I didn't get what I hoped for. I hadn't considered England-international ultrarunner Nathan Montague or, to a lesser extent, Patrick Devine-Wright (a good friend of Alex's), who I would place joint second with. Nathan has since become a good friend and is possibly the nicest guy in ultrarunning. He's consistently the first person to message me after a race or challenge and his gratitude and enthusiasm seem relentless.

The following April, Patrick would run a new record on the South West Coast Path, followed a few weeks later by Mark 'Bez' Berry (who I'd met at the Spine): two record attempts I followed with intrigue ...

6

THREE BIG ONES AND AN FKT

'You must have had some pretty shit holidays.'

I couldn't bear the idea of the 2015 Spine Race happening without me. As well as a desperation to be part of the Spine bubble experience again, as the author of the official Pennine Way guide it felt important to be on the Pennine Way in the fiftieth anniversary of our oldest National Trail. It was a big moment in the history of the outdoors in Britain and though my personal history with the trail wasn't even five years old, it already felt intense. This was a personal way of celebrating it.

Matt Green and Ellie West, the hard-working and talented couple behind Summit Fever Media and race photographers the previous year, were also crowdfunding a film about the race. Later in the year I'd appear in a BBC documentary about the Pennine Way with Paul Rose. Though, oddly, me saying 'I love Hawes' was left on the cutting-room floor.

The first year had been merely about completing the Spine. Now I was in Edale to compete. Instead of a giant step into the unknown, I had a good idea about all the gloriously hurty, half-asleep bog-trotting ahead. I revamped the comprehensive kit list (which in 2021 now stands at a whopping twenty-nine items), obsessing over the weight of everything, my spork included.

However, due to a gluteus medius strain (yes, a bad ass), I wasn't able to train properly until six weeks before the Spine. There were no back-to-back-to-back long runs this time. I went out for an all-nighter once, though, clocking twenty-eight miles from home; then, in an effort to 'sleep deprivation train', based on no science whatsoever, tried to go straight into a normal family day. I was in bed at 10 a.m. and a wreck for the rest of the weekend; while bivvying out in the back garden overnight, to test kit, was a confusing sight for my neighbours.

The start was delayed for two hours due to strong winds and they tore into us on the Kinder plateau, turning the Kinder Downfall waterfall into Kinder Upfall. When I complained to Richard Lendon about some private areas becoming uncomfortably cold he callously failed to offer help. This time I kept pace with Pavel Paloncý, Eugeni Roselló Solé and an Irish guy who chatted away amiably. 'Pah. I can beat Pavel,' said Eoin Keith at one point. I thought he was delusional, that Super Pav was invincible. But Eoin would make me eat my thoughts a year later.

At the first main checkpoint, Hebden (forty-six miles in), Pavel snuck out quietly while the rest of us were eating. Eugeni invited me to run with him. I was in awe of the 2013 Spine winner and felt flattered. As we skimmed across fresh snow on the silent moors, we lacked a mutual language but entertained ourselves with a shared joy of what we were doing. '*Soy contento* [I am happy],' said Eugeni. And I felt the same. But a knee problem was getting worse for the Catalan. At the Malham Tarn checkpoint, not unusually, Eugeni was soon stripped down to his little white pants. A medic explained he might have ligament damage and should stop. He was distraught and it was a tearful goodbye. I was in second place, feeling excited but out of my depth.

On Cam Road West it felt like a jumbo jet was trying to land on me. A cannonball of wind sent me tumbling ... uphill. The wind pushed me around like a hairdryer on an ant. It was unlike anything I'd experienced in the Himalaya, the Andes or the Antipodes. Pavel would report seeing rabbits blown through the air. This was before storms in the UK were given official names like Karen or Colin.

At Hawes, the second major checkpoint (108 miles), I asked for a weather forecast. 'Shit!' announced Nici Griffin. 'It's not fucking Barbados, you know.' I'm unsure of Nici's meteorologist qualifications, but she had a good point. I went down for a short nap but woke to discover the race had been paused, due to weather. When we were allowed to continue, I was faffing with kit as Eoin snuck efficiently out the door. The road was flooded. The fields were flooded. At the top of Great Shunner Fell the wind hurtled me along the icy flagstones like I was a shopping trolley. Leaving the summit, I was sent flying into a bog, breaking a pole. I lost sight of Eoin.

The race was paused again at the Middleton-in-Teesdale checkpoint, just over halfway. When it was restarted, I ran with Pavel, my good friend and fellow Bat Tim Laney, and two strangers, Beth Pascall and Mark Townsend (as usual, Eoin had snuck out before us). I was still with Mark and Beth, oblivious to the huge roles they would play in my running career, as we approached a snow-covered High Cup Nick and the sky lightened as a gang of semi-wild ponies galloped joyfully across our path.

Up on the Cross Fell plateau, everything for miles was a perfect white. The wind ripped into us on Little Dun Fell, barging us like we were prop forwards. Wimpishly, I suggested a detour around rather than over the summit. But the other two remained unruffled, jogging stoically onwards.

After barely two hours of broken kip at Alston (180 miles), I learnt Beth and Mark had already left. Because of the race pauses, I had an approximate three-hour advantage over them, so I couldn't let them get far ahead. I was desperate to cling to third place. My ankle had other ideas. 'It's tendonitis, from all the sticky mud,' a medic said, 'possibly ligament damage too'. He suggested I stop. But he taped me up and put me on medication anyway.

The sleep monsters hit hard. I was so tired and paranoid that after receiving a text telling me someone was close behind, I thought a local in Slaggyford was trying to send me the wrong way, helping my pursuer (who turned out to be Tim). When he caught up, my fellow Bat told me he'd recently run into the side of a cow. The fact this wonderfully comical incident didn't even register as amusing at the time perhaps illustrates my state of mind.

We tackled a snow-smothered Hadrian's Wall. Despite another incredible breakfast at Horneystead Farm, I was being overtaken by snails. As well as the shin, which painkillers were failing to mask, I'd succumbed to something much worse: self-pity. I contemplated giving up.

I'd only ever cared about getting on the podium; I'd already proved I could complete the race. In my head I started composing a DNF Facebook update, full of faux-heroic excuses. Arriving at Bellingham checkpoint (forty-three miles to go), I was hoping a medic would advise me to stop again. More than anything, I needed a good snooze and a gallon of tea. I was told the race had been paused again. Best News Ever.

Roomed up with Mark, Beth, Tim, Pavel, Eoin and soon Dales ranger Matt Neale in comfy cabins for some sixteen hours, I slept, ate, showered, slept, ate, had a confusing half-awake paranoid conversation with Tim where I thought everyone was leaving without me, slept, ate, apologised to Tim, then saw a medic. After popping a blood blister under my big toe, she thought I was okay to carry on; more tendon than ligament damage, probably.

At 8 a.m. on day six, the front seven left together, joking about getting to Kirk Yetholm's Border Hotel in time for closing. I'd soon broken two more poles, both Mark's. The ice-cold bogs were an excellent anaesthetic for my throbbing shins and elephantine feet.

Up in the Cheviots, our old foe the wind returned. Then the snow came. 'The conditions were astonishing,' a member of the Border Search and Rescue Unit would later tell *grough.co.uk*, 'possibly the most severe I've ever experienced.' Flagstones became treacherously icy and we took it in turns to tumble over and bump into each other. I felt alive with adventure.

It was dark by the time we reached the second emergency hut and we shared food inside. I felt a little shellshocked. 'This has been one of the best holidays I've ever had,' said Matt. 'You must have had some pretty shit holidays,' retorted Mark. Back outside, the drama increased as Mark complained of heart issues (which were frighteningly real – he had an operation weeks later). 'You're not alone,' Tim reassured him. Feeling helpless, I offered him a gel.

At about 8 p.m., the five of us ran into Kirk Yetholm side by side. I was awash with euphoria and relief, hugging and laughing and smooching the Border Hotel wall – a tradition of mine few have copied. Then inside for ale and chips by the fire, and the far warmer glow of a very testing challenge completed. 'Some of the worst moments of my life have been on the Spine Race,' I wrote in a magazine. 'But so too have some of the very best.'

In Summit Fever Media's film, Beth, looking inexplicably fresh as she's interviewed in the Border Hotel, admits to tears in the race. The Spine, she says, was 'awful'. Then her eyes light up and a guilty smile creases across her face. 'But it was amazing.'

I babbled something semi-drunken about how people need more peat bogs in their life. It would be seven weeks till I could run again.

* * *

After a satisfying podium place at the Spine, I was curious to see how I could do at the Dragon's Back Race, a 180-mile, five-day, multi-stage race down the mountainous spine of Wales. The race had only happened twice before, so there was a real buzz around it. It's generally seen as Britain's next-toughest race, but it's a very different style: navigation is important (you're only handed the map a few minutes before the start each day), it's on proper mountains (by UK standards), but it's definitely a fell race not a trail race (as the race website warned).

A much stronger line-up than the Spine included my friends Lizzie Wraith and Beth Pascall, future Spine-winners Carol Morgan and Sabrina Verjee, GB athlete Joanna Zakrzewski and someone called Jasmin Paris. The men's race included my marathon-running buddy Jez Bragg, Spine-winner Pavel Paloncý, Swedish ace André Jonsson, multi-ultrawinner Ed Catmur, future Fellsman-winner (and future husband to Jasmin) Konrad Rawlik, record-breaking fell runner Jim Mann, and future author and sausage-roll-scoffer Ally Beaven. I was star-struck. Top ten was the height of my ambitions and seemed a long shot.

Mark had urged me to take my training more seriously and get a coach, this time a proper one. GB athlete Marcus Scotney was winning races, including the 2014 Spine Challenger, and seemed a logical choice. Once I could run again post-Spine, we did a lactate test on a treadmill in Sheffield and he created a plan based on heart rate. We got on well (still do), but he (rightly) didn't want me racing yet. So when I did a sneaky local half marathon (and won) he said he'd normally sack someone who did that. I thought he was joking, but he confirmed years later he wasn't.

He also wasn't impressed I was doing a Long Distance Walkers Association 100-mile event just four weeks before the Dragon's Back. LDWA100 was for a magazine story, but I'd thought it a good last 'long run' before my A race. But it was a dumb decision. I was lackadaisical about the challenge and wore the wrong shoes (giving me blisters and Achilles issues and making me slow), the weather wasn't kind, there was pesky navigation involved; and though the event itself had a lovely atmosphere and sensational aid stations, I had a fairly miserable time and couldn't run for a week afterwards. I'd thought it would be comparatively easy (when is running 100 miles ever easy?). Always better to assume these things are going to be really fecken awful, then when they're not, you'll be smiling. It never always gets worse.

'Sixty finisher medals have been made,' Dragon's Back race director Shane Ohly told the 139 competitors, who responded in nervous titters. (He would be only five medals short.)

On an early summit in the clag I was about to head one way when I spotted two runners going in the opposite direction. I sheepishly followed them. 'Them' turned out to be Jasmin and Konrad. When we hit notorious knife-edge ridge Crib Goch, Jasmin disappeared along the top of it into the mist, while the rest of us hugged the rocks like they were our mothers.

I placed fifth on that first day (sixth overall). Day two was going brilliantly (I think I was second in the men's race) till late on, when I made a hilarious nav howler and lost time and placings. Tendonitis started to kick in and I had doubts about finishing.

I had to trim my ambitions. The last three days were spent mostly with Pavel and Beth, a Spine sub-group. Halfway through each day the Jim–Jasmin juggernaut would charge past, and Pavel, like an overexcited puppy, would try and keep up with them. And I'd try and keep up with him (he's good at nav). It could be an uncomfortable hour or three. At one point on day four we passed a guy belting out 'Why, Why, Why, Delilah' as he ran.

Life became wonderfully simple: get up, eat, run up and down some mountains without getting too lost or hurt, get a massage, eat, socialise, eat more, sleep. If I didn't miss my children so much, I could have happily done that for the rest of my life. The scenery was stunning, the weather was mostly brill and each afternoon we tucked into piles of chips, bathed in cold rivers and sat around yakking. The race has numerous wonderful touches, like vegan cuisine, but I especially loved the post-race shindig where, in front of the rest of us, every finisher was individually presented with a much-treasured baby dragon medal. I was very happy to finish third (fifth overall). But more than that, I'd enjoyed the social side of it.

* * *

With podium spots in the two races generally considered to be Britain's toughest, I was feeling content with my year. But I still had Ultra-Trail du Mont-Blanc (UTMB) to come, my first international race and the Champions League final of mountain ultrarunning. My preparation was mostly not doing much running, after knee and tendon issues from the Welsh mountains.

I was looking for opportunities to both get a last long run in and generate a story from a family holiday on the Isle of Wight. I'd been hearing a lot about FKTs on podcasts such as Talk Ultra. US ultra star Scott Jurek had just set a new record on the 2,189-mile Appalachian Trail, the holy grail of FKTs, which had garnered a lot of attention. I'd enjoyed (well, mostly) the South Wales Traverse the previous year and the DIY adventure concept was exciting, more independent and empowering, more of a personal quest than simply signing up for a race and letting them do everything for you bar the running. I noticed the Isle of Wight had a Coast Path. At just over sixty miles (if you don't research it properly) it seemed achievable. And it had no recognised record. It was an FKT open goal.

I didn't treat my first record attempt with the respect it deserved. Firstly, I wasn't sure of the exact distance, which does on reflection seem kind of important. Assuming sixty miles, I hurriedly calculated I could maintain six miles per hour and be back in under twelve hours (error number two). Which is what I told Amy (error number three), who understandably wasn't fully enthused about me leaving her with both children for a full day of what was meant to be a holiday.

I started my attempt from St Helens at 5.50 a.m. There's something deliciously secretive about going out running before everyone else is up; you're experiencing something almost no one else is. Plus there's no one to laugh at your compression shorts. The sun rose from the ocean, bleeding pink and orange across the sky. But I lost the path temporarily in Nettlestone, and doubled back, frustrated. I was irked again in Cowes, having to wait for the chain-operated water taxi. As usual, my emotions mirrored the terrain: up, down and all over the place.

At twenty miles, leg soreness and stiff hips kicked in. At around 11 a.m. I arrived in Yarmouth, at the western end of the north coast, and went into the first shop, emerging with four different types of drink, salty nuts and a quiche. I crested a hill to a wonderful view of The Needles, the island's Stonehenge, and hordes of tourists (yuk). From there I enjoyed a long run along the clifftops. At a campsite, unprompted, a man offered me water. I looked that bad, huh?

My naive optimism has served me well down the years (I wouldn't have signed up for the Spine if I'd pored over the details), but it has got me into trouble too. Amy knows that if I say something is 'about five minutes away', it means twenty (we timed this once to check). After eleven hours of running, at around 4 p.m., I counted the kilometre squares on the map and it turned out I wouldn't be finishing soon. The route was in fact seventy miles and a bit more – another fifteen at least. I wasn't going to see my kids again that day and Amy wasn't thrilled with my incompetent maths and parental neglect when I phoned her. We were both disappointed in me.

Motivation nosedived. I wasn't getting the feedback I'd normally get in a race: supporters, friendly aid-station staff, other runners, knowing I was in a good position. I was on my own. When a local jogger ghosted past me, I looked at my Suunto to see I was doing nine-and-a-half-minute miles, compared to the seven-minute miles I started off at. My iPod Shuffle failed to defibrillate me, as did a gel when I bonked. After some sulking, the golden evening light lifted my mood as I looked back along Whitecliff Bay, knowing I was nearly done. A sprint finish (of sorts) got me back to my start point at 7.59 p.m. There was no one to applaud my heroic/idiotic achievement. Though I quite liked that. It had taken me thirteen hours and forty-nine minutes to run the seventy-three-mile Isle of Wight Coast Path: a stunningly average and eminently beatable time. But, for now at least, it was my FKT.

My debut FKT adventure got better with every flashback. Life is good when all you have to do is run and scoff Mars Bars. Though when I humble-bragged about it on Facebook, Lizzie Wraith rightly questioned how smart it was just eleven days before UTMB.

* * *

You can't do a race in the UK without hearing someone mention UTMB points. The 105-mile circuit from Chamonix, France, through the French, Italian and Swiss Alps on the popular Trail du Mont Blanc hiking route, is so popular you need to earn qualifying points from other races. Everything about UTMB is big: the course (with 32,000 feet of ascent – more than Everest), the crowds, the competition, the whole experience. There are some 2,300 runners in the main event. It's the de facto ultra-, trail- and mountain-running world cup and the best mountain ultra-runners in the world go there.

The UTMB start was like nothing I'd experienced before. Streets and balconies were full to bursting. Anthemic Eurotrash blasted from speakers. Cameras and smartphones were pointed at us like we were famous. In the elite section ahead I spied South Africa's Ryan Sandes, America's Sage Canaday, Spain's Luis Alberto Hernandez and some others I half recognised. (As a football fan I could never be on the same pitch as Thierry Henry, Robert Pires and Nelson Vivas.)

The sun blazed down. A tame eagle soared above our heads and off into the big blue nothingness. Nervous anticipation fizzed and crackled in the air. Finally, the irresistible hum of 'Conquest of Paradise' started, a moment I'd watched countless times on YouTube. There was a countdown from ten. Oh holy crap. And we were released.

I couldn't believe how many people had turned out to watch. Crowds were five or six people deep on either side of the street – waving flags, cheering, filming, ringing cowbells. Car horns tooted. UTMB's hullabaloo is notorious for shooting people off at a kamikaze pace. So I took it easy and only, um, passed 200 people or so in the first five kilometres. My aim was to finish in less than thirty hours, which should get me into the top 100. My good friend Allan Cox had warned that might be a bit too ambitious.

In no time we'd reached the first major checkpoint, Saint-Gervais (twenty-one kilometres), which felt like a music festival. The entry and exit areas were thick with people, bigger crowds than at most UK marathon finishes. The air was heavy with cowbells and shouts of *'Allez, allez, allez!'*, *'Bravo!'* and *'Bon courage!'* I frequently responded with 'merci', which increasingly sounded like 'mercy' as the race went on. Even after dark families were gathered around open fires to cheer us on. I could have been 30th or 300th. It was liberating not knowing. As I power-hiked with my poles, silhouettes of big jagged mountains were on either side, a long line of head torches stretching behind me. I felt good on the climbs, passing people, even if half of them got me back on the subsequent descents.

On the rising road out of La Balme at around forty kilometres, a full moon lit up snow-covered peaks, light enough for me to turn my torch off and rather surprise a peeing Frenchman. I still felt suspiciously good, so I continued to make my way up the field, with a nagging whisper that I might pay for it later. I knew daytime would be hot and I don't like heat so much, so reasoned it'd be smarter to get some miles in before then. I passed perhaps ten people on the climb out of Les Chapieux, including Robbie Britton and Danny Kendall, two of Britain's best ultrarunners. I shouldn't have been ahead of them.

High in the mountains I passed Nathalie Mauclair (who would win the women's race). I started to feel a bit spent on the impolitely steep descent through the trees down to Courmayeur, nearly the halfway point. I'd never run a descent that long before and my legs were groaning. For my sub-thirty-hour schedule I had to get there by 8 a.m. It was 4.30 a.m.

It was surreal suddenly being indoors with bright lights and lots of people, and I felt weary and confused. Trying to refill soft flasks with unsteady hands, I spilled water over the biscuits and the staff were annoyed with me, swearing in Italian. I stayed for twenty minutes, eating a big plate of pasta, but still felt bobbins on departure. I'd been drinking okay but sweating constantly and ten hours in I'd only urinated once. Then I stopped sweating.

After a torturously long climb, across the valley the sun was just starting to illuminate the fearsome Mont Blanc and a fantastical crown of mountains. I stuck my headphones in and, as if by divine intervention, Bruce Springsteen's 'Born to Run' pinged triumphantly into my ears. I checked my phone for the first time. 'You were fortieth at La Balme,' said Allan. 'You were thirty-second when I went to bed,' said Amy. HOLY CRAP, BATMAN! This wasn't meant to happen. I felt really excited. But also fearful. I was out of my league. But damn, it felt good. The good news gave me some zest for the long descent to La Fouly (108 kilometres), where it's said the race really starts. What?! I was wrecked. My quads were sorer than they'd ever been.

I saw Robbie Britton again. 'How are you doing?'

'Bad,' he said.

We ran together. He talked a lot, but I could barely muster conversation. My urine was brown. Not a mellow brown, like Jennifer Aniston's hair. A disturbingly dark brown, like urine definitely shouldn't be. Robbie told me all the terrible things it could be. Did he say imminent kidney failure? Or was my liver buggered? Did Dr Britton (who has become a good friend, something of a coaching mentor and confidant at times) just say I had three minutes to live? I needed to get it checked, but I didn't want to get pulled from the race.

At Champex-Lac (122 kilometres), I semi-reluctantly looked for an English-speaking medic. Charitably avoiding the obvious 'urine trouble' pun, a medic asked me several questions, including: 'Have you been drinking any sports drinks you wouldn't normally drink?' Bingo! I'd been quaffing cola, which I wouldn't normally touch with a trekking pole.

After an awkward scramble-climb section, there were views of a valley a long way below. 'They can't possibly be expecting us to go all that way down there?' I said to myself. Oh but they did. Ouch. Ouch. Ouch. I'd been on my feet for about twenty hours. Still, just one more big climb, right? An English supporter told me that, actually, there were two. I think I kind of swore.

I was out of water on the steep climb from Trient (129 kilometres). It was stinking hot. I wasn't sweating or pissing. I felt dizzy and strange. At the top, Spain's Uxue Fraile Azpeitia (who would finish second lady) caught me. Conveniently ignoring the fact she was probably just as thirsty as me, I felt a growing fury that she wouldn't give me her water. Couldn't she see I was struggling? Thankfully, there was a surprise extra water station. Slurp, slurp, slurp ... burp.

After cursing another quad-crushing 1,000-metre descent to the Vallorcine checkpoint, I saw a runner who had surged past me before Courmayeur, now in tears. His race was over. The lucky git. It was an effort to get going again. But a gaggle of Brits (Richard Ashton's wonderful cheerleaders), spotting the Union Jack and name on my race bib, chanted 'Damooo! Damooo!' I felt so thankful I could cry. But I soon felt dejected again. I must be, what, thirty-ninth? Yet another runner passed me on the penultimate ascent. I was pathetically slow.

I was into the last 10k. I had to cling to fortieth place. It became everything. I kept looking back to see two guys hunting my top-forty spot. Quads. So. Sore. Everything. Sore. In the woods on the final descent my big, soon to be black, toe met rock. I broke a pole. I shouted out loud. Frequently. Some twenty-six and a half hours since I left Chamonix, just as it started to get dark, I was back.

The finish is like the London Marathon, but just for you. The route takes you around the town centre, so you can soak up the atmosphere. People in restaurants, in cars, in the streets applauded and cheered. I was fighting back tears as I high-fived kids; people were taking my photo like I'd won the thing. Richard's cheerleaders were at the famous dark blue arch, as were Allan, his wife and daughter, and my room-mate, photographer James Carnegie.

I had thought about reaching the arch many times over the last twenty-six hours. For reasons that escape me, somewhere in the middle of the night I'd decided to mimic the *Platoon* film poster: on my knees, arms raised, head back. So I shamelessly milked the moment. I thought I was fortieth, but I'd actually placed thirtieth in the men's race (later bumped up to twenty-ninth after Gonzalo Calisto's failed drug test) and third Brit, albeit over five hours behind the winner, Xavier Thévenard. In the results, Allan loved seeing 'Corsham Running Club' next to my name while every runner near me had a sports brand.

The next morning, after checking my urine was back to normal, I met Mark for breakfast. I was so hungry that as we waited for our food, I cleaned up a plate of half-eaten pancakes left on our table. It was inspiring watching the final finishers come into Chamonix, some on their feet for forty-six hours. One of them was seventy-three. The celebratory atmosphere continued into the afternoon as the top ten men and top ten women were presented on stage, getting prizes and applause, including Thévenard, David Laney and Gonzalo Calisto. I stood in awe, worshipping gods. I could never do what they'd done. But I could probably do a bit better. I already knew I'd be back next year. I'd got a new obsession to replace the Spine Race.

To my surprise I was invited on Talk Ultra; wasn't it for proper ultra-runners? Afterwards I asked Ian Corless what races I should think about doing next. He suggested I should largely ignore the domestic scene and concentrate on the more competitive European races.

As luck would have it I was invited, as a journalist, to run The Coastal Challenge, a 240-kilometre multi-stage in Costa Rica, in February 2016. It's not the type of race Ian was suggesting, but it did look likely to be an amazing holiday. As she seemed to know a thing or two about multi-stage races in hotter climes, I asked Elisabet Barnes to coach me and she prepared me well.

The scenery was straight from *National Geographic* and the experience was magical, often camping by the beach as the sun set into the sea, after half a day of running through jungles and up and down little green mountains. The race attracts a small field but some classy runners, including Spanish Olympic marathoner Chema Martínez, South African two-time TCC-winner Iain Don-Wauchope, Portugal's Carlos Sá and Ester Alves, and Ecuadorian Gonzalo Calisto (before his doping ban).

I learnt that these elite, sponsored runners took their refuelling, rest and sleep seriously, but also raced with an attritional intensity. I'd start out each day trying to stick with them, but they'd usually drop me within the hour, and I ended up fifth overall. I grilled them about their training, and especially Gonzalo about UTMB, where he had placed an unfathomable fifth the year before. He told me he ran up hills with a pack on for strength gains. He neglected to mention he'd also taken banned substance EPO.

At a post-race dinner, TCC-winner Ester Alves and I compared racing histories. Impressed with my debut time at UTMB she said, 'Damian, I think you should stop being a journalist who sometimes runs. And instead be a runner who sometimes writes.' The idea percolated in my head on the way back.

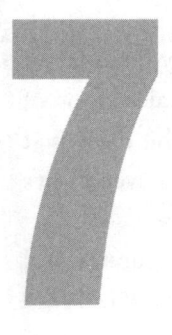

7
FEAR AND LOATHING ON THE SOUTH WEST COAST PATH

'There's something wrong with us. We're hurting ourselves. And we're hurting ourselves because we enjoy it.'

It wasn't like normal snot. It was thicker, slimier, stickier. Like the stuff slugs secrete. And a new colour too: a deep, dull green. I was morbidly intrigued. I honked on my hooter again, but my new-found thrill was short-lived. Now the stuff coming out of my nose was red. More morbid than intriguing.

I had an equal array of unusual colours, textures and smells coming out of the other end too. 'If you get diarrhoea, you've either eaten your own shit or someone else's,' Mark Townsend, medical qualifications unknown, had warned, nine days ago. 'Better if it's your own.' For the first time in my life, I hoped I'd eaten my own shit.

The previous night in the van I'd done a blow-off so powerfully toxic that Mark and Tom Jones (not that one) hadn't found it remotely funny. Three men in a van for over a week and the classic male bottom-burp humour was wearing thin.

My tongue was spotty too, swollen and weirdly tingly. My lips, burnt by the sun, felt twice their normal size and like they were covered in glue. I'd recently also been told my breath was – again without humour – 'rancid'.

As I pulled on my inov-8 Race Ultras just before 5 a.m., they felt like they were full of broken glass. Tendonitis on my shin and heel was being particularly needy. My knees throbbed. Not just when running – all the time now. A previous gluteus medius injury was back.

When I stumbled from the van, groaning like it was my final day of life, I needed trekking poles just to get the biomechanical actions of forward motion going. And it wouldn't be long before the day's first power sob, a new but crucial part of my morning routine. It never always gets worse? Death was fractionally more appealing than this.

'There's something wrong with us,' GB ultramarathon runner and climate activist Dan Lawson would say in 2020 after his LEJOG. 'We're hurting ourselves. And we're hurting ourselves because we enjoy it.' I've since realised I enjoy hurting myself because it makes me feel alive. I wasn't enjoying (feeling alive) that morning.

This was day ten of our perverse and savage quest to set a new speed record on England's longest National Trail, the South West Coast Path, which goes all the way around the country's sticking-out-leg bit, 630 miles from Poole on the south coast to Minehead on the, er, top of the south coast. The distinctly not-flat trail amasses around 115,000 feet of ascent (nearly four times Everest, to use the universal benchmark).

It's rare you get such a strong feeling that your body is unmistakably adamant it doesn't want to do something. That something was getting up and out of the VW Transporter that morning, after just two hours' broken sleep. To run, or at least hobble, along that never-ending, cruelly uppy-downy coastal path.

It was all Mark Townsend's fault. When he first suggested running the South West Coast Path, my initial response was along the lines of 'I'd rather rub my eyes with a cheese grater.' Many times I've wished that, like a vacuous TV quiz show host, he had accepted my first answer.

Mark had run it in 2013 with Julie Gardener, setting a record of fourteen days, fourteen hours and forty-four minutes. If the Bob Graham record is in the Premier League, the SWCP is probably in the Championship (the second division). In April 2015, the south-Devon-based, excellently surnamed Patrick Devine-Wright (who I'd placed joint second with at 2014's Cotswold Way Century) ran a new record of fourteen days, eight hours and two minutes. Little over a month later, north Devon's Mark 'Bez' Berry (who I'd met at 2013's Cotswold Way Century and the 2014

Spine Race) knocked a whopping three days off, completing the trail in eleven days, eight hours and fifteen minutes.

I emailed Patrick to break the news to him. He took a few days to respond and was, understandably, disappointed. It's a tiny bit mean, isn't it, breaking someone's record before they've even uploaded it to Strava? 😉

Mark Townsend was the co-owner of Contours Walking Holidays and wanted to promote his company's new arm, Contours Trail Running Holidays. But, more than that, he wanted the record back. He saw me as an insurance policy: if he couldn't get round, I might. He offered to pay for food, accommodation, petrol for the support van, and even funding for a crew person. This made me suspicious. I hardly knew him. What did he want in return? But he's just one of those really generous people. He also paid for me to be coached by US-based 100-mile ace Ian Sharman. I'm lucky to have met him, and feel really grateful for the input he's had on my running.

Even though Bez's Facebook updates and podcast interviews made running the South West Coast Path sound deceptively like a jolly holiday, it was hugely intimidating. The Spine Race, a mere 260 miles, had steamrollered me. Also, Bez had helped me when I was struggling in the same race, so going for his record seemed like stabbing him in the back.

Cleverly, Mark didn't try to twist my arm when I said no thanks. He just left me to think about it. He also pointed out that runners break friends' records all the time. Later that year Karl Meltzer would break his mate Scott Jurek's on the Appalachian Trail, while in the UK Jasmin Paris would do the same to Nicky Spinks. Over a week or two, the appeal of a huge running adventure superseded the idea that running 630 miles was sheer lunacy. The ideas that scare you are the ones you should go for, right?

I discussed with Amy and my parents whether being absent from my young children, then aged two and five, for two weeks – but hopefully returning with something worthwhile if intangible – was good or bad parenting. Thankfully they all voted for the former. So I said yes. We fixed dates and recruited Tom Jones to crew.

It's hard to find someone who is free for two weeks, let alone understands just how smelly, grumpy and ungrateful the people they're acting as a servant for are going to be. If it was a job advert, no one would apply. Tom, who I'd met briefly at my first Spine Race, fitted the bill perfectly. He was a runner and had no permanent job or home – by choice. He knew the South West well and was passionate about the idea from the off. Which was a relief, because we had no back-up option. We were all set. But wider dramas were happening.

Mark Vaz (what is it about Marks and long-distance running records?) had just been outed as a cheat and it felt like a new era for FKTs. I was frustrated that we didn't have a tracker, to appease any suspicious minds. Mark Townsend hadn't been keen, because it encourages people to join in, which can be a distraction (Karl Meltzer thought the same for his Appalachian Trail FKT), or lead to overexuberant pacing. This was primarily Mark's trip, so I deferred to him. Mark and Tom felt comprehensive notes, photos and gpx tracks were perfectly sufficient, though I also intended to upload to Strava as we went.

I still felt guilty about Bez, and emailed to apologetically let him know about our attempt on his record. He came back full of enthusiasm and said he'd love to join us, though Mark wasn't keen, so I let it slide. Bez had averaged fifty-five miles a day, but two weeks before our attempt Royal Marine 'Baz' (and you thought all the Marks was confusing?) Gray attempted to run the path in ten days. So we had to plan to do the same. Baz looked on target for a few days, but was sadly forced to give up on his fifth day with a knee injury, which was both a relief and a worry (Mark made a sizeable donation to his fundraising).

We too were wary of injury, so our strategy was to move at an easy, sustainable pace, no faster than four miles an hour. Aiming for sixty-three miles per day would only allow for about three hours' sleep a night, we calculated. But injury struck before we even started. With cruel comedy, someone ran a mobility scooter into Mark in a supermarket, knocking him flying, with soup tins bouncing down the aisle. Like something out of *Little Britain*, the perpetrator then legged it. I offered to delay the attempt, but Mark said no.

I was half bricking it and half excited about my longest ever running holiday as we set off from the big blue sculpture by the beach at Poole that signals the official start of the SWCP, at 5.01 a.m. on Saturday 14 May. Tom would drive on ahead, prepare huge scrumptious meals and copious cups of tea, shop for supplies and massage our sore legs (though that bit wasn't contractually binding, he said). The early days of an FKT attempt are like the group stages of a football World Cup, Tom said. 'It's just getting the job done. No need for surprises or overextending yourself.'

That first day was jubilant. We clocked up 66.5 miles (a 3–0 win) in the sun as the path rose and fell beside the Dorset sea all the way to Abbotsbury. Tom kept spirits high with fish and chips in the evening (kept warm in his down jacket) and general puppyish enthusiasm. He would go to huge lengths to get our van parked as close to the path as possible – often befriending local fishermen and even traffic wardens. Locals would turn up with hot food or hand me cash for my fundraising (for my godmother, who was dying of cancer in America). All Tom's doing. Finally getting our heads down some time after midnight, my Suunto helpfully recommended 111 hours of recovery time. We'd allowed ourselves a generous four hours' sleep. It felt like the start of the perfect running adventure. We'd never do so well again.

Day two felt tougher, predictably, as muscles and tendons announced their reluctance to repeat the task. The afternoon heat didn't help; nor did countless steps, which made my right knee wince worryingly on descents. But the scenery was wondrous: steep sea-batted cliffs to one side; gorgeous, curvy greenery to the right.

I loved the glorious simplicity of having no other task to do all day than simply run. Trail running keeps you in the present – Buddhists would approve. The mind wipes clean and starts over, with dive-bombing seagulls, sunbathing seals and mischievous clouds replacing previously nagging concerns about unanswered emails and unpaid credit-card bills. None of the rabbits or bees expect anything from you. The cliffs don't care who you are. There's little to distract you from the task at hand. In a happy daze we ran past coy coves, wild sand dunes (infuriating to run in, mind) and timeless beaches.

That said, we weren't exactly stopping to build sandcastles. The pressure to keep miles ticking over was ever present. The SWCP is relentlessly up and down, which makes for some slow going. In fact we were finding that rather than trying to keep below four miles an hour, it was hard to reach that target. Still, we accumulated 57.3 miles to Sheldon, a perfectly acceptable shift.

On day three we managed just fifty-three miles, to Salcombe. We attributed this to a lost hour at a ferry crossing at Dartmouth. Indeed, ferry crossings were an unwanted complication. If a boat wasn't running when we needed it, we'd drive round to the other side – as previous SWCP FKT runners had done – which always took longer. The heat and long sections on tarmac slowed us too, and made our feet sore. Mark is an insomniac and hadn't slept at all the previous two nights.

Devon-based *Running with the Kenyans* author Adharanand Finn joined us for a bit on day four and told us he was researching for a book on ultrarunning. We were very tired, doubtless smelt like a tip, and I'm surprised we didn't put him off. We only managed forty-five miles. As well as ferries, we blamed wretched, grey Plymouth and all its tarmac. We scrapped the madcap ten-day idea and just aimed to remain ahead of the FKT, which we'd slipped behind by a couple of hours. Mark's beleaguered knee was kicking up a fuss. We had a full five hours' rest in an effort to help it mend. He got about an hour's sleep.

It was on the morning of day five, coming into Looe in the rain, that Mark first talked about quitting. Three times that day I insisted it shouldn't be an emotional decision; we should think it over; he should keep going while the record was still possible. At one point he told me to 'Go on, fuck off.'

We laughed, though, after a misunderstanding at a toilet stop. While Mark splashed his boots, I decided to grab us some refreshments, without telling him. I was stuck in the queue when I saw Mark leave the toilets, look around, decide I'd gone on ahead and give chase. I followed as soon as I could, spilling hot takeaway tea down my arms. It took me at least a mile to catch him.

Mark's incredibly determined. Dragon's Back, Tor des Géants, he's done all the biggest, baddest races, and once refused to give up during UTMB after a mid-race stroke. I hated the fact I sometimes secretly wanted him to quit now. He'd been so kind in funding the trip and inviting me along, but we were slipping further behind Bez's record. And he might be doing himself some real damage. Finally, five miles short of halfway, after two days of limbo and our lowest mileage, Mark announced that he was stopping.

It was really emotional, in that awkward, British, male way. 'You'd better fucking set this FKT now,' he said. And he wasn't joking. That phrase ricocheted about my head over the next few days. I didn't need reminding of his emotional and fiscal investment. I wanted success too. It wasn't an easy time for my wife, at home with two young children. Or for Tom, who'd slept as little as me, and worked even harder. I owed it to them to do all I could.

Matt and Ellie Green from Summit Fever Media arrived late on that sixth day, to make a short film, *Salt & Dirt*. It was a welcome distraction and they freshened up the dynamic. We'd all been getting on each other's nerves a bit and there was some friction as Mark muscled in on Tom's crewing. After some sleep, a refreshed Mark was back to cracking jokes about how awful my breath was.

I felt paradoxically both liberated and pressured. I had to clock up sixty miles a day for the next five days to be sure of a new record. My first full day solo, day seven, was beautiful, with beaches stolen from the Mediterranean. Passing bleak Land's End, I saw a fox chasing a rabbit in the thick mist. It felt like the edge of the world.

It felt otherworldly running past huge eerie lighthouses on the Lizard peninsula late at night, their haunting sirens and expansive sci-fi disco lights filling the sky. I thought I was comfortably on track for sixty miles. My reward would be bed before midnight – the biggest treat I could imagine at the time. But Mark had miscalculated. Actually, I needed to do not six more miles but eleven – which could be three hours. I felt overwhelmed by the task and I was worried about wet clifftops and tired legs in a storm. I thought of worst-case scenarios and of my children. We didn't fall out as such. But we didn't depart on good terms.

The three hours to tiny Zennor were some of the worst of the lot. It was 2 a.m., raining hard, boggy, soggy, confusing nav, dispiriting in every way. Heroic Tom thoughtfully ran out to meet me. Seeing I was rattled, Mark said, 'I'm sure Amy must be really proud of you.' All I could think was, she'd probably rather I was at home, helping with the kids.

Amy can gauge how well a running challenge is going by how soon the emotional SMS texts start arriving. If she gets none, she knows everything's okay. 'Hey honey, how are you? Have the kids done any wees in amusing public places today?' means I'm getting a bit weary. 'I love you all and miss you all' means, oh crap, things are really bad. She got a text like that that day.

She should of course have said something like, 'Shut up, you pathetic wimp. You're always going on about how much you love running and now you're getting the chance to run all day, you're whinging about it. Pull up your big-boy pants and get on with it.' Instead she was supportive, sending me funny pics of our kids and telling me all the amusing public places they'd urinated.

I got used to starting at 5 a.m. and not always being done by 2 a.m. Mark, usually obsessive about details due to his Asperger's, never got the mileage wrong again. He was the run's mastermind, calmly explaining at midnight that if I wanted to set a record I needed to go out for a couple more hours. Sometimes I did and sometimes I didn't. It was a record so few people knew about, let alone cared about. But in our bubble of crazed sleeplessness it had come to mean everything.

Day eight, from Zennor to Porthcothan, was more runnable, apart from the cursed sand dunes. I was treated to pizza in Newquay, though it was a culture shock to hit it on Saturday night and be surrounded by what you might euphemistically call revellers. I can't express how badly I longed to get to the van. Once I was asleep it felt like only minutes before the cruel alarm went off. But the ten or twenty minutes from arriving at the van to when I lay down, spent eating, drinking and trying to make my feet look like feet again, were so precious – the only time I wasn't either moving or sleeping.

We knew the Padstow ferry might be a tricky transition point and

Mark and Tom drove ahead to suss it out. Mark phoned to ask how far away I was. The ferries weren't regular and one was waiting. I could see houses ahead, so I said, 'Maybe five minutes?'

'Okay, we'll hold the ferry.'

Ten minutes later, when it had clearly transpired that those houses were not Padstow, Mark called again. 'Er, how far away now?'

'I don't know! Another five?'

For the next ten minutes, I did some of my fastest running (in truth, probably eight-minute miles at best) of the whole South West Coast Path.

When I finally tumbled on to the small passenger ferry and breathlessly apologised to the patient crew, I'd kept them all waiting for twenty-plus minutes. Thankfully the passengers were endurance junkies too, of the two-wheeled variety, and peppered me with questions.

I never genuinely thought of giving up. It just wasn't an option. I was doing it because Mark couldn't. But I got pretty despondent. Day nine's huge cliffs after atmospheric Tintagel, each one like an individual mountain, slowed me up again and I needed a gentle talking to that evening. Mark was good at that.

'You're doing well, really well,' he would say in an avuncular tone. 'But if you could just be a tiny bit quicker, just get a handful more miles out of the day ... '

The four-miles-an-hour/sixty-miles-a-day target was a millstone, always just out of grasp. It felt like I'd never get to Minehead, a place I was beginning to think didn't really exist.

I can't remember which day I first cried on, but it was probably that one. I was tired. I missed my children and had become convinced being away from them was abysmal parenting. My power sobs lasted just five – okay, ten – seconds. The catharsis was immediate. The mornings became my golden time. The previous day's niggles would magically vanish and I'd feel like I could run forever. On day eight I remember feeling almost alarmingly fantastic. My body had admitted this was what it did now.

Endurance challenges are mostly psychological. I didn't have any real physical problems, just niggles. I'd remind myself both Mark and Tom would love to swap places with me and this was the sort of thing you daydream about when enslaved by a desk. People were so kind too, donating to my fundraising, giving free food and ferry rides.

I had enemies, though. Shuffling along a narrow cliff path way past midnight, I rounded a corner and belatedly realised a hedgehog was about to offer a test of penetrability for my Race Ultras. At the last moment, I enacted a clumsy jump-swerve to avoid the little ball of pain, and almost ended the record attempt and my life by plunging off the cliff. The lethality of hedgehogs is underrated.

There was another late-night altercation the next day, in Bude. A lone local was up on the clifftops after pub closing and, surprised by a bright head torch suddenly heading towards him, shouted 'What are you, a bike?' 'I'm running,' I replied, not wanting to be delayed by inane questions. 'Wait!' he said. But I ran on. 'Come here!' he yelled, aggressively, as I passed him. 'I used to run too!' he said, whipping his top off. (Er … ?) 'I'm coming for you!'

He was drunk and it was dark, so I wasn't too concerned. I was more frightened about losing precious time. I kicked up a gear. But we were going downhill on an uneven field. My foot punched air and I went crashing to the ground. When I say the ground, I mean a bramble thicket.

On the floor I'd be disadvantaged in the fight I assumed was coming, so I quickly turned my torch off to give myself time and surprise him.

'Are you okay?' he yelled, to my surprise.

'Er, yeah,' I replied, coursing with adrenaline but relieved he wasn't going to delay me further. I flicked my light back on and jogged on.

'Sorry!' he called after me.

The adrenaline had all gone when I reached Tom and Mark in town. I desperately wanted to get into the van and curl up in the foetal position. The brambles had redecorated my leg with Freddy Krueger-esque slashes. Spotting fresh blood on my hands, Tom was tireless in attending to me. I wasn't as grateful at the time as I should have been. 'Better get going,' said Mark, 'before you get cold.'

I went on till 3 a.m. and had just two hours' sleep. I was ahead of the FKT by a handful of hours. But we wanted it to be certain. I was paranoid that without a tracker we didn't have enough proof. Especially in Cornwall we didn't always have good enough internet reception to upload my gpx data at the end of the day. I'd try for ten minutes, then remember how precious sleep was. Mark and Tom had kept a logbook, I'd taken ample photos, and they both reassured me no one would have good reason to doubt us.

The start of day ten was my lowest point. I felt, and probably looked, like an arthritic ninety-year-old. Two hours' sleep isn't sustainable, regardless of running nearly sixty miles a day. The flat section from over-eagerly named Westward Ho! to Barnstaple was tarmacky and tedious. On Bideford's horribly flat cycle path I finally got four miles to an hour, but I remember pausing, letting my hands slide to my knees ... then the sound of whirring bicycle wheels woke me. My head was slumped sideways on a low wall. How long had I dozed? Ten seconds? Ten minutes? Longer? Balls!

Getting to the van at around 10 p.m., I had another power nap – a planned one this time – fifteen luxurious minutes. And then my secret weapon: custard. Friend and sports dietician Renee McGregor had advised me to eat at least sixty grams of carbs an hour, but to also remember fat, protein and salty foods. I took that to mean just eat all the food: it was often three breakfasts, two lunches, grabbing ice creams, milkshakes, pasties, fish and chips en route. After a few days I was yearning for fresh fruit, then cheese, milk and yoghurt, then salad, fried chicken, avocados ... custard. Tom's special sauce came in paper cups and there were lumps in it. He wouldn't tell me what they were – and still won't. But I ate them all. And I survived. I ate an alarming amount of custard. It may have been what got me through it.

By bedtime at 3 a.m., I'd cracked it. It was the sixty-mile-plus day we'd been waiting for. I had two hours' sleep for the second night in a row. Probably less, as my sleeping mat wasn't thick enough and I'd wake regularly. But finally I'd built a safe twelve hours between me and the current record. With less than fifty miles left.

I left the VW van for the final time. The sun shone and there was celebration in the air as I revisited cherished family-holiday destinations of Woolacombe, Ilfracombe, Lynton/Lynmouth, Exmoor. I gave it everything in those last twenty miles. Well, I went faster than four miles an hour for a bit. I wanted Mark and Tom to be proud of the FKT. My – *our* – time was everything.

I reached Minehead at 8.19 p.m. on Tuesday 24 May, setting a new record of ten days, fifteen hours and eighteen minutes – knocking nearly seventeen hours off Bez's previous best. Sorry, mate.

Beth Pascall's Somerset-based parents and two of their running friends were there. I didn't feel triumphant, really. Just relieved that I could sleep for more than two hours that night. And that the next day I didn't have to run.

That feeling when you're physically spent and so many bits of you are hurt and misshapen and weirdly coloured, and you're close to being psychologically broken, is hard to describe. But it's the best feeling in the world. You've achieved something difficult. It's about feeling alive. And the colour of your snot matters not.

Till then I was really curious about what was possible; in other words, how far could I go? But now I knew the answer: there was no limit. I could go as far as my mind wanted or allowed me to go (with a few caveats about needing cake and legs not falling off).

The drive home was emotional, realising the bubble of adventure was about to pop. There was a definite feeling that I would be doing more things like this. It was an extra dimension to racing. It felt like so much more of an adventure. Naturally we discussed follow-up options and Mark suggested the Pennine Way. My gut reaction was, no way!

It was the first time there had been some media interest in my running. Albeit partly self-instigated, admittedly, to try and promote Contours, which had kind of been forgotten in the deranged hedgehog-dodging saga. I got in the *Telegraph*, the *Guardian*'s running blog and the usual magazines, plus the popular Marathon Talk podcast.

In August 2018 I received an entertaining email from a self-styled adventurer, life coach and personal trainer claiming a new 'Best Known Time'(?) three hours quicker than mine, despite being self-supported (carrying sleeping kit) and stopping at his home in Devon for twelve hours.

The times and dates in his email didn't match those claimed on an Instagram post or his website. But I congratulated him and politely said I'd be intrigued to see his data. (He must have shifted like a, er, cheetah.) Regrettably he didn't have any, but magnanimously was 'Happy to call [mine] an unofficial time ... I didn't use any means of data timing. Not necessary. My life's about the journey.'

Hmm. I left it there.

8

TURNING 'PRO'

'It's only a race.'

If I was going to start taking this long distance lark seriously – to try and compete in rather than just complete the toughest races – I needed a coach. Or at least Mark Townsend said I did. As usual, my surrogate (running) dad was right.

I effing love running and have never had a problem with motivation: 6 a.m., 5 a.m. and even 4 a.m. alarms were common at the time. But without a structured plan I ran mostly aimless miles, which gets you aerobically fit, but doesn't necessarily help you break into the top twenty at UTMB. That needs smarter and more specific training. I needed guidance. But I couldn't afford it. Amazingly, Mark offered to pay for me to be coached by Ian Sharman (and did the same for Beth Pascall). I was uncomfortable with the idea at first. But it was hard to turn down the opportunity.

US-based Brit Sharman is one of the best 100-mile runners around and teaming up with him made me start thinking of myself as an athlete rather than an (over)enthusiastic hobbyist. I even bought one of those foam rollers with knobbly bits on. If I was trying to do this stuff seriously, at forty, I probably didn't have much time before I'd be past my peak. I'd finally found something that seemed to suit me. But I'd found it late in the day. I wanted to be the best I could be ASAFP.

Lee Procter from inov-8, a British running shoe and clothing brand, had given me bits of kit before to test for magazine stories. When he offered me gear for the year, I'm sure he saw me more as a journalist who would appear in magazines and write about the kit I'd used, rather than a record-bothering athlete. But I told myself I was now a sponsored runner, which gave me another level of motivation. Plus some fancy new daps.

The big goals for 2016 were UTMB and the South West Coast Path. But when I learnt the Highland Fling, a popular fifty-three-mile race in Scotland, was to double as a trial for the GB trail-running team, I couldn't resist entering. I still felt bruised from my bellyflop at 2014's Lakeland 50 and this was a chance for some level of redemption, even if I'd still shown no pedigree at the sub-100-mile distance.

In what feels now like a crucial moment, I cancelled a trip to Turkey for a race just two weeks before the Fling. If I was serious about doing my best, I needed to race less. Thanks to a full year of uninterrupted training, some super-compensation from The Coastal Challenge and fifty miles over a weekend on the Ridgeway with Bevo (for a magazine story), I felt fitter than ever. The fitness cake was iced with productive long runs with Lizzie Wraith in the Brecon Beacons and Nathan Montague on the Ridgeway. Crucially Ian Sharman lectured me on how to race. 'Typically in competitive ultra races, the person leading at halfway doesn't end up being the winner,' he said. 'It's more likely to be the person who slows down the least, who has a stronger second half.'

'The depth of talent is arguably the best that any UK ultra has ever seen,' read a Highland Fling preview in *Athletics Weekly*. 'The men's race is stacked … at least ten athletes will be vying for that record of 7:02:50 and the UK title.' They included GB mountain runner and 2:20-marathoner Joe Symonds, Lakeland 50 winner and GB ultrarunner Kim Collison, GB ultrarunner Robbie Britton, UTMB-winner Jez Bragg, Lakeland-50-winner Jayson Cavill, Lakeland-100-winner Paul Tierney and multi-ultra-winner Donnie Campbell. Unlike them, I'd never won an ultra, so I was flattered by a namecheck in 'Other names of interest'. I'd be chuffed with a top ten placing. 'You're just as good as any of them,' Mark SMSed me the night before.

On a deliciously crisp morning, we started from a Milngavie car park and flowed out along the West Highland Way. A group of eager speedsters, including Britton, Collison and Campbell, steamed off. I let them go. I felt unerringly calm.

I fell into stride with Ireland's Eóin Lennon, who had an excellent habit of arriving at gates just before me and opening them. On Ian's advice, I tried not to know my placing, but it was hard not to guess; we were around fifth or sixth.

Over the crest of Conic Hill, Loch Lomond spread out before us, completely still, like glass. The peaks behind were dusted with snow, the sunshine blasting everything into full HD. Eóin was great company, and holding conversation was a sign I wasn't overdoing it. At thirty-four miles, we were eight minutes from the front. Which felt top banana. A relatively technical section – roots, a few boulders, some steps – reminded me of boulder-hopping as a child on rivers in Devon. After a while I realised Eóin was no longer with me. Then I passed Joe Symonds. 'If you've paced it right, it'll feel like others are slowing, coming back to you,' Ian had said.

At the Beinglas checkpoint (forty-one miles), I was in fourth place. It was beyond my expectations. I hadn't considered it till then, but the first three places automatically put a runner forward for GB selection for the IAU Trail World Championships. The idea I would represent my country at anything other than the Hilariously Bad Haircut World Championships was frankly loopy. But there was a slight possibility ...

'How far to the front?' I asked a checkpoint volunteer.

'About ten minutes.' That seemed like a big gap. I felt a little deflated. I was tired. My hips were stiff, my legs heavy. Unknown to me, though Donnie was ten minutes ahead, the other two were much closer. Matt Green from Summit Fever Media was filming the race and I half-heartedly asked how far ahead the next runner was. 'Only about three minutes,' he chirped. Game on!

From that tiny bit of positive information, everything changed. In fact it may even have been the biggest sliding-doors moment in my running career. Tiredness vanished from my legs. Suddenly running felt easy. Round the corner I spotted the ponytailed Robbie Britton. 'You again?' he said, referring to the previous year's UTMB. I was apologetic, but he was a good sport.

TURNING 'PRO'

Adrenaline was pumping as I caught Kim in the woods. We chatted for a bit, before I gradually edged away. Then I had to pause at a road crossing and he caught back up. Which was awkward. Er, hello again. But with just three miles left, I couldn't believe what was happening. This was a British Athletics national championship race and I was second. One day I'll tell my children about this, I thought, how I ran for GB. I felt tearful. Focus, man. Focus!

After what seemed like an eternity, I heard bagpipes. Could it be? I rounded the corner to a red carpet lined by international flags. I charged down it, fighting back sweaty eyes and shouting something indecipherable, fists in the air. I tumbled over the line after six hours, fifty-eight minutes and thirteen seconds, hyper-alive with the drama of the race and giddy with redemption.

Team GB officials were there and I was a new name to them. They made it clear selection wasn't guaranteed and we still needed to apply. I guess the result looked like a fluke, but when I put my application together I realised it was a culmination of several years of passion, curiosity and expert input. I'd worked with four coaches plus a technique coach in Shane Benzie. I spoke to Renee McGregor about nutrition, now saw a physio regularly in Matt Holmes, and had built up four years of barely interrupted training, gradually building to average seventy-plus miles per week. And now Ian Sharman had taught me how to race.

Although it's not my most prestigious result, 2016's Highland Fling is still my best performance. Never has a race gone so smoothly. That day I learnt how to be the fastest tortoise (well, second fastest, after future Munro-record-smasher Donnie Campbell). It was a breakthrough. Was I a 'pro' ultrarunner now? I didn't make a penny from the sport. There's good money in the US and elsewhere in Europe, but the scene is still niche in the UK and from what I can gather (we tend to keep the information close to our chests) there are very few full-time ultrarunners here. Most coach as well, to subsidise moderate sponsorship funding (when I mocked Robbie Britton's big orange cap, he retorted, 'Hey, I get paid to wear this'). Nevertheless, I did what seemed to be the most important thing other elite ultrarunners did: I started up Strava and Instagram accounts.

Two weeks later I was on the South West Coast Path. What a deranged adventure that was. I had loved it, really, I would realise in time: the power sobs, the deceptively dangerous hedgehogs, all that custard. I had another adventure lined up, the daddy of all UK mountain-running challenges: a Bob Graham Round.

Nicky Spinks would be horrified about this. And don't get me wrong, I'd been excited about attempting a Bob ever since – cliché alert – reading *Feet in the Clouds*. But I'm a little bit ashamed to admit I saw the fabled lumpy loop primarily as a training run for UTMB, rather than a goal in itself. My glaringly obvious take-home from the Alps was that I needed to spend more time running in mountains, bashing my quads up on the longest possible descents, the sports science theory being that those myriad micro-tears grow back stronger. UTMB has 32,000 feet of ascent (or vert, as the Americans call it) and the BG has 27,000, though the terrain is much rougher: rock and bog and long wet grass, as opposed to fairly manicured trails. I lived in the Cotswolds and needed to get my legs (and head) used to bigger lumps.

Tradition dictates that a BG is a year-long project, with a recce of each of the five legs de rigeur. 'Unless you immerse yourself in it you will never succeed,' warns Richard Askwith in *Feet in the Clouds*. Indeed few things seem to irritate Lakeland locals more than clueless southerners popping up to have a crack at a BG on spec. I have sympathy for the traditional ethos. However, for me, and most people from the south, that means a lot of time on the M6 and a lot of greenhouse gas emissions, and lot more erosion on the route from all the recces. Plus learning the route beforehand diminishes the sense of adventure when you do step on those hallowed fells for the real thing – as of course does having an entourage of supporters to carry your sangers and do the nav. Though these variables are exactly what attract so many of us to these DIY adventures; you can do it your way, tweaking the jeopardy dial either way. I respect the Bob Graham traditions. But I respectfully disagree with them too.

'I don't think people should put the BG on a bucket list alongside, say, the London Marathon,' says Nicky Spinks. 'They wouldn't be embracing the challenge. They are the sort of people that would like to be able to pay someone to guide them around to simply tick it off. That's not what the Bob Graham is about to me. If you want to do it, you want to do it properly, showing respect for the mountains, the tradition and the challenge. Recce it, find your own support and create your own schedule.'

Luckily I knew Charlie Sproson – not perhaps the most popular name in Bob Graham Club circles. Charlie is a mountain guide from the Lakes, and his company Mountain Run offer guided recce runs on the Bob. He's fully aware this is controversial, a commercialisation of the mountains that some inevitably rally against. But the Lakes has its own microclimate of ethics. GPS watches, trekking poles and course markings are all uncontroversial elsewhere in the UK and even Europe, but somehow irritate some Lakelanders.

It would be just Charlie and me, except for one leg where a friend would join us purely in a social capacity, and we'd have access to kit and nosh at road crossings (bar Wasdale) courtesy of photographer Mick Kenyon. Okay, Charlie was doing the nav. But I didn't want anyone carrying my kit for me. That felt too anaesthetised.

Finally seeing the famous blue door of Keswick's Moot Hall felt like a moment. I'd seen so many photos of fell runners standing weary but triumphant in front of it, not least Jasmin Paris and Nicky Spinks, who'd both broken Bob Graham records in the summer of 2016. We weren't planning on any record-bothering – we started at 8.06 p.m. on a twenty-three-hour schedule. As people leisurely wandered about town on a sunny evening, two grown men dressed like five-year-olds headed off to get muddy in the mountains all night.

Behind Skiddaw the setting sun pierced through the clouds, spreading orange across the fell sides. The rocky, wet descent from Blencathra was just at the edge of my comfort zone and for a moment Hall's Fell had a chance to be nicknamed Hall Fell. At Threlkeld, James 'Pup' Harris joined us, with the sort of annoyingly muscular legs you only get from daily fell running. He admitted to an 'unhealthy obsession with the Bob' and regaled us with tales over the next few hours.

Charlie's nav expertise really came to the fore in the dark and the clag (a Lakeland word for 'you can see bugger all and it's quite cold now').

Everything looked the same to me: long wet grass on steep slopes, little visibility, only occasional trods (alleged paths a fell runner can see but you can't). I didn't especially warm to Fairfield, but when the clag dispersed, it was a beautiful night. Light on the horizon revealed long silver puddles way below and an army of behemoth shapes emerging from the darkness. We said goodbye to James at Dunmail Raise, the changeover between legs two and three (out of five), at about 4.30 a.m. James cycled back to his van and went straight to work for the day, without sleep. I guess that's just what fell runners do.

On leg three bright sunshine blessed the soft lumps around us. But there were effing loads of 'em. Surely we didn't have to summit all those? Oh. Feck. Summits were mostly called Pikes and Stickles. I liked Pike of Stickle, sticking up like a swollen thumb. Blissfully, there was no one else about. It was a lot rockier along there and while Charlie skipped effortlessly across loose stones, they slowed me down, even if my football background came to the fore with a penchant for kicking them.

It was my first time up Scafell Pike, England's highest summit, without getting a soaking. I wasn't looking forward to the notorious scramble at Broad Stand, where people's lives have ended. But with Charlie's calm guidance I survived a climb up the large natural step without a panic attack. We were fifteen minutes ahead of our twenty-three-hour schedule most of the time, but had secretly hoped to pick up the pace. I just couldn't seem to get going. The endless descent to Wasdale was a few metres shy of 1,000 metres, then I spied the monstrous climb up the other side. 'Yewbarrow is one of the key moments of the round,' said Charlie. 'A lot of people give up here.' I could see why.

Yewbarrow took nearly an hour of puffing, panting and cursing. But from the top we could see magnificent Lakeland castles – magnificent till you reminded yourself you needed to go up them all. Especially the nightmarishly massive Great Gable, which we'd been circling flirtatiously for some time. The novelty of going up, up, up, only to go down, down, down, had worn off. 'How many are left, Charlie?' I ask. 'Three or four?'

'Seven.'

Oh FFS. I felt the BG gods mocking me, a bucketlist-ticking southerner dashing up for a quick BG and failing miserably.

We tumbled down to Honister and Mick's mobile tuck shop. Fresh socks and a scoff of Charlie's tofu stir-fry perked me up. Barring disaster, with only three summits left, we would finish under twenty-three hours. Sub-twenty-two was an outside chance. The climb up Dale Head wasn't so bad, knowing it was the last big one.

After dropping sharply down into a picturesque valley, five miles of road felt like fifteen. When we finally reached the edge of Keswick my legs were stiff and my glutes howled. But we legged it down the high street to Moot Hall to tag the famous blue door in a thoroughly unimpressive but perfectly satisfactory time of twenty-one hours and fifty-seven minutes (exactly the same time as Bob Graham Club member no. 82, Charlie Ramsay).

We hugged and I was soon flooded with the familiar cocktail of sweet exhaustion and ouchy euphoria. The resultant fish and chips were the best I'd ever tasted, their enjoyment dampened only temporarily when Pup texted to tell us the tracker showed us missing a summit. In panic, we verbally ticked them off ... then realised he was pulling our legs and sent him some deserved abuse.

I was thrilled to complete a Bob Graham Round, the king of UK off-road running challenges. But over time that morphed into slight disappointment. Mark Townsend said his BG was one of the two best days of his life, alongside his wedding. For me it was a cracking bimble in a lumpy place with fine folk. But by treating it as a training run, I hadn't immersed myself fully in the challenge, in its culture.

When my Bob Graham Club certificate arrived that autumn, it felt anticlimactic and a little bit fraudulent. Maybe it was because I hadn't, as Nicky and Richard warned, really got to know it, or given it my all on an athletic level.

* * *

My attention turned firmly to UTMB and I began visiting the Brecon Beacons regularly, sacrificing a day off work rather than neglecting family at weekends.

I met Dan Doherty in the Beacons. He's basically a monster, who's represented Ireland numerous times at both the mountain (i.e. fell) and trail-running world championships. He was Welsh Fell Running Champion and has placed fifth at the unimaginably ouchy 205-mile Tor des Géants. Dan gave me a proper beasting on our first run together, later admitting he reserves a special route for Beacons virgins. He's been a firm friend ever since (even when I stole his South Wales Traverse record in 2020, though it's merely on loan).

The highest climb/descent in the Beacons is well below 500 metres, while UTMB's are consistently around 1,000 metres, which are hard to replicate in the UK. But Snowdon/Yr Wyddfa, the highest peak in England and Wales, comes closest. I copied Jez Bragg's idea and did reps on it. I woke at 4 a.m., drove for four hours, power-hiked up it in the clag and ran down it four times, then drove home.

The journey home turned into a bit of a nightmare due to roadworks on the M5. The already stressed and weary tendons on my right leg were working the accelerator for hours. A few days later I had to admit I had an Achilles tendon issue and, with both UTMB and the Trail World Championships looming, back off my training.

Yes, four years after running my first marathon dressed as a toilet, I was to represent Great Britain at the age of forty. That was just plain ludicrous and I still didn't believe it would actually happen. But it threw up some complications.

The Trail World Championships is a strange beast. It's a newish concept, in a different place and a different distance every time (sometimes, bizarrely, 50k, just eight kilometres longer than a marathon), your sponsors aren't that interested (because you're wearing another brand's kit), and ultrarunning fans aren't that interested (because it's an exclusive one-off race they can't be a part of). But you do get to represent your country and get a big blue suitcase with a Union Jack on it.

It wasn't till mid-July that the three of us in the team also doing UTMB were asked if it was 'really advisable', having previously been told it was fine. My UTMB obsession was at an advanced stage. I daydreamed about the race every day, watched YouTube videos of Xavier Thévenard arriving triumphant in Chamonix on repeat. I'd long since persuaded Amy we should all go there for a 'family holiday', with travel and accommodation booked. I had work (magazine stories) agreed around it, inov-8 liked that I was doing it and I was fully committed. If forced to pick between the two, I'm not sure I would have picked the Trail World Champs. UTMB is the real world championships. Is it smart to run 100 miles eight weeks before a fifty-mile race? If the second race is the most important, no. But the concerns were being raised too late in the day.

The implicit disapproval of the GB selectors, my ongoing Achilles niggle and lingering fatigue from the South West Coast Path conspired to work against me physically and mentally during UTMB. The elite pen is like a doctor's waiting room on steroids (actually, hopefully not steroids), sizzling with fear, nerves and eyes that say, 'I don't want to be here; my sponsors made me do this.' The idea was to run the first half conservatively, ignore splits and placings, and be stronger in the second half, when others slowed. That approach had been working well for me.

The first climb from Les Houches felt interminable, though, when the previous year it'd been a breeze. My visor dripped with sweat. As I overtook Jez Bragg he joked with Mike Wardian and Rory Bosio that there were already 200 ahead of us. At Saint-Gervais I felt dazed and confused. Trying to release air from my soft flask bulging with fizzy cola, I squirted a spectator full in the face.

I had told myself not to check my phone to see my placing until Courmayeur. But three hours in, I couldn't resist. Ninety-fifth! Blistering barnacles, I'd taken the relaxed approach too literally. I'd be lucky to get in the top fifty. Darkness brought coolness and I began gradually making my way up the field. But on the zigzags down to Les Chapieux my adductor spasmed alarmingly, causing me to cry out and stop.

As the race got quieter in the small hours I found that elusive sweet spot towards the top end of my comfort zone. Dawn revealed huge heroic peaks all around and a spectacular cloud inversion. But it was unbelievably hot climbing up to Champex-Lac. The shadeless climb to La Giète was worse. I was twentieth, and being top twenty felt like everything. I hammered the downhill to Vallorcine, which hurt like hell. Robbie Britton sponged me down. Just one more climb.

I passed a hobbling Caroline Chaverot before the steep climb up La Tête aux Vents. She was struggling with cramps and had DNFed in this same spot last year. She wasn't giving up this time. In fact, she nearly caught me back up. Chamonix glistened below in the magnificent early evening sunlight. If I ignored the hurt, it felt magical beyond description.

My selfish fantasy had been that my two kids, aged two and four, would join me for the last 100-metre run-in. 'This is where you can meet Daddy and run the last bit with me,' I'd said the day before. 'Would you like that?'

'No,' they replied in unison. Why would they? Climbing frames and ice creams are, understandably, many times more appealing than a short jog with a very stinky Daddy. So I didn't think they'd be there. But as I rounded the bend, 'Conquest of Paradise' thrumming through the air, my son was bouncing up and down with excitement (I have a photo of the exact moment on my desk now). He charged at me, almost rugby-tackling me to the floor, closely followed by my daughter, who grabbed my hand and ran. I hoisted my son up, but he wriggled to be put down and run.

Crossing the line with the two of them was the best feeling in the world, the ultimate combination of the things I loved most: my children and, paradoxically, the obsession that so often took me away from them. I was living the fantasy that Allan Cox had put in my head years before. I had finished nineteenth, in twenty-five hours and twelve minutes. I had improved significantly, without breaking myself. Tortoise tactics paying off.

In the late afternoon sunshine, the crowds seemed bigger and louder than the year before. I wasn't in a hurry to move on. I wanted my children to remember it. After a short while, a staff member whispered that perhaps I could consider moving along now. The first woman was about to finish, France's Chaverot. Of course, most of the crowd were there to see her.

TURNING 'PRO'

* * *

When your GB kit arrives in a big blue suitcase it's a special moment. You are an international athlete. Obviously most of it you'll never wear and much of it doesn't fit. But it's still special, trying on the same shorts as Mo Farah wears (they look a lot better on him).

In late October, a male team of six (Tom Owens, Andy Symonds, Donnie Campbell, Kim Collison and Tom Payn) and a female team of five (Beth Pascall, Jo Meek, Sophie Grant, Sally Fawcett and Jo Zakrzewski) with three volunteer support staff travelled out to Braga, Portugal. At Gatwick in my gleaming white GB tracksuit, occasional strangers asked what we were up to and wished us luck. It was a good feeling. At the opening ceremony I felt self-conscious waving our flag so soon after Brexit. But no one booed. Everyone had a cheap chuckle when Andy threw a banana skin in front of the French team.

Peneda-Gerês National Park's 85.5-kilometre course had 5,000 metres of ascent. With the sheer depth of talent and the relatively short ultra-distance I knew a top twenty finish was unlikely. I hoped for something in the twenties to forties, to help the GB team to the podium, where they'd finished in 2015. Some 260 head torches of athletes from thirty-eight countries jostled on the start line and at 5 a.m. we were set free into the darkness. The front runners charged up the first climb with teeth-gnashing ferocity. I hung back a little, to play assassin in the second half.

As sunlight arrived, so too did beautiful mountain scenery. I began making my way through the field. Temperatures would rise to 10 °C hotter than forecast and a section between aid stations seemed longer than anticipated with several of us complaining of dehydration. I passed Kim and Donnie, who were dropping out. Once replenished, I hit a long gradual downhill hard, my chance to make up those places. But then: disaster.

Cramps. I froze. I literally could not move forward. Spectators laughed at me. Finally one of them gave in to the pitiful sight, said she was a 'therapist' and offered help, performing a much appreciated massage on my adductor, which enabled me to shuffle on.

Cramp would return intermittently and I spent the rest of the race meekly letting runners pass me and occasionally stopping to shriek a bit and put myself into various comical shapes to try to stretch out cramping muscles.

I'd learnt to love running partly because it's a solo endeavour. You only let yourself down. But here I was back into team sports. The first three finishers' scores counted towards the team's total. I was in fourth, so it didn't matter hugely that I was having a mare. But then the GB male ahead dropped out. There were only three of the six British males left in the race. Suddenly my placing mattered a lot. The two guys in front were in good positions. I was letting the team, and my country, down.

Dropping out was never an option. But the combination of a profound feeling of disappointing others and my inability to move at any pace faster than a drunken ninety-year-old spiralled me further into what you might euphemistically call a bad mood. I placed fifty- or sixty-something and the GB men's team was just eleventh.

'It's only a race,' said Kim. 'Don't lose your passion, your fire.'

It was the first time I'd had cramp as a runner and sports scientists don't agree what causes it. Though it definitely had something to do with dehydration and lack of electrolytes (when I spasmed at the finish line, salt relieved it instantly), it probably also had something to do with beleaguered muscles from UTMB and a huge year.

I was invited to apply for the team again in 2018, so I did. On Sunday night at the end of the official selection week, I learnt I had been selected. But as a reserve. One of the team needed surgery and if he didn't recover in time, I was in.

I understood their thinking. But I had been in limbo for six months, unable to plan, to commit to other races or even family holidays. And now I was being asked to wait for another three months.

I hated the idea of stalking my mate on Strava too, half-hoping to see missed or aborted runs. I thought about it for a week; then, echoing a decision I made as a seventeen-year-old, I told the selectors no thanks, knowing I probably wouldn't get a chance again.

I didn't have a grudge. And didn't necessarily think I should have been selected (the team went on to win silver medals). I just didn't want to be in limbo any more.

The big blue GB suitcase still sits on top of my wardrobe, mocking me. It's the first thing I see each morning when I wake; a reminder of a humbling high-level bellyflop and a pretty good motivator for getting me out the door on dark mornings.

9

HIGH ON CHARLIE

'Whose fucking idea was this anyway?'

My Achilles tendon got worse over the winter. Being forced to take six weeks off running allowed residual fatigue from the South West Coast Path and a huge year overall, racing from February to October, to finally clear. Aside from Spine recovery, it's been my only significant break from running in eight years.

I resumed full training just five weeks before the Marathon des Sables (MdS), a week-long, 250-kilometre multi-stage race in the Sahara, the ultramarathon best known to the wider world. When I first told my brother-in-law, James, about the Spine Race he said, 'Yeah, but what about that one in the desert?'

MdS wasn't a race I'd been looking to do. Mostly because it costs over £4,000, but also because the one thing that unites most ultrarunners, other than an out-of-control nut butter habit, is snobbery towards the 'Toughest Race on Earth'. That was the name of a TV documentary which followed Olympic gold-medal rower James Cracknell as he took on MdS, and the hyperbolic phrase rightly annoys ultrarunners. There are many, many tougher races. It also has a reputation, this time unfairly, for being a holiday for CEOs. However, via the incredibly generous Mark Townsend, I had the offer of a place.

I came thirteenth, which I was fine with given my limited training. The social side of things made the experience memorable, though, and I had a blast in our tent, with the likes of Twitter's Susie Chan (whose face

I sneezed in in my sleep), sweary Jeff Mitchell and my old buddy Nathan Montague. The best moment of each day, especially towards the end, was waiting for the last tent member to finish, which could be really emotional. Conditions were extremely rudimentary by western standards (we slept in eight-person, open-sided tents, queued up for drinking water and pooed in bags) and I pondered why we'd paid so much to live like really poor people. What did that say about our modern lives?

While we're pondering the bigger questions, surely MdS is an event that can't continue, ethically, in its current format. As well as the flights (almost all of the 1,000-plus runners fly there), around 100 SUVs help transport the camp to a new spot each day, often only a few kilometres away, plus two helicopters circle overheard. The carbon footprint must be unforgivably huge. Similarly, the World Marathon Challenge, where rich or well-sponsored contestants run seven marathons on seven continents in seven days – with a hell of a lot of flying in between – surely can't continue as it is.

My big goal for 2017 was UTMB again. As usual, I'd come away from Chamonix in 2016 with hugely positive vibes but also a nagging feeling I could do better. My training would include Lavaredo Ultra Trail, fast becoming a UTMB dress rehearsal, and a Charlie Ramsay Round, an experience that couldn't have been further removed from a desert full of noisy vehicles.

* * *

Charlie Ramsay completed a Bob Graham Round almost by accident. Having left a family camping holiday in the Lakes in 1977 for a jog up Skiddaw with his mate Boyd Millen (the first person to run a Double Bob Graham), Charlie unwittingly became a mule on Chris Brasher's third attempt at the famous challenge, he told David Lintern in *The Big Rounds*. Brasher dropped out on Yewbarrow, along with Paddy Buckley, but Charlie and a couple of others carried on, returning to Moot Hall in twenty-one hours and fifty-seven minutes. At a celebratory meal afterwards, Chris asked Charlie if there was a Scottish equivalent of the Bob. It got Charlie thinking ...

He had completed the Tranter's Round the same year. With nineteen peaks, thirty-six miles and 20,000 feet of ascent, it wasn't quite the same level of test as a Bob Graham. But Charlie saw how extending it to twenty-four summits and approximately fifty-five miles with 28,500 feet of ascent, would bring it close enough. The following year he completed it, in twenty-three hours and fifty-eight minutes.

Ramsay's Round is harder and at least an hour slower than the Bob. Close to 2,500 people have completed the Lakeland loop. Just ninety-seven people had completed the Ramsay when Charlie Sproson and I set out on our attempt in May 2017. It's significantly more remote than the Bob, with fewer support points. We were attempting it 'on sight' – something Charlie takes deserved pride in – and self-supported (one drop bag). We weren't chasing records. We were chasing adventure.

It was a relief to be underway at 7 p.m. after days obsessing over weather forecasts. 'Are you going all the way?' asked a hiker coming down from the snowy summit of Ben Nevis. We just said yes. It didn't seem like the best use of time to explain our full intentions.

After the dislocated dragon's back of Càrn Mòr Dearg Arête, we tumbled down to an idyllic col where two wild campers were enjoying dinner at dusk. I felt jealous of them being able to linger and enjoy the magical spot. Especially as the huge green wall of Aonach Mòr was ahead of us. The last light of the day painted broad strokes of pink and gold across surrounding peaks, jagged and full of glorious menace. The fact that the handful of people who knew what we were doing were hundreds of miles away felt both liberating and unnerving.

It was getting dark as we tagged Sgùrr Choinnich Mor. On the way to Stob Coire an Laoigh we got trapped in a tosser of a big-block scree field, loose rocks snapping at our ankles. The sky cheered me up, revealing bright sparkly stars reflecting back from the frosty floor, and, later, an extraordinary blood-orange half-moon. This is why we do it.

Dawn started on the distant horizon before 2 a.m. After a long, fun descent to the Loch Treig Dam at nearly 4 a.m., we were twenty minutes behind schedule (which I'd long since dropped – but thankfully I had a photo on my smarter-than-me phone). Spirits jumped when we located our drop bags. I crammed down custard (cashback!), blueberries, flavoured milk, a pastry, several fistfuls of salty nuts, and two cups of tea. And felt sick for the next hour as we climbed Stob Coire Sgrìodain.

Neighbouring peaks were bathed in warm gold. Mist filled the valley bottoms. We shared the magical mountains with a herd of red deer as we plummeted 500 metres down from Chno Dearg and my quads started complaining. Beinn na Lap is another knee-to-chest slog, followed by the most enjoyable, gradual descent of the route. A new landscape was ahead, softer and less jagged, splashed in morning sunlight. 'This is the most beautiful valley I've ever been in,' declared Charlie.

The sky darkened. Volcano-mimicking Sgùrr Eilde Mòr was energy-sapping. We were some twenty minutes behind schedule and going nowhere fast. Niggles, soreness and the increasing difficulty of maintaining good fuelling and pacing were coming into play. We still had ten peaks and 10,000 feet of ascent to drag our protesting backsides up, in about eight hours. It was on Binnein Mòr, though, that our attempt nearly ended.

Charlie's navigational skills were unerringly excellent. But I'd started to feel guilty that he was doing it all. So I started making suggestions. Instead of cutting across a small boulder field to a good ridgeline path, I proffered, why don't we just head straight up the face of Binnein Mòr? It might save time. Charlie must have been very tired, because he foolishly listened to me. It was really, really steep. There was very little to grab hold of: moss, slabs of rock, loose stone. I slipped. Charlie slipped. We both halted our falls. But we could have gone a long way. I didn't make any nav suggestions after that.

My knees were whimpering on the descents. One trip on An Gearanach's (peak eighteen's) out-and-back technical ridge would have been life-insurance-invoking. The inevitable question got asked: 'Whose fucking idea was this anyway?' I told Charlie it was his. (It was probably mine.) He now had a hacking cough and paused regularly to do a cough-dry-puke thing, although some cunning contouring saved us ten minutes and gave us a boost.

But after Sgùrr a'Mhàim (peak twenty-two) we were twenty minutes down on schedule again. The time mattered to us. Sub-twenty-four hours was a huge point of mutually understood pride, the athletic mountain-running standard. But we faced cursed ascents and knee-shuddering descents, false summits, unpronounceable names, sore legs, hail and snow.

Then suddenly there was only one hill left, a benign Mullach nan Coirean. And a rainbow. And glorious early-evening light splashed across curvaceous lumps. Somehow we were back on target and all was right with the world. Not just right, but ruddy-fucking amazing.

As we pelted along the road to the Glen Nevis Youth Hostel, twenty-three hours and twenty-one minutes after we left it, hatred had become happiness, torture had turned to triumph. I may not have enjoyed every single minute of it, but the mental and physical struggle had made it all the more satisfying. It was the perfect combination of a beautiful and remote landscape with a timed challenge, testing enough that there was always jeopardy. We may have had doubts, but we got our reward.

* * *

A month later, standing in a crowded, noisy elite pen in Cortina, Italy, at 10.50 p.m., awaiting the start of the seventy-five-mile Lavaredo Ultra Trail, the contrast couldn't have been more stark. The Ramsay had been just me, a mate and a shedload of big lumps. This was me, a shedload of big(ger) lumps (the Dolomites) and people squashed together like cattle in a market. The 1,500 head torches and reflective attire made Cortina's narrow streets feel like some kind of polite and slightly anxious rave. I won't pretend I wasn't enjoying the ramped-up sense of event and competition.

Lavaredo was a Ultra-Trail World Tour event, the Champions League of global ultra races, attracting the circuit's best. The men's race included America's Seth Swanson, Lithuania's Gediminas Grinius, France's Julien Chorier and Sébastien Chaigneau – all UTMB top ten-ers – plus Norway's Didrik Hermansen and New Zealand's Scott Hawker, who'd had equally impressive results in other international races. Oh, and some guy called Pau Capell.

We were released into the darkness at 11 p.m. and a six-minute-mile dash through town ensued. I tried to keep up, but backed off on the first climb as poles came out with a vengeance. It was annoying losing at least ten places and my old friend Negative Voices started up: *What are you doing here, you imposter? How can you expect to compete with runners who train in the Alps when you live in the Cotswolds?* That happens every race.

Still ascending, we crossed a road where a 100-plus crowd was ringing cowbells and clapping. The descent was gloriously runnable, zigzagging singletrack and I just about managed to hold off the pesky European mountain goats behind. On the second major climb everyone was hiking – quite slowly too. I began to pass people. This was more like it.

When I heard alarmingly loud puffing and panting behind me I recognised the sound. It was the incredible Caroline Chaverot. She doesn't half work hard and she doesn't half make a noise as she does. As she overtook, with her unique hobble style, I stuck with her to see what I could learn. I learnt she was a fast descender, as she bombed the next downhill, making me go faster than felt comfortable. But maybe I wasn't gung-ho enough sometimes? This was a B race. Let's experiment a little, I thought, be less cautious and see what happens. I left her behind.

I love running in the woods in the dark, chasing a pool of light I'll never catch. It was rare I saw anyone or anything but trees, rocks and mud. I had to keep reminding myself I was in a race. I first noticed the altitude as I overtook Scott Hawker. At 4 a.m. as the sky lightened slightly, I passed five or so runners, all suffering. As we reached the mythical towers of the Tre Cime di Lavaredo, the most photographed rock formation in the Dolomites, the sky turned an ethereal silver. Lights from distant small towns twinkled mischievously far below. I was passing sponsored runners. I felt top banana and my instincts told me to go with it. I tried to keep up with Julien Chorier as he torpedoed a long, zigzag descent.

At the halfway checkpoint I was tenth. That was exciting. But I was suddenly anxious too. Now I had something to lose. Sometime later, at a minor checkpoint, staff said I was sixth. That couldn't be right.

There was a mountain stream so cold and pure it was the most delicious thing I've ever drunk (you'll have maybe noticed I tend to think this at least once in every race). I was gaining on a guy ahead, but also being pursued by someone close behind, who turned out to be Romania's Robert Hajnal.

'My best friend is called Damian,' he said, spying my race bib.

'My first cat was called Robert,' I offered in return. 'Let's run together.'

He was out of fuel, so we shared my gels. Whacked up on caffeine and sugar, we approached the final crest. Before us was a sensational scene, a bowl of mountains ringing a deep valley, and at the bottom, lovely Cortina. But Didrik Hermansen was chasing us down hard.

We thundered down the mountain. In trees with no views, the fear of being caught grew. I let Robert go on. He'd insisted we finish together, because I'd shared my food with him, but I didn't want to hold him back (look at me, what a hero). It was painfully steep. Hermansen finally thundered past. I had no hope of matching him.

As we finally emerged from the woods into the edge of Cortina, locals had erected a shower. Ahhh, bliss! But as I stood under it, I saw Sébastien Chaigneau not far behind. Gah! Round the corner I spotted Hermansen again. The three of us raced through town. It was strange and stressful to suddenly be amongst traffic and people. But crowds from local bars cheered as we approached the final stretch, still in the same order, just twenty seconds apart. I tumbled across the finish line in seventh place, exhausted but ecstatic. I can't quite believe it: a top-ten placing in a UTWT race.

For the first time in a mountain ultra my legs, while heavy and grumpy, weren't sore as such. I hadn't blown my quads. It was a breakthrough moment physically, but mentally too. I'd beaten runners who if I'd been a little younger would have been in posters on my wall. They weren't invincible. Even though I felt like an imposter at the next morning's podium presentation, the outlandish idea entered my mind that a top ten at UTMB might just be possible ...

Although maybe not. While UTMB is traditionally the most competitive race of the year, 2017's jamboree was even more so. Kilian Jornet, François D'haene and Xavier Thévenard – who'd won it seven times between them – all returned, joined by American stars Jim Walmsley, Zach Miller, Tim Tollefson, David Laney and Sage Canaday, plus just about anyone who was anyone in the world of ultrarunning. Influential

US-based website *iRunFar.com* hailed it 'the best field ever assembled for a trail ultramarathon'.

I didn't see myself competing with these supermen (my ITRA race ranking was eighty-fourth). My fascination was simply to see how close I – at forty-one (but only five in running years), with two young children, working typical self-employed hours, living in Wiltshire – could get to the professional, full-time runners, with sub-2:20 marathons and regular big-mountain training. I was an outsider, an underdog. I had some rough splits planned. At the top I'd written, 'No pain, no apathy allowed. Smile, you idiot.'

'ATTENTION snow > 2000m and temperature felt -9 °C' said the SMS message from UTMB HQ on race morning. I was thrilled. I'd struggled in 30 °C temperatures previously and classic British conditions suited me. As well as the weather and my best training block, I had another secret weapon: fell-running ledge and fellow inov-8 athlete Nicky Spinks crewing for me – the first time I'd been crewed. I couldn't believe my luck. Until I got to Les Contamines and she wasn't there.

Unknown to me, Spinksy had abandoned her car in unexpectedly heavy traffic and sprinted a kilometre with my heavy crew bag to try and get there. It was my fault, really (and it wasn't a problem). I was ahead of my splits. This time, if I was to do better, I needed to be more ambitious early on – which brought more risk, of course. I enjoyed sharing early miles with fellow Brits Danny Kendall and Andy Symonds. I high-fived my kids at Les Houches, where we'd been staying. With the superstar line-up, the crowds seemed twice as big as usual.

As it got dark and we got into the mountains proper, temperatures dropped. Rain, sleet and snow tested us. I ran with Andy, each reminding the other to hold back a little. Then it began to get surreal. We passed America's David Laney (who'd placed in the top five for the last two years). Then Sage Canaday. Just seeing Nicky in Courmayeur (seventy-eight kilometres), knowing she had my back, gave me a lift. You can't whinge about a sore glute to someone who holds the Double Bob Graham record, has survived cancer twice and bosses cows around all day, can you? You have to feel good leaving Courmayeur. And I did.

The undulating plateau usually has sensational views of Mont Blanc, but it was still dark this time. I passed a few runners, trying not to get overexcited. The arduous climb up to Grand Col Ferret (2,500 metres) gave me a reality check. But I love the long descent to La Fouly, better still in cold wet fog. At the aid station I was in twelfth place. The news was exhilarating and frightening. I remember glancing at my packet of what should have been six macaroons and was confused to see a couple missing. I couldn't recall eating any.

At Switzerland's pretty lakeside village of Champex (123 kilometres), things were getting difficult. I was told there were two runners just ahead, including Spain's Jordi Gamito. I felt obliged to catch them and my poles tangled in their legs as I passed. The climb up La Giète was torturously slow. At the top I got caught by a rejuvenated Gamito. When his jacket dropped from his pack, I stuffed it back in for him. I never saw him again.

I was in a funk. Nicky and the inov-8 guys were so supportive at Trient (140 kilometres). But I was moving slowly. It's clear retrospectively I simply wasn't eating enough. At Vallorcine (150 kilometres) Nicky magicked chips out of thin air, like Jesus. I was still only five minutes from tenth place with one more climb and descent – about two hours – to the finish. I was told Zach Miller wasn't far ahead and looked, according to Robbie Britton, fucking awful. But I could hardly run on the flat. Scott Hawker caught me just before the final descent. Twelfth is okay, all considered, my defeatist mind decided. I just wanted to see my kids. I felt like I'd been 2–0 up but conceded two late goals.

Crowds lined the streets, despite the rain. People in restaurants rose from their tables to applaud. Cowbells rang. They made me feel like I'd won the thing. Amy and the kids had been waiting patiently in the rain, bribed with ice creams. When they rushed to meet me I nearly exploded in tears. We ran the last stretch together, to that hallowed blue arch. I paused to walk the last few metres, trying to make the moment last.

Twelfth is better than nineteenth. Every runner ahead of me was a star name, full-time pros, younger, mostly childless. It felt like a moderate win, especially as the next day I went up on stage to receive a prize for being the first finisher over forty, ahead of US star Jeff Browning.

But I had been in tenth. Despite the stellar line-up, a top-ten place had been possible. That thought would gnaw at me for twelve months. My UTMB obsession, more specifically now an obsession with getting into the top ten, only magnified.

My other thought was, 'Who ate my macaroons?' It must have been that rascally Spinks! Nicky had originally been put in the unenviable position of crewing for two people and when the other guy was struggling, she'd swapped, she claims, some of my macaroons for some of his gels, to try and get him going again. You can, dear reader, believe it was an act of kindness. Or you can believe she's a dyed-in-the-wool macaroon thief. I'm sure I'd have held on to that hallowed tenth place if I'd just had one more macaroon ...

Sometime that autumn Amy would overhear our daughter say, 'Actually, Daddy did quite well at UTMB because there were over 2,000 people and he was the twelfth one.' That broke my heart with happiness.

* * *

I was happy to go self-coached. I wanted to do some higher mileage, more weeks above seventyish miles, to see if it worked for me. I'd occasionally heard other runners mention things like 'six by 600', which meant nothing to me. So that winter I started going with Alex and Otto Copping to Team Bath Athletics Club's state-of-the-art running track.

It was well weird. Coached by Bath Bat Paul King (whose gruelling trunk-training sessions have been a weekly staple ever since), we stood in a line and did funny dances. I think they were called drills. Then we ran round an oval one and a half times, uncomfortably fast, with only very short breaks. We did that five times.

'How many are we doing?' I asked. 'Six, was it?'

'Twelve,' came the reply.

Oh FFS.

It was horrible. But exhilarating, in a way. I was desperate to stick with the others. I was sustaining speeds I hadn't been able to sustain for any length of time on my own the week before. Running with others – crucially, fast others – helped make me run fast (go figure). I liked the slight friction that existed between us. We weren't competing. But also we were. We all shook hands afterwards, after a bit of dry-retching.

2018 kicked off with the irresistible opportunity to run Beyond The Ultimate's Ice Ultra, a five-day, 230-kilometre, multi-stage race in Arctic Sweden, a kind of Marathon des Sables with frostbite. Snowshoes, glow sticks and tampons (excellent kindling, apparently) were on the mandatory kit list. 'This is a very dangerous race,' warned the chief medic at the pre-race briefing, before going into detail about how to avoid frostbite, including susceptibility in men's intimate regions.

Indeed some runners went home early with frostbite, and at the end of the first day's running I found a woman's foot stuck firmly in my armpit, attempting to thaw it out. Even locals called us crazy when it got as cold as -36 °C one morning and Shane Benzie threw hot tea into the air only for it to come back down as snow. On that day I ran with my hands under my armpits to try and warm them, a frozen energy bar sticking out of my mouth.

For the first time in an ultra, I felt pressure to win. It was a small field and I was an invited runner. I needed to prove that status wasn't a laughable mistake. There was one more invited runner too, German paratrooper and obstacle racer Fabian Breitsamer. I identified him pretty quickly, as he shot off from the start line like he'd pickpocketed me. His youthful overexuberance burnt out and unfortunately he developed an injury early on – though he recovered to give me a race on the following days.

The scenery was beyond magical, woods like Narnia, glorious snow everywhere. I saw reindeer and met indigenous Sami herdsmen. Most nights were spent by roaring fires in little log cabins and we were repeatedly told we might see the Northern Lights. After a few nights of skygazing I grew bored of dashed dreams and retired early, prioritising real dreams and recovery. Naturally, the next morning everyone was raving about the incredible streaks of ethereal green across the skies. I won the race (my first ultra win), but I felt like a bit of a loser.

I had the seventy-two-mile Madeira Island Ultra Trail (MIUT) and Mozart 100 (kilometres), both Ultra-Trail World Tour (UTWT) races, as B races to help prep for 2018's UTMB. The first represented a three-quarter UTMB, the second a faster trail race to try and give me some oomph.

In the lead-up I ran a PB of 2:38 at the Manchester Marathon. It was a long way from the sub-2:20 the likes of Tim Tollefson were capable of, but suggested I was in decent shape and the track sessions were paying off. It also qualified me for the England V40 team and gave me another chance for me to reject the establishment, in a statement of rebellion right up there with anyone who's ever worn odd socks.

I loved MIUT. The pre-race music and local dancers, banter with friends, fast and furious early hours. I love night running – the silence, the visual and sonic simplicity of the world, the way no one can see if you've got snot smeared across your face. When it rained, I welcomed the typically British conditions. Daylight brought views of huge green, steep mountains and I gradually moved through the field to fifth place.

That felt huge. I was ranked twenty-third. Another UTWT top ten would prove Laverado wasn't a fluke. I welled up at the thought of reaching the finish line in the top five and telling my kids about it. Even given their standard response then – and now – of 'Shut up, Poo Head'. I was running in spectacular mountains and everything felt right and good. It lasted for a long time. But not forever. Suddenly I was in sixth.

It was a blow. I was mentally tired. I had déjà vu from UTMB, where tenth place had slipped agonisingly out of my grasp.

In the next hour, as the course descended towards the finish in Machico, my mood did the same. Three more runners passed me. It wasn't just that I was sliding down the placings. Or that people could see from the live tracking how badly I'd misjudged my race. Or that the Trail World Championships were two weeks later and it might have been nice to show the selectors what they were missing. It was that the four runners were going so fast and looked so fresh. I felt crushed.

My foul mood dissipated a little as I reached the finish. And when a guy with a microphone said, 'Congratulations, you've finished in sixth place!' I nearly kissed him. It's not fifth. But it's not ninth either. What I had forgotten, in my weary, gel-fuelled, race-obsessed state, was that several shorter races took place at the same time on the same course. Almost all that self-loathing I'd gorged on was groundless. Instantly I was back in the dream-like happy state. Dammit, I love this shit.

I'd been working on my descending – my clear weakness at UTMB – with Shane Benzie, and MIUT felt like vindication. I don't normally pay much attention to Strava, but a glance at my race upload showed I'd accidentally nabbed a long descent segment from previous MIUT and UTMB winner François D'haene. Something was working.

In my last warm-up race before UTMB, Mozart 100, I was thrilled to place second, despite cramping issues. Florian Grasel saved my race by sharing his salt tablets, even though we were fighting for first place, although he couldn't save me from dad-dancing to a Eurotrash soundtrack next to him on the podium later that evening.

I don't know when it was exactly. But I can see how that sometime around 2017 or 2018 I fell in love with what coaches call the process. The races were going well, but it was more about the training, big fun days out in the Beacons especially. At the beginning it had been all about the races. Now I raced to train. It felt like some momentum was building.

10

UNDERDOG AND UNDER BOG

'If you're coming up here tomorrow, bring a body bag.'

If I was to compete with full-time runners at my fourth UTMB in 2018, I needed to be a full-time runner too. Yes, I needed better snaps for Instagram. But I also needed to work less so I could train more and have adequate time for recovery. Else I'd snap.

Fortunately my work (running coaching, freelance writing and subediting) was all remote, so in July and August I went to the Brecon Beacons twice most weeks. Trying to mirror the lumpy UTMB course, I often summited Pen y Fan three times before a twenty-mile run with heavy legs. I turned work opportunities down if they might get in the way of training – not easy when you're battling credit-card debt. I recced the route over three days with Beth Pascall, Jim Mann and Jo Meek. On a family holiday in the French Alps I got up at 5 a.m. to run for three to six hours each day. As usual, I'd given up alcohol, and I trained harder than ever, getting in regular 100-mile weeks with 20,000-foot vert. I almost overdid it. There were hints that UTMB was starting to dominate the family's summer, so I promised I wouldn't do it in 2019.

The obsession felt beyond my control. My cousin's wedding would clash with the race – not just some distant cousin but one I really like (sorry, Tara). Matt and Ellie from Summit Fever Media wanted to turn my UTMB quest into a film. Working with them always just feels like hanging out with (cheese-obsessed) mates. But the success of the project, an expensive gamble for them, would live or die by my race performance.

I seemed so busy in Chamonix: filming, staying on top of coaching work, and appearing at inov-8 events, where Lee introduced me to a crowd saying I was aiming for the top ten. *Trail Running* magazine asked me to write about my preparation for UTMB, in which I made the rookie error of declaring my top-ten ambition. People were shouting 'Good luck for top ten!' across the street.

'One person to watch is the UK's Damian Hall,' read Ian Corless's race preview. 'He is super motivated this year and although I don't think he will make the top five, the chances are high for him to fulfil his top-ten dream.'

It all felt a bit claustrophobic. My final, tension-relieving, run was a little too long and fast. My resting heart rate the day before the race was disconcertingly high and I was a bit tetchy with my film-maker pals. I had no right really, aspiring to be top ten. ITRA ranked me fiftieth.

We went up La Flégère to film and found ourselves in the same cable car as US ace Zach Miller and film-maker Billy Yang, whose film about 2015 UTMB I've watched precisely 17,003 times. The respective camera-fondlers spotted each other's tech and got talking, while I exchanged words with Zach. He'd been there for a couple of weeks and run the route three times. I was a little star-struck. 'Have a strong race, man!' he said as we parted ways. I said I hoped I didn't see him, as it'd mean he was having a bad one.

I possibly didn't sleep at all the night before. But when the day finally arrived, the weather forecast was perfect: rain, below 0 °C, just like the Beacons. I forced myself to watch *Chariots of Fire* to try and relax, and reminded myself this whole situation was my choice. I loved doing this shit.

Chamonix was electric, a sea of smartphones held aloft. After the goosebump-triggering 'Conquest of Paradise', we were off.

Having analysed previous results, I knew I needed to be more ambitious early on. It was ace to catch up with Scotty Hawker as we belted down the Chamonix valley in the peloton with the likes of Miller and Kilian Jornet, Jim Walmsley peacocking out front. The first big climb stretched the field out. I was with Ryan Sandes and Alex Nichols (who would both DNF) in fifteenth place coming into Saint-Gervais.

Top left: Playing at being Robin Hood with my friends Arthur and Tangwyn.
© *Tangwyn Andrews.*

Top right: Summiting Tocllaraju in northern Peru in 2007.

Middle left: Running like I've stolen a drink at the 2011 Bath Half.
© *marathon-photos.com*

Middle centre: Looking a bit flushed at the 2012 Brighton Marathon.
© *marathon-photos.com*

Middle right: A first full experience of the Pennine Way.

Left: Hitting The Wall.
© *Rat Race Adventure Sports.*

Top left: Back on the Pennine Way for the 2014 Spine Race. © *Summit Fever Media.*

Top right: Finishing the 2015 Spine Race, with Beth Pascall, Mark Townsend, Matt Neale and Tim Laney. © *Summit Fever Media.*

Left: Knocking back the nosh on the South West Coast Path, with Summit Fever Media. © *Tom Jones.*

Below: Climbing towards the Minack Theatre on the South West Coast Path. © *Summit Fever Media.*

Top left: A humble and dignified race finish at the Highland Fling. © *Graeme Hewitson (monumentphotos.co.uk).*

Top right: Representing GB at the Trail World Championships with Beth Pascall.

Right: Getting minus points at the Ice Ultra in Arctic Sweden. © *Ice Ultra/Mikkel Beisner.*

Below: With Beth again on the Cape Wrath Trail.

Top: The Bob Graham with Charlie Sproson. © *Mick Kenyon*.

Left: The Charlie Ramsay with Charlie Sproson.

Above: Noodling along with Nicky Spinks on her Double Paddy Buckley Round. © *inov-8.com/Lee Procter*.

Top: Chasing a record with Michael Corrales on the final leg of the Paddy Buckley Round.

Above: Back on the Paddy, this time solo and chasing the winter record. © *inov-8.com/Lee Procter.*

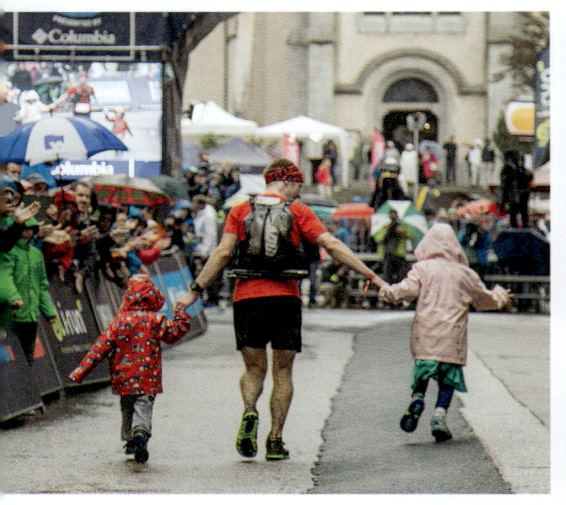

UTMB

Top left: Finishing the 2017 race.
© *Andy Jackson.*

Top right: Hugging it out after a tough one.
© *Matt Brown/inov-8.com*

Right: 'Yeah but have you got any macaroons left?'
© *Andy Jackson.*

Below: The 2018 men's podium.
© *Andy Jackson.*

Pennine Way

Top left: Wall-bothering in Kirk Yetholm. © *inov-8.com/ Dave MacFarlane.*

Top right: Being led over Blenkinsopp by John Knapp. © *inov-8.com/Dave MacFarlane.*

Left: Approaching Snake Pass and silently cursing Nicky Spinks a bit. © *inov-8.com/Dave MacFarlane.*

Below left: Tea at Tan Hill. © *inov-8.com/Dave MacFarlane.*

Below right: After a failed snooze at Hardraw. © *inov-8.com/ Dave MacFarlane.*

Top: At the Old Nags Head, Edale, with my children's XR flag. © *inov-8.com/Dave MacFarlane*.

Above: Three wall-botherers – with Mike Hartley and John Kelly. © *inov-8.com/Dave MacFarlane*.

Then things started to feel difficult. It was dark, raining, my legs felt empty, my pack heavy. Time to back off a little. I got passed on the climbs – including by my buddy Robert Hajnal from Lavaredo.

Finally we got away from the noisy towns and up into the proper mountains and I reminded myself there were twenty-plus hours to go. And that's part of what I love about 100-mile races. They're like a game of chess: you have to keep an eye on your pacing, fuelling, hydration, sodium intake; manage your body's response to climactic conditions and sleep deprivation; problem-solve when one of those isn't working out; manage your mindset throughout – and it all gets increasingly difficult as you tire and get emotional.

There are four different movement skills: running uphill, hiking uphill, running downhill and running on the flat. Hardly anyone excels equally at all four and everyone usually has at least one clear strength and weakness (hiking was my strength; uphill running my biggest weakness). So if someone has a sub-2:20 marathon, as many elite ultrarunners do, they will have an advantage of genetic aerobic talent that I can't compete with. But if they misjudge any of those factors – and in a 100-miler it's a matter of how badly or how long you misjudge them for – someone with less aerobic talent but who has managed their chess pieces better could surpass them. Part of the tactic is remembering to play the long game.

It was deliciously cold, with drifting mists, flickering stars, a big white moon, snow gleaming on big triangles, frost glittering on the ground. I gradually felt better. In fact, I felt ace. At 3 a.m., forty-five miles in, descending to Courmayeur, I passed race joint-favourite Walmsley. I was shocked but excited. Courmayeur is usually DNF Central for kamikaze runners. The race doesn't start till there.

I was buzzing when I reached the Italian town in thirteenth place, bang on target. I was lucky to have Spinksy crewing me again and just seeing her gave me a lift – even if she did leave me hanging on a high five. I ran with super-bearded Florian Grasel, who'd saved my race at the Mozart 100 (I'd brought spare salt tablets this time, I told him, to return the favour). In that cold frosty night, it felt like we were a team. But I was feeling mysteriously good, so I pushed on.

Glimpsing a light up ahead, I couldn't resist a bit of head-torch chess, turning my head torch off and on again as I heaved myself up to Grand Col Ferret. I passed Scott Hawker, who'd pipped me the previous year. He was having tummy issues, poor chap. At La Fouly, I learnt I was seventh. I hadn't dared dream I'd ever get that far up the placings. I hadn't passed anyone else, but there'd been more DNFs ahead.

I still felt pretty good at Champex-Lac, seventy-five miles in. The two ahead of me looked good too, I was told. Less so the two ahead of them, though, Tim Tollefson and Zach Miller. I needed to keep focused on the basics: eating, drinking, pacing. Knowing I couldn't simply come back next year and put things right if I slipped up – as I had last year – kept me honest, as did the frustrations of last year. At the risk of cliché, it was now or possibly never. There'd be people behind me running well. Indeed, a rejuvenated Hawker shot past me on the next climb. But then I caught Miller. He was limping and babbling semi-coherently. 'Where is everyone?' he asked, presumably meaning Walmsley and Jornet (who'd DNFed after a bee sting caused an allergic reaction). He said he might DNF. I thought that might be the best thing for him (and me).

I was surprised to re-catch Hawker on the descent and felt guilty about capitalising on his misfortune, his tummy issues returning. The steep climb to Les Tseppes was soul-destroying. Last year I had been overtaken by snails here and lost my precious tenth place. Focus, don't be lazy, I told myself. The crowds seemed to grow at every checkpoint. Nicky had bought me chips again at Vallorcine, to go with tea, chocolate milk and boiled spuds in mayo. But this time I couldn't face the French fries. I couldn't bring myself to tell her, though. So I took them anyway, before shamefully chucking them in a hedge.

On the next interminable climb, I saw Ellie crouched in a bush, camera in hand. I'm surprised she saw me, because she was accidentally wearing my, weaker-than-hers, contact lenses. She would later tell me she was 'literally crying my way round in a cross-eyed way, with double vision. I saw two Damians!' One of me said 'I'm fifth!' in disbelief. 'I know,' she beamed back.

On the final climb, I had a cushion of twenty minutes on the guy behind.

I relaxed. Too much. Just before the last decent, I glimpsed a runner behind me. I really liked fifth. Top five is a thing. Top six isn't. My face must have showed dismay, because Matt, who was filming me, said, 'Whatever happens, mate, I'm proud of you.' I almost burst into tears. I felt desperate, primal. I tripped and cut my hand and knee. Idiot!

The lower reaches of the descent were lined with spectators. Strangers ran with me. In the streets, there were hands to high-five everywhere. I felt so much emotion as I rounded the corner to the hallowed arch. It'd taken four years and an exhausting amount of hard work and focus, but I'd got there. And it felt really fucking good.

Matt had joked I had to celebrate, to create good film footage, but I didn't need encouragement. I milked it like I'd won it. It was a self-centred socio-psychological orgasm, the closest I'll ever get to the feeling of scoring for Arsenal or being Matt Berninger and hearing a crowd sing 'Mr November'. Sweetly, you see Spinksy shedding tears in *Underdog*, which went on to win the People's Choice Award at Kendal Mountain Festival.

It was the best placing by a British male for eight years, and I was thrilled to learn Grasel had finished ninth and Hajnal second. 2018 was the year of the underdog. When I went up on to the podium on Sunday afternoon, to be one of those 'superstars' I'd worshipped four years before, it felt like it wasn't really happening. I was also invited for a video interview with Bryon Powell for *iRunFar.com*. I'll admit the social media buzz you get after something like that is hard not to enjoy. Hobbling happily back from town in a dream-like state, my new trophy swinging in my hand, I passed Tollefson and Miller with Yang and self-consciously hid my bounty behind my back. I've tried to think of a better way to sum up my 2018 UTMB experience, but I repeatedly come back to the feeling that it was simply really bloody satisfying. I made sacrifices (though they were always choices), I went all in, and it paid off. I did feel some pressure, but it was all self-created. Plus people like inov-8, Nicky Spinks, Summit Fever Media and Shane Benzie (who was in Chamonix too, cheering me on from many an aid station – a reminder to 'load the bow' and get my lazy arms swinging) all believed in me. That's not pressure. That's people willing you to do well. You think of them when it gets ouchy.

* * *

After a run ending somewhere so noisy, I sought something rather more quiet and remote. Running the Cape Wrath Trail in winter was Ellie's idea. Many months before, we'd been batting winter adventure-film ideas about and she blurted out 'Cape Wrath!' The trail in Scotland's northwest is Britain's wildest, remotest and some say toughest. In fact it's not even a trail. The unmarked route winds 230 miles north from Fort William through spectacular and rugged Highland lumps to a huge lonely white lighthouse atop the epic cliffs of Cape Wrath, the northwesternmost point of the mainland. We knew instantly that the idea couldn't be bettered. The conversation ended right there.

Matt and Ellie were a bit bored of filming me banging on about bimbles, my midlife crisis and how trail running is an antidote to the ills of modern life, so they invited Beth Pascall along too, to freshen things up. She'd had a sensational year placing fourth at UTMB, we're pretty compatible runners and pretty compatible people (she doesn't seem to outwardly hate me, anyway), and better still, she's a doctor.

We didn't know anyone who'd run the trail in winter, which made it all the more appealing. The record, according to *fastestknowntime.com*, was seven days, nine hours and thirty-one minutes, set by Przemysław Szapar. Judging by online pics, he's more of a fastpacker than a runner and we felt respectfully confident we could take a chunk out of his time. More than that, it just felt like a big wintery adventure in the UK.

But was that the record? Someone mentioned GB trail runner Katie Kaars Sijpesteijn might have run it recently with her husband, Casper, so I dropped her a line. 'Yep, 7+ days is not the fastest!' she said. 'Guess I'll just have to tell you when you are done … makes it more exciting for you hey ☺'.

That idea didn't seem particularly exciting, to be honest. Or very fair. We would be in the unique position of going for a record without knowing what it was. 'I'm not just trying to be a dick not telling you,' she said. 'It's just that's not why we did it. We … didn't want our time to be a target for someone to "beat". So when you go faster than 7 days you will have the FKT because no one knows how long it took us and we are cool with that.'

Yet when inov-8 posted my pre-run blog on their Facebook page, she was one of the first to comment: 'Fastest KNOWN Time 😉'. It was confusing. Did she want to keep her run a secret, or not? Putting it politely, neither Beth nor I thought that withholding information was in the spirit of things. Still, it added a little extra motivation.

'It is hard to improve on this pithy warning,' says Iain Harper in his excellent guidebook, *The Cape Wrath Trail* (Cicerone). 'This is rough, unforgiving country that should not be underestimated ... often there are not even any clear paths, only bogs and leg-sapping terrain. This is absolutely not a route for beginners or those unfamiliar with remote, rugged mountain areas.'

The river crossings made me nervous – people had gone for swims in them that required no towel. I spent hours on the phone to Gary Tompsett, who works on the Cape Wrath Ultra. He knows the route intimately and was really generous with his time. He also knows about crossing rivers safely: if they're above waist height, they aren't safe to attempt, he warned. The prospects of being knocked off our feet, drowning, smacking a head on a rock or getting hypothermic from a 3 a.m. dunking were not as distant as I'd have liked. The route is often many hours from a road and there's little to no phone signal. Tim Laney, a mountaineering guide and ex-army officer on top of his vast fell-running nous, warned me not to go.

We would carry Open Tracking GPS trackers with an SOS button to alert Mountain Rescue if things went haggis-shaped. Beth and I would be self-supported, meaning we could pick up supplies en route. Matt and Ellie would give us nothing but the occasional word of abuse. We spent a day driving ahead and depositing boxes full of snacks. It rained most of the time and we could see rivers bursting their banks, as my nervousness also rose towards bursting point. Beth seemed calm as a cucumber.

'If you're coming up here tomorrow, bring a body bag,' said a gamekeeper cheerily. Maybe he was trying to scare the tourists, but the Scottish Environment Protection Agency website, which gives real-time river-depth data, rated a river we needed to cross as two metres high in places. I'm not even nearly two metres high. We agreed to postpone the start by a day and hoped that was enough for the rivers to sink to non-murderous levels. To keep ourselves out of mischief we ran up a snowy Ben Nevis.

Sunday morning was chilly but rain free. We started our Suuntos as the ferry left Fort William in the dark for Camusnagaul. It was a relief to get going, but I was nervous about the river crossings and soon felt the weight of my pack. I was too much of a daydreamer to be in charge of navigation, so the ever-focused doctor took over. The terrain switched abruptly from good, fast trails to boggy or rocky ground, often fun (at first) but slow.

We planned to stay in bothies, but there wasn't a convenient one until eighty-two miles in, which we hoped might take us about twenty-four hours. We turned into Cona Glen, the type of glorious glen that would characterise our trip: remote, mysterious and, to paraphrase Icelandic pop pixie Björk, oh so quiet. We soon became blasé about seeing huge stags. At around 8 p.m. we stopped for dinner (okay, two dinners). It was a huge relief to find the first serious river crossing, River Carnach, barely knee-deep.

We climbed mountains in gentle snow, miles from civilisation. After sixteen and a half hours' darkness, we felt weary, and opted for the first of many fifteen-minute power naps. We just plonked ourselves down on the trail – I didn't even remove my bag – set an alarm and dozed.

It was already really hard work. But the scenery was to die for. The morning brought sunshine, snow-dusted summits, more long golden glens and huge herds of deer – the stags forming a protective barrier around the does – and finally the Maol Bhuidhe bothy, where we were greeted by Matt and Ellie. Said to be the UK's remotest, the white bothy is surrounded by snow-dusted lumps, the sort of place you fantasise about escaping the zombie apocalypse to. We'd hoped to get there for around 5 or 6 a.m. and sleep, but it was already 10 a.m. and wasting precious hours of daylight seemed folly. We battled knee-high tussocks mounted on deep bog. One Cape Wrath mile was worth three English miles. It was frustratingly slow going. Then I did something quite stupid.

I couldn't be bothered to go as high up as Beth and stubbornly decided to stick to a lower contour ... until, er, I couldn't see her. Maybe I was ahead of her? I waited for a bit. No Beth. Now I didn't know if she was ahead or behind. I headed for the higher ground. Still no Beth. I shouted. Silence. No sound or view of human existence. For the only time in my life, I used one of those emergency whistles. No response. I shouted again. Nothing. If we couldn't find each other it was probably mission over. I wasn't panicking. But I was worried and angry with myself.

Should I go back, continue, or stay where I was? Knowing that the smartest thing was probably to remain still, I gambled and ran ahead, shouting and whistling. After another five minutes, I heard a shout. Beth was ahead, waiting for me. I apologised. She was more forgiving than she should have been.

Despite several days and nights with almost no one else around, we didn't talk a great deal. But when you run 230 miles with someone you don't need conversation to get to know them. (And she'd already learnt I could be a bit of a muppet.)

Fast, hard trails followed, then energy-sapping, trackless bog, all the way to Strathcarron, where we found an open pub! As locals eyed us with friendly suspicion and forgave our unconventional aromas, we downed pints of lemonade and pots of tea, and cleaned the establishment out of Double Deckers and ready salted crisps (even if I initially asked for 'salt and onion'). Interviewed by Matt, Beth said it was now Type 3 fun, while I pretended it was still Type 2. We badly needed sleep.

We reached Coire Fionnaraich bothy at around 5 p.m., ninety-three miles and thirty-three hours in. We lit a fire, warmed dehydrated meals and lay down, with an alarm set for three hours later. My frail sleeping mat was my only kit fail. Hard floorboards and sore limbs aren't a pleasing mix. 'We lay on a hard floor and felt everything hurting and then the alarm went off,' is how Beth remembers it. 'Another half hour?' I croaked. I felt cold, damp, stiff, achy. We jogged on, along undulating rocky single-track under another clear night sky.

We wanted to stick faithfully to the CWT route (there are various variants) detailed in Iain Harper's guidebook, but even he had recommended we skip the section around the back of Beinn Eighe. But we wanted our possible record to be transparent and replicable, so we stuck to it. Beth – you would hope, with her vocation, not someone prone to exaggeration – called this section the 'slowest terrain of my whole life'. We moved at one mile an hour. We were mostly going sideways across very steep, rocky, uneven ground covered in high heather and peppered with tank-sized boulders. There was every chance of broken ankles. There was no path. There were of course the usual river crossings to soak and freeze us. Everything there seemed to hate us. The fact our battle took place between about 1 and 5 a.m. probably didn't help matters. To top off our foul moods, when we finally reached Kinlochewe and the promise of a box full of treats each hidden in the undergrowth, Beth's was missing. After some searching, thankfully we found it, unopened. Presumably a local badger had shown an interest in Beth's M&M's.

We had two schedules, one labelled Optimistic, one Pessimistic, and we were on the latter. We would still break the record if we could stick to it. Leaving Kinlochewe at about 7 a.m. we paused for another power nap. Then, as often happens when you're at your lowest, the natural world gave us a gift. The sun came out to cast gold on our treasure, another long glen carrying us to Lochan Fada. Mini pools of iced water glistened all around us, snow hovered above the heather and in every direction were bold mountains and huge lochs.

As usual, a big moment of wonder was followed by a reminder of just how long this effing trail really was. The journey to remote Shenevall went on for yonks. The bothy, where we stopped for lunch, was another magnificently remote spot: yellow and white mountains, yet another long loch. 'Just a UTMB to go,' said Beth. The climb out zigzagged between ice pools and denuded rocks, their skins scraped off by glacial ice. I didn't want to carry on. I was happy there. We had another power nap at dusk, always a hard time mentally. We were entering sixteen hours of darkness and I hit my lowest point.

I'd been foolishly holding out a hope of getting back to Wiltshire for my children's nativity play, my four-year-old son's acting debut (he was playing a pig). It was now obvious – because of the delayed start and the terrain being so much slower than anticipated – that wouldn't happen.

I felt like a bad parent. I sulked. I may have sobbed too. A long zigzag climb in pine woods from Inverlael didn't enhance my mood. Neither did a broken pole. Or the endless bog-slogging in long yellow squelchy grass with the wind howling at us. Or several hours tumbling through an infuriating peat-bog labyrinth. We sat for a quick snack and I fell asleep.

We reached Knockdamph bothy at about midnight, fifty-nine hours and 153 miles in, and discovered … mattresses! It was the happiest I've ever seen Beth. Sure, you'd walk out of a hotel in disgust at the sight of them in the Other World, but to us they were the best present possible. We agreed on five(!) hours' sleep and at least one press of the snooze button. 'This is one of the best beds in the world,' said Beth. 'And one of the hardest to leave.'

Indeed, at around 5 a.m. it was a huge effort to swap the desperate comfort of warm sleeping bags for horrible wet socks, wet shoes, wet tights and wet bogs. But light came quickly and for once good trails took us all the way to the River Oykel. Glenmore Forest is an epic, U-shaped glen with giant-steep sides and no forest. It was so rare to see people that we instinctively stopped to talk. When a young gamekeeper learnt what we were doing he instantly donated his sandwiches. We must have looked hungry.

I swore I saw a huge eagle land nearby (Beth was sure I was hallucinating), and an orangey-gold sunset sent us down towards Inchnadamph. Huge lochs glistened, the mountains purred. I felt happy and alive. Matt and Ellie were filming and I idiotically ran a little too hard. Not long after, tendonitis announced itself down my right shin.

As it got dark again, the wind came in from the Atlantic. The next few hours, on rocky, narrow, clifftop paths, were accompanied by constant angry white noise. When we finally got to Glendhu bothy we tried to sleep, for about three hours. 'I kept waking up,' said Beth. 'The pain in my feet was so intense.'

Ominously we needed a power nap not long after leaving the bothy. Beth had developed copycat tendonitis on her shin, making downhills painful for us both. After a couple of hours bog-trotting in the windy dark, the sky exploded into gold and pink, like I've never seen before.

We saw Matt and Ellie again too, which perked us up. In their footage there are tears streaming down my face. I've always insisted it was the wind, but it did feel emotional, knowing we were (barring disaster) into our final day. I felt an eagerness to return to family, but also a sadness that our adventure would soon be over. There's a risk I've made this run sound unrelentingly awful, but I promise it was often amazing too: the scenery, the stags, the sense of space and remoteness, the quiet companionship, the peace.

As we reached the wind-battered village of Rhiconich around lunchtime, seventeen miles still felt a long way to go. I was the main instigator in our hunt for tea and we quickly gave in to the additional offer of chips in a cafe, which tasted sensational. But it felt weird to be somewhere civilised.

The last few hours of daylight were sucked up by yet more squelchy bogscapes. Though my lower-leg tendons were angry and I was whacked up on Pro Plus and paracetamol, reaching the delicious curve of Sandwood Bay at dusk was a moving moment. 'It feels like we're running to the end of the world,' said Beth.

The bogs and peat hags only got more charismatic. I plunged into one up to my waist and squealed as I rolled an ankle. Finally, we reached a track, which felt like alien terrain. It couldn't be far now, surely? 'Race you to the finish,' said Beth. I tittered. I bloody well hoped she was joking. But we both sped up.

Suddenly there were buildings, lights, a handful of vehicles and a huge lighthouse. We touched the wall four days, nine hours and forty-three minutes after we'd started, even if that felt like weeks ago.

I was going to miss the sense of empowerment and self-reliance, the edge-of-the-world frisson, the absence of screens, how pleasingly uncomplicated our lives had become and, above all, the thrilling remoteness. But the adventure wasn't over.

We fell into a minibus with Stuart, our driver, Matt, Ellie and two lighthouse workers, intending to head back to civilisation. I tried to swig whisky (when in Rome …) as we drove along a rough track. A bumpy, burpy hour led to a launch point for a small motorised boat and a ferryman visibly anxious to get going. Waves splashed us as we slid out into the ominous choppy waters of the straight. The motor spluttered like a cough as we tipped from side to side. Our captain looked agitated and was muttering to himself. 'I don't like this,' he said. 'Does this seem safe to you?'

I'm as knowledgeable at seafaring as I am about Albanian opera. But when the captain of a vessel asks if you think it's safe, then it definitely isn't. I was very happy to return to land. Mission aborted, we drove the hour back to the huge lighthouse.

Keeper John, who lives there year-round, often on his own, and his visiting daughter Angie very kindly put us up in makeshift beds and fed us a very welcome feast of macaroni cheese and tomato soup, which I wolfed down in minutes. In a smoke-filled room, we sat and chatted, a unique gathering of folk with little in common but Cape Wrath itself. A bonus night of adventure was a helpful bridging moment, lessening the blow of the sometimes abrupt transition back to 'normal' life.

As usual, I returned home with cuts, bruises and a mutilated ankle, but with an incredible sense of peace and fulfilment. To be a good ultrarunner you need three things. One, a high pain threshold. Two, a bad memory. And three … I can't remember what the third one is. As with all of these ultra-distance races, challenges and training runs, the memory plays tricks and you very quickly forget the discomfort, the yearning to finish, the inability to walk in a non-comical fashion the day afterwards; while memories of the happy stuff linger far longer.

Nevertheless, the Cape Wrath Trail run was the very best type of running adventure, the perfect mix of an athletic deadline that was comparatively comfortable (we beat Przemysław Szapar's time by almost three days, and as Katie Kaars Sijpesteijn didn't make any further comments on social media, we can only assume we beat her time too), and a real sense of jeopardy and adventure.

11 CREW TO BE KIND

'It's all a little bit odd, isn't it?'

Back in December 2017, I was as excited as a badger come mating season when I got an email from Her Royal Fell-Running Highness, Nicky Spinks. Did I want to support on her Double Charlie Ramsay Round record attempt? Did I ever! At football, a supporter mainly shouts rude words and eats lots of chips. Is it much different to that? (Not really, it turns out.)

After selecting a challenge and a date, the third big decision is what style to do it in. The ultimate satisfaction comes from being solo and unsupported: no one helps you; you must carry everything you use except water. But the glory and deeper satisfaction is all yours (though your photos will be mostly selfies).

Self-supported means you can pick supplies up en route, whether that's from shops or stash boxes, like Beth and I did on Cape Wrath. That helps keep your pack weight down if the route is longer.

Supported is the option most people go for, because it carries the most advantage. Other than having to organise everyone and less flexibility with dates, it usually means having crew support at road crossings and support runners on the hill. Frankly this makes things easier, safer and more social. Plus to have a Bob Graham ratified by the highfalutin BGC, someone has to verify the runner reached each summit, so pacers are essential if you want a fancy certificate. But this is where it starts to get muddy again, because the BGC and Charlie Ramsay don't recognise solo round completions. The Paddy embraces it as almost the truest ethos of the Snowdonia circuit and our buddies in America do too, and you could still get these runs verified by *fastestknowntime.com*. Indeed, they record a best time for each style, and even a team/pairs option. You could in theory have a solo BG ratified by *fastestknowntime.com* but not by the BGC, which hasn't caused any notable problems, yet ...

Wait, did Nicky's email say 'double'? I hadn't known a double round was a thing until 2016, when, to celebrate ten years since she was diagnosed with breast cancer, Nicky ran a Double Bob Graham Round. Yep, two consecutive Bob Grahams. That's 132 miles, 54,000 feet of ascent and forty-five hours and thirty minutes on her feet, with just one ten-minute power nap, breaking a thirty-seven-year-old record. Since then I've watched from afar as several men have attempted the same feat. None have got close. No one was known to have ever attempted a Double Ramsay Round (forty-eight peaks, 116 miles, and 57,000 feet of ascent).

Spinksy had crewed me at UTMB in 2017, so I owed her one. But I was flattered to be asked, fascinated by how the Queen of the Fells repeatedly went about making history, and saw it as a sort of entry to the fell-running world, which still seemed like the Freemasons to me. Above all, I wanted to see what snacks of hers I could snaffle, for some post-macaroongate revenge.

I was curious about these wonderful selfless people who make up the invisible armies of supporters on other people's rounds. They seemed to be like Santa's elves. But did Nicky know she was hiring a naive newbie? I wasn't going to tell her. She's famously picky about her teams. 'I like to get half a dozen key people in place, people who really know me, who really know what I'm like when I'm good and when I'm not,' she says. 'They can help pull you around when you're feeling bad.'

For Nicky, being a good supporter has very little to do with someone's running CV. 'You don't know when you enlist support who's going to be good or not. The quietest people can turn out to be the most wonderful support. Mountain Rescue people, who you expect to be part of a team and so on, can be rubbish! They'll run on ahead with all your stuff! You learn. Now I don't enlist people I don't know.'

She knew me well enough. You don't get to know someone any quicker than crewing them over 100 miles, watching them turn from would-be hero to blubbering wreck over twenty-four hours. Nicky's straight-talking, doesn't suffer fools and can seem a tiny bit Eeyore-ish at times, but is deceptively funny with a beer in hand. We'd got on well, I thought. If Mark Townsend is my surrogate running dad, Spinksy is my auntie. Which makes Tim Laney, Alex Copping and Allan Cox my irresponsible uncles.

You won't find pacer guidelines or etiquette written down anywhere. Was I meant to recce my leg? I'd done a clockwise Ramsay, but my designated section was anti-clockwise, in the dark. I couldn't justify two trips all the way to Scotland. I'd just have to wing it. Was I meant to tell her to hurry up if we were slipping off schedule? Was I meant to bring macaroons?

A support runner is a serious role, for a record attempt anyway. 'It's a job, not a jolly,' Nicky told me. 'People are relying on you ... A good supporter wants to do everything they can to help. It's annoying when they don't want to do a night leg or a difficult leg.'

A bad supporter has come along more for their benefit than yours, she says. 'They only have room in their rucksack for their stuff; they haven't looked at the map or the schedule. They will probably ask you to sort out their lift to/from the start/end of their leg two days beforehand. They want to be involved to say they were there when you broke such and such a record. They don't realise that by not contributing they are a drain on the attempt. They may not do it on purpose, but they don't know the etiquette. I can't assess how every person will act. It's usually about how willing they are to learn and be better, which determines whether I'll ask them again.'

Gulp. It felt like an audition. And I didn't know the etiquette.

I started getting emails from Charmian Heaton, Nicky's de facto chief of logistics, arranging transport from the ends of our respective legs back to our vehicles. It was a massive jigsaw puzzle and required numerous people doing numerous unglamorous tasks. In this mostly amateur sport, it was a military-level operation. I've still not supported on another challenge as well organised. I was the new kid in class again, desperate not to stuff up. Especially as 'Some of her hill supporters have reported some memorable strops!' Charmian told me (though she added, 'I can honestly say that I have never seen this side of her'). I'd been assigned the first leg, an eight-hour run through the muscular Mamores mountains, starting at midnight.

Inside Charmian's camper van was fell god Joss Naylor, inadvertently making people whisper reverentially. Charmian gave me a bundle of spare kit to carry. But after Spinksy's additional huge picnic was shared out roughly equally between four of us, the other supporters came to me separately and asked, 'Erm, I've got a bit of a dicky [insert name of tendon here], would you mind carrying a bit of this just in case?' They handed over the nosh till I had pretty much everything. I didn't mind a heavy pack, though, as I assumed the pace would be fairly relaxed. Error number one.

Bang on midnight, we set off from outside the Glen Nevis Youth Hostel. My nervous energy made me witter away inanely. But Nicky wasn't in a talking mood. There were records to be broken. When the gradient got steep, Nicky powered on ahead and dropped two of her pacers, hitting the first peak ten minutes up on schedule. Her pace was scorchio. I was working effing hard.

My second mistake was that my bag didn't have many accessible pockets, meaning every time Nicky wanted something, I had to stop, take off the pack, tip the contents out, rummage through the pile in the dark, find the elusive rice pudding, repack, then catch Nicky up. Which took a comically heavy-panting effort and up to ten minutes. Her Royal Spinksness had made very good progress but – in my head at least – had grown a little impatient with having to wait for her simple requests for water or jelly babies to be fulfilled.

A full moon lit the sky and it never seemed to get properly dark. An orange glow appeared on the zigzaggy horizon before 4 a.m. Nicky mentioned some twinges of cramp, and giving her some of my salt tablets – which worked! – gave me a buzz too. I'd helped a bit more efficiently this time. I much preferred the physical stress of muling to the cerebral stress of not getting lost.

Once the sun was up, nav was easier and we all felt a little more relaxed. I was curious to get to know Nicky's other supporters. Jean Brown had known Nicky for years, but Paweł Cymbalista, a last-minute substitute, knew her less well than I did, even if he knew this leg incredibly well because it was his twelfth support on the round.

'My wife says there are three people in our marriage,' he chuckled. 'Me, her and the Ramsay.' (Later he sent me a list of all his support runs: names, dates and whether they were clockwise or anticlockwise.)

Paweł's Ramsay romance started back in 2016 when his friend Helen asked if he wanted to 'help two guys "do a crazy thing". We arrived at Fersit Dam one hour before scheduled, set up a wee camp and waited. I was very excited. It felt like a secret mission. When they arrived, they got quickly reorganised, got some food in and off they went. I felt inspired and I said to Helen, "One day I will do a Ramsay too."'

Paweł, who lives fifty minutes away from Fort William (close to the Ramsay's start) in Mallaig, became 'absolutely obsessed' with the round. 'I wanted to know everything, meet everyone, help everyone and one day do it myself. I started helping people. Secretly I was hoping they would come and help me one day too.'

Indeed after a failed attempt in 2018, he returned in 2020, 'much stronger, with an amazing team of friends and strangers, and got it in the bag, which was amazing!' But he's more excited about helping others. What does he get from it all? 'The experience of being out in the hills helping others fulfil their dreams. Seeing smiling faces at the finish is the biggest reward. I think supporting people on this round will be my life-time commitment. I can't imagine a year without at least three support rounds.'

The Highlands saved his life, he says. He used to be sixteen stone, smoke twenty cigarettes and drink four pints a day. 'If I hadn't moved here I would be an alcoholic now.'

Running friends are different. I know a whole bunch of people who don't know my birthday or my children's names, but ask them to meet me at 3 a.m. on Helvellyn in a blizzard and bring four litres of custard, and they'll be there (as I would be for them). Paweł reminded me of

Victoria 'Tory' Miller, a South African Lakes-based fell runner. Despite only being in Cumbria for two years, Tory has supported on at least ten Bobs ('I've lost count'), two Wainwrights, two Steve Parr Rounds and others. She rediscovered running after a divorce from a marriage where she 'felt very trapped'. It made her feel free and she soon made the natural progression to trail running. But when she visited the Lakes, running off-trail reminded her of the childhood joy of playing in the mountains in South Africa. 'I fell in love with running in the Lake District,' she says. She was coming up nearly every weekend, so when a job came up she jumped at it.

Within a year of starting running she completed the Dragon's Back Race in 2017 (and was driven straight from the finish line to hospital: 'My feet were absolutely shot'). 'I'm a fell runner, not a fell racer. I just love being on the hills.'

She became known for liking long days out. 'A friend messaged me saying their friend needed some help on leg three of the Bob Graham. I needed to be at Dunmail [between legs two and three] at 1 a.m. or something stupid. But I just thought, "why not?"'

She was meeting a group of strange men at a mountain pass in the dead of night. 'My South African upbringing had me very safety-conscious – thank goodness my parents didn't know what I was doing! I got there and there's this knock on the window by this burly guy. I thought, "Crikey, what am I doing?" But he got in the car and he was lovely and friendly.'

She could barely keep up on the first summit. 'I remember feeling overwhelmed and a bit pathetic, like I was a burden.' But she ended up being the only supporter who visited all the summits on leg three and went on to do leg five too. 'I was hooked.'

Leg four has become Tory's specialist leg. She loves the scenery and climbs, but also the drama of it being the make-or-break moment for most attempts.

So what's the secret to being a good support runner? 'A good level of being encouraging and kind, but also knowing when to kick someone up the backside. It's finding that right balance and it differs for everyone.

And you've got to be efficient – you can't faff around with nav ... I love the fact I'm not only doing what I love but I'm helping someone achieve what they want to achieve. I'm not just going for a run, I'm doing some good at the same time. You could say support is selfish, because by giving to people I get back. It gives me an immense sense of gratification.'

Meanwhile, on the Ramsay, Nicky was focused and positive when we got to the changeover point, a tent erected in the middle of nowhere to protect from midges. It was a source of pride that we'd delivered her to the next pacers seventeen minutes up on schedule and without any dramas, except my comical routine for locating her rice puddings. It was mind-blowing to think she was set to continue for another forty hours.

On the long drive south, as I munched on one of the Tunnock's bars that had accidentally fallen into my possession, a warm gooey feel-good sensation spread through my body, mingling with the normal peaceful weariness. Whenever I stopped for tea I checked Nicky's progress. She remained ahead of schedule for over thirty hours. Unfortunately, on Sunday she gradually got behind and it became clear she wouldn't be able to complete the double round before her deadline. Did she give up? Did she heck. She's Nicky fucking Spinks.

After fifty-five hours and fifty-six minutes of continuously moving in the mountains, she finally sat down in a foldable chair to bacon and eggs at the bottom of Ben Nevis. To me, by stubbornly refusing to give up, she had achieved something even greater than she set out to do.

What gave me a bonus gooey feeling was just how many people wanted to help. There was an almost tangible tidal wave of goodwill pushing her along, both in the Highlands and online. It felt good to be part of a team again, doing a team sport without an opposition. Isn't that the best type of sport? No one really loses (except some toenails).

More recently I asked Nicky about her best moment as a supporter. 'Andy Plummer was on my first BG, but we got separated in the mist. I got round and he didn't,' she recalls. 'Things just kept going wrong on his attempts. He's not the greatest at organising and he's a bit nice to people. You have to be a bit selfish ... On his fifth attempt, I did leg three and four and it was obvious he'd do it. I was in tears watching him go up

Dale Head. We've got pictures from Moot Hall and I couldn't have been grinning more.'

'It's a privilege to be invited on anyone's round,' says record-breaking fell runner Jim Mann. 'Whether it's a record attempt or just someone trying to complete a BG, it's a shared experience. It's so nice to play a small part in helping someone complete a personal challenge. It's also nice when it's your day and people come and help support you to do something you have invested a lot of time in. They are giving up their time to help you achieve a personal goal which is often pure folly.'

It's like being invited to someone's birthday party, one with a zero on the end.

* * *

Presumably forgetting all about bag-gate, Nicky recruited me again to support on her Double Paddy Buckley Round record attempt in May 2019. I was assigned two legs (a promotion!), including the first again. All was top banana as I clocked off at Llanberis. When I checked the tracker at 6 a.m. the next morning, though, things had changed.

Nicky was over an hour behind schedule, due to some topographical confusion in the clag and dark between the Tolkienesque summits Bryn Banog and Moel Hebog. It was unlikely now she could do a double in sub-forty-eight hours. Nicky looked tired and fragile as she came into Capel Curig to complete half her double. She quickly hugged her brother Charlie, got into Charmian's van and ate a full breakfast. Which soon came back up. Her power nap also failed.

It's very different pacing when it's business time. The first leg is the cheat's leg: everyone's fresh and happy and there shouldn't be any dramas. Nicky was very quiet. 'I honestly can't remember a lot of [the next] leg [clockwise from Capel Curig],' she wrote on her blog (*runbg. co.uk*). 'I've never wanted to be one of these people that do very long things very slowly and then complain about the whole experience – but that's what I felt like I was doing. I felt like I had let everyone down …

'I decided to voice my plans to quit to Adam, Kirsty and Damian. If they immediately agreed then it would strengthen that argument.

Of course they didn't! Kirsty said no one thought I was wasting their time, that everyone was there for me and it didn't matter how long I took. That I would do the same for any of them. Damian said "you would only come back and try it again" [something I remembered she'd said about a previous record attempt], that it would make a rubbish film [Summit Fever Media were making one], that I'm achieving something great by even trying it [defo this] ... We continued to climb Moelwyn Bach.'

We needed to get her eating. She'd had almost no calories since her rainbow yawn in Charmian's van. Luckily noodles did the trick and I became her Noodle Man, carrying the open bag. Nicky had a ten-minute snooze in a bivvy bag at the quarries. As we continued, she gradually came back to life. She was more talkative, moving a little better, talking about the next leg ... It was a full-blown resurrection. I told you Nicky was like Jesus. Some of the old cast-iron resolve was definitely back when we said goodbye at Aberglaslyn. It was emotional and inspiring. The things worth doing aren't the easy things.

She did it, of course. In fifty-seven hours and twenty-five minutes. Again, not the time she wanted. But she'd completed an unprecedented hat-trick of record doubles on the Big Three rounds. It was a genuine honour and a thrill to play a tiny role in something epic and historic. It was a more wholesome elation than a good race result (which ultimately is all about you).

Being a pacer may seem selfless, but it's a role many willingly do, because above all else it involves running, usually somewhere priddy and with like-minded loons, plus you're often accruing supporter credits or at least karma for when you want to do something similar. The real unsung heroes of these shindigs, though, are the road crew. They don't even get to run.

The road crew have the stress of repeatedly being at the right place at the right time at some very unsocial hours, organising hot food and drink with strict specifications, potentially reorganising pacers when a schedule goes out of the window, troubleshooting if a supporter drops out at the last minute or, worse still, if the protagonist's favourite pizza is unavailable. They might have to deal with tears, vomit and blood.

The equivalent in the non-running world would be offering to help with a house move, where the person moving only shows up four times in twenty-four hours, smelling like mouldy death, is grumpy, downs a cup of tea, half spilling it everywhere, knocks back two doughnuts, dumps a handful of rubbish and some muddy socks on you, and buggers off again, without saying thanks. After a bit, most reasonable people would lose some enthusiasm for shifting their boxes about.

There's no road crew Open University degree, recruitment agency or union. There's no money in it. And you have to hang around with lots of smelly runners. Not only is crewing the hardest and least celebrated part of the whole jamboree, but the amazing people prepared to wait around at remote car parks making vegan hot chocolate at 4 a.m. are the most interesting ones ...

At the 2012 Dragon's Back Race, Charmian Heaton volunteered as a marshal while her partner Steve ran it, as did Nicky Spinks. Charmian and Nicky hit it off: 'She always had a ready smile and seemed so modest and friendly,' says Charmian. When Nicky asked Charmian if she would support her 2013 Paddy Buckley Round record attempt she readily agreed.

Fans of nominative determinism may be equally thrilled and frustrated to learn Charmian is now chairman (not chairperson, she corrects) of the Fell Runners Association. But long before that, she was 'bone idle' at school. 'I used to ride horses, but I found running a mile really hard!' But she gradually became interested in mountaineering and climbing Munros and started running to get fit for that, and eventually joined a Nottinghamshire running club. Some folks there were into fell racing and she started going to the odd race. 'I just enjoyed being off road. I'd developed my love of hillwalking to running, albeit mostly at the back of the pack.' Sometimes when Steve raced she would volunteer at the same event. But the responsibility and pressure of being a small part of a large organised team is very different to being sole road crew for a record attempt.

'As we drove to Wales, Nicky asked, "How many of these rounds have you supported on?" I said, "Oh. I've never done it before." And the colour drained from her face! We drove around the checkpoints [again, more thorough prep than anyone else I've heard of] and she gave me a Nicky Spinks Masterclass, explaining what was in each of her bags and what she might need at each changeover.'

Charmian was learning on the job. 'One of her supporters ran into Aberglaslyn saying "She wants the green, long-sleeved top!" And I thought, "Shit, where's that?!" For the next stop I had all the gear laid out!

'It can be stressful. You probably see that person for a couple of minutes at each changeover. So you're putting in an awful lot of energy and organisation into very little time, which is quite critical. I do take it seriously and I must have done an okay job, because she keeps asking me back. You learn by experience. She's pretty easy, really: supply her with beans and rice pudding and she'll be okay.'

There's nearly always a curveball, though. On Nicky's second BG record attempt, 'she fell and cut her hand, so that was a quick patch-up exercise at Threlkeld. You have to be flexible and deal with things as they happen. On her Double Ramsay I'd promised her a cheese and onion pie at the dam, but I'd left it at home. I sent Steve to Fort William to try and get another one, but the Scots don't do pies. All he could get was some sort of macaroni cheese pasty thing. It didn't go down very well – she wasn't very happy. I just said, "Well, that's all there is, so get on with it." If I'd done that at the Paddy Buckley, I might not have been asked back!'

Something about their dynamic obviously works: 'We are both straight-talkers and she will tell me if I put too much milk in her tea. "When I get tired and I'm under stress I have been known to sort of snap at people," Nicky told me, "and I don't want to fall out with you." I said, "You won't fall out with me because I don't take offence at things like that." And we never have ... She can be a hard taskmaster – she is so focused on what she's doing – but afterwards she's usually much more understanding.'

Charmian, a former accountant, is more deeply involved than most road crew, even poring over Nicky's maps while in hospital recovering from surgery. 'I love the logistics side of it. I like to be organised: spreadsheets, working out where everyone needs to be, how people are getting to and from places, making sure there are no cars left in [remote] Wasdale. Nicky's super-organised, but for a record attempt she has enough to think about already. She doesn't need to know that somebody's dropped out the night before, that's an extra level of stress. So if I can take care of that and arrange lifts for everyone, if she trusts me with that, that's just something I can offer. It's quite a big responsibility. Staying calm under pressure is the key skill. And not getting distracted. It's a job, not a jolly.'

When Charmian attempted a solo Frog Graham Round (a forty-mile run and swim challenge with 15,750 feet of ascent and four lake swims), Nicky surprised her by turning up to canoe across Derwentwater (a crossing that's nigh-on impossible in the dark) on compass bearings, to show Charmian the way, otherwise she probably wouldn't have finished. 'I'm getting emotional just thinking about it now,' says Charmian.

Charmian has also supported other runners. 'Everyone's different and you have to get used to each person.' Rob Allen's Lakes, Meres and Waters (approximately 100 miles) took him around twenty-nine hours, and from Friday to Monday Charmian drove 302 miles with no sleep. 'It's got to be the hardest support work I've done. It was a bit of a bad time because Steve's mum died that week and I did think, "Do I really want to do this?" But it was good for both of us to get out. Steve did a long cycle in the night supporting Rob and that helped kind of take his mind off things. I've no regrets. But I was completely knackered.

'I'm just pleased to be able to help people to achieve their dream. When Paul Tierney sees me now, he comes over and gives me a big bear hug and you know how much it means to them. Nicky doesn't say a lot, but when she turns up with a bunch of flowers you know she's really happy with what you've done. People are really, really appreciative and it always feels worth it.'

When I contacted Matt Neale about crewing me on the Pennine Way in 2020, he cc'd his mate Jess Palmer, offering him up for crewing duties. Jess even offered his house as somewhere my crew could sleep and shower. I wanted to keep my team small and preferably people I knew. But I was amazed someone would be so generous to strangers, during a pandemic too. Mark and Tim agreed having a substitute tea-maker would give them a rest (they're getting on a bit and need a mid-day nap) and make them safer.

Back in 1976, when Jess was just eighteen, he hiked the sixty-one-mile Fellsman race in the Yorkshire Dales. 'It was a friend's idea – we'd done the Yorkshire Three Peaks and it was just a completely random thing to do,' he told me in his rich Yorkshire accent. 'It was quite a shock to the system and half killed me! But I must've liked something about it, because something stuck. Underneath all that pain, it gives you a real buzz, dun't it? It was so far beyond what you're used to, it takes you to another place. It got me hooked on the idea of pushing yourself in extreme situations. I had my long-distance walking background and there was the 1980s running boom and the two just fitted together.'

In forty-five years, he hasn't found anything that gives him the same excitement. 'Running gets you fit, it gets you out in the fresh air, you meet people, all those things. You can get that from a five-mile fell race or a ten-mile road race, so why do you have to do 100 miles, why do you have to do 268 miles non-stop? They are the questions that are harder to explain to other people, aren't they? Is it a good thing or a bad thing that I get more excited the more distance and pain is involved? It's all a little bit odd, isn't it?'

He completed more races and challenges, a Bob Graham and 'twenty-odd' Fellsmans. He was good too. 1996 was his best year, placing fourth at Fellsman and just two weeks later running a Long Distance Walkers Association 100 in around twenty-three hours. 'It was the early nineties and we hadn't invented the word ultrarunning yet. It was just long-distance running. I got to a respectable standard ... and bang, my world turned upside down'. He was diagnosed with chronic fatigue syndrome. From the age of thirty-nine to forty-nine he wasn't able to run or hike any real distance. He's been able to get back into things more recently and is planning a third go at the Spine Race. 'But my body can't take it now.'

Hundreds of amazing people turn up to help at events such as the Fellsman each year, to marshal at the top of mountains, often in inhospitable conditions. 'It's still nice to get out and enjoy it and there are other ways to get involved. I had been on the receiving end of all that support. After the diagnosis, I couldn't do what I used to do. But I could turn up and help someone on a Bob Graham or sit in a tent on a mountain at the Fellsman [which he's supported on eight times]. It kind of escalates then, dun't it?'

Jess's wife Andrea became interested in supporting, and five years ago they retired and bought a camper van. 'It went a bit bonkers then. We turned semi-professional for a while,' he laughs. 'We were doing support every few weeks: a Paddy Buckley, Bob Graham. Matt [Neale] does a lot and we've gone and helped him a lot, and we got to know Adam Perry on five of his attempts at the Lakes 24-Hour Record. Adam was running for twenty-four hours and we probably saw him for seven minutes. So you do get that feeling of pressure.'

Jess is a former psychiatric nurse, while Andrea was a nurse and a teacher. 'That's probably why we make a good support crew. I suppose the skills of looking after people and being able to understand what they need might come from the nursing toolkit. Looking after you on the Pennine Way and looking after psychiatric patients over the years, there is an overlap, in the nicest possible way.'

What do they get from what seems on the surface like a huge amount of tiring, mundane, unpaid work? 'It's another way of being involved,' says Jess. 'It fulfils a lot of the same needs, I think. The basic human needs, to be part of a group, the belonging, all the obvious psychological stuff. But you can get that in lots of ways. Whether it's running or supporting, there's something about putting yourself up against something that's more extreme than normal, that's going to stretch you, and stretch you quite close to your limit.'

It's not just altruism, he insists. 'There is an awful lot to be gotten from it as a supporter. That is the payback. People are grateful. I don't need a massive amount of thanks. If you get it right, it makes a difference. The runner couldn't do it without us. We make a difference and that's the satisfaction. The Pennine Way record had stood for over thirty years – and there's a reason for that. So just to be involved in that in some way, that's a buzz.'

Jess and Andrea have sold their camper van now and 'only' support on ten to twelve challenges a year. 'It's a bit more under control now. We're dealing with the addiction.'

Sometimes it takes someone from outside to show us what we've got. America's John Kelly wrote about 'the passion and selfless support of the fell-running community' on his blog at *randomforestrunner.com*, after his first encounter with Britain's hill runners on his Grand Round 1.0 in May 2019. Even if he seemed slightly bemused by our insistence on carrying his spare kit and exotic array of sugary snacks.

'I'm still in a bit of disbelief at their generosity, and I come from a place that I'd say epitomizes southern hospitality ... I had never experienced anything like this, where there was such a shared sense of pride in achieving the goal ... Over two dozen people were supporting me on this adventure. People I had never even spoken to before. People who deep down inside may have thought my crazy goal was impossible, yet were still taking time out of their lives to show up at all hours of the day and night in absolutely horrid weather to help some crazy American pursue that goal.'

In this fucked-up world of ours, in an age of divisive politics, hate-mongering and social media mobs, it's worth remembering there are still some fundamentally good and very kind people around. And a lot of them are runners.

12

BLOWING HOT AND COLD

'It was never intended to be an easy day out.'

2019 started thrillingly. Not just for me, but for fans of the long game everywhere. One of my female coaching clients did rather well at the Spine Race, winning overall and breaking the overall course record by a not-to-be-sniffed-at twelve hours. Oh yeah, while expressing breastmilk at aid stations. It was one of those rare moments where our niche sport exploded out of its soft flask and made a mess everywhere. The story was on TV, on the radio, in *Vogue*, from Australia to the US. Barbra Streisand tweeted about it.

Jasmin Paris doesn't need a lot of coaching. The then-thirty-five-year-old mother and small-animal vet was already beating the men at most things (including me, at the 2015 Dragon's Back Race, where she was second overall; she had the overall record for the Charlie Ramsay Round too). Jasmin would routinely get up at 5 a.m. to train before a busy day as a PhD student and mother to a one-year-old. Like a few successful ultrarunners, she has no TV.

Women beating men in ultras isn't new. Pam Reed won the 135-mile Badwater Ultramarathon outright twice. Mimi Anderson won the 350-mile 6633 Arctic Ultra. Ann Trason twice placed second at the very competitive Western States and once at 100-mile Leadville. Lizzy Hawker placed third overall at the 155-mile Spartathlon. Courtney Dauwalter and Camille Herron win races outright in the US. It happens in ultra-distance cycling and swimming sometimes too. But Jasmin's bimble was such an emphatic win in such a tough race that it revived the fascinating debate about gender differences in endurance sports.

When it comes to the long stuff, women have several physiological advantages over men. They tend to have more slow-twitch muscle fibres, which are more fatigue-resistant. They have a larger surface area to mass ratio, which means heat dissipates more easily and they cool quicker. It's also thought they handle cold weather better: insulating subcutaneous fat layer under the skin is twice as thick as men's. During lower-intensity activity, women derive significantly more energy from fat, meaning consistent, almost limitless energy release, while carb-reliant men are more likely to bonk (suffer energy crashes) – especially as they're likely to run faster.

Indeed, several marathon studies have shown that women are better at pacing too. Men tend to 'believe a bit too much in their abilities' and start out too fast, says statistician and former pro runner Jens Jakob Andersen. There's not yet any convincing evidence that women have a higher pain threshold. But anecdotally, many would agree the version of the species capable of giving birth is the tougher of the two. There's no DNF option there. I've seen two births and I'd much rather run 100 miles.

However, despite the performances noted above, when the best in the sport race each other at Western States and UTMB, it's very rare that a woman places in the top ten. Why? Because men have advantages too. They, on average, have bigger hearts, greater strength and a greater capacity to get oxygen to their muscles (a higher VO_2 max). I'm also told breasts aren't particularly performance-enhancing and the menstrual cycle can throw a curveball.

But let's look at it another way. With 100-mile races, for most runners, finishing is success. Only a small percentage are really racing. 'How come nearly all the women finish Leadville and fewer than half the men do?' asks Christopher McDougall in *Born to Run*. Ultra race results frequently show a similar pattern. Women often have a higher finisher rate.

'The longer the race, the greater the chance for women to shine,' says Ian Corless, Talk Ultra podcast publisher and a photographer often found clicking away at the sharp end of ultras. 'Watch any ultra race and men charge off the front and the ladies play it far cooler, with a more relaxed long-term picture. When the men drop out through exhaustion, the ladies come running by looking fresh as a daisy.'

And then there's the mental side. 'About fifty per cent of running long ultras well is about your head,' says Jasmin. 'The longer you go, the less it's about aerobic power and strength. It's about what's in your head, about looking after yourself, being able to multitask. Even if they're just ten per cent of the field, women are usually better prepared. And they're less likely to have a macho attitude of "I can do this! How hard can it be?"'

'The guys who cane me over 10k, I might have a shot at them over 100 miles,' says Sabrina Verjee. 'No one can run all-out for 100 miles. That top pace gets taken out of the equation and it becomes more about a disciplined pace, looking after yourself well, eating, drinking, looking after feet, pushing through any pain barriers.'

Indeed, there isn't anything much more painful than childbirth, says Sophie Power, who gained attention for breastfeeding at aid stations during 2018's UTMB. 'So maybe we handle pain better and keep a positive attitude. I can't ever remember attempting to convince a woman not to quit a race. But I've done that to plenty of men.'

The first person to complete a Paddy Buckley Round, Wendy Dodds, is more direct: 'At a non-elite level, I have observed in a number of different endurance sports that men are more likely to give up when the going gets tough.'

Nicky Spinks agrees. 'Mentally I think we're stronger. We don't tend to mope so much when things aren't going right. We tend to think about what we can do to put things right. And then get on with that, however unpleasant it is. There's less feeling sorry for ourselves.' (Wait, who's she talking about here?!)

Nicky thinks women are also better at organisation and self-discipline. 'Over the longer distances there's more to go wrong,' agrees Sophie. 'I think women are better at handling themselves when there is more to think about than just running. We are usually more practised at multitasking, more organised, have planned better and are maybe more in tune with our bodies – knowing when to push and when to stay within ourselves.'

Alex Hutchinson, author of *Endure: Mind, Body and the Curiously Elastic Limits of Human Performance*, 'mostly agrees' with the idea ultra-marathons are close to being a gender-neutral sport. 'At a 5k or even a marathon, physiology tends to trump everything else,' he says. 'Men tend to have a bunch of traits that give them an edge over women. But the longer the distance, the harder it becomes to predict on the basis of physiology alone who's going to win. It's a bit of a cliché, but ultra-distance races are fought more in the mind, and I think it's fair to say that puts men and women on a more even footing.'

He suggests we should appreciate an individual's accomplishment, 'rather than using it as a bludgeon to make broad points about sex differences. Which, I guess, is another way to say that we can perhaps consider ultra events as, if not gender-neutral, then at least far closer to gender-neutral than shorter events.'

It's frustrating that the start line for most ultras is usually only ten to twenty per cent female. But that ten to twenty per cent are probably better prepared than a lot of the men. Women only apply for promotion at work when they believe they meet 100 per cent of the requirements, according to an internal report by Hewlett-Packard to investigate why more women weren't in top management positions; whereas men apply when they meet sixty per cent of the requirements.

I'm not meaning to stir up a gender battle, but when I think about who's impressed and inspired me the most – for a variety of reasons – in this madcap sport of ours, the first names that spring to mind are Lizzy Hawker, Nicky Spinks, Jasmin Paris, Beth Pascall, Carol Morgan, Lizzie Wraith, Jo Meek, Helene Diamantides, Clare Gallagher, Rory Bosio ... Compared to that fearsome bunch, and I am falling into clumsy generalisations here, some elite men seem flaky and foolish, trotting out the same excuses on social media after the same mistakes (usually, letting their egos dictate their race speed, then being surprised when they blow up and DNF).

I love that on the start line of a 100-miler you can't tell from appearances who is going to finish. Rather than the knuckleheaded 'man up' mantra, it should be 'woman up'.

* * *

2019 wasn't a good time to be an inov-8 athlete, because the brand's others runners were knocking it out of the park. The ruddy gits. After Jasmin's internet-breaking bog-bothering, Nicky would set her Double Paddy Buckley Round record in May, while in June Paul Tierney would break the Wainwrights record, running the 214 Lakeland peaks in six days and six hours – seven hours quicker than Steve Birkinshaw's 2014 time. Meanwhile, I was scoring own goals.

All self-coached, 2018 had been my best running year, climaxing in UTMB. Was I an international elite ultra-trail runner now? Should I start referring to my sponsors as 'my family' (before switching to another family the following year)? I still felt like a balding, middle-aged father who enjoyed a lumpy bimble. But UTMB was a sea change of sorts.

Talking of sponsors, there was firm interest from a big American brand. But I couldn't bring myself to think seriously about running in anything but inov-8 kit. The underdog company had backed me when I was bobbins, had gone out of their way for me, is full of fine people who care about the right things (more anon), and their gear just works for me. Plus there's very little pressure to do social media or steering me towards particular races, unlike some other major running brands (hence why you see so many DNFs from their ambassadors at UTMB).

Unusually, I received prize money from UTMB, and I was being interviewed in the same magazines I used to interview runners in. I received more bookings for talks (which still terrified me) and more coaching enquiries, and my Instagram following doubled overnight (woo-fucking-hoo). Incidentally, if you ever feel you have too many followers, simply post a pic of a recently detached toenail – that tends to sort the faithful from the tourists.

I won't lie. I didn't mind the extra attention. It's good to feel you've done okay at something.

I was often asked in interviews if I could do any better at UTMB, but in truth I felt I probably couldn't. I was still an hour and fifty minutes behind the winner and my 2018 time wasn't that much better than 2017 (course tweaks make direct comparisons tricky). It felt like a good time to move on – I'd promised Amy that. I wanted to test myself at some of the world's other biggest 100-mile races.

Hardrock 100 and Western States, the world's oldest 100-mile trail race, were highest on my wish list. But due to land regulations in the US, the fields are small, making it verging on impossible to get places, especially for foreigners. For States, other than the lottery I enter annually with 6,000 others, the only entry option was via a Golden Ticket race. These are all in the US, tend to be 100k or less, and you need to place in the top two. It may sound like splitting hairs, but running sixty miles is a very different type of race to 100 miles. It's like using half marathons to see who the best marathon runners are (it's rare a Golden Ticket entrant does well at States). I don't have that genetic talent and raw speed, so longer distances seem to suit me better.

Regardless, with inov-8's help, a trip to California in April beckoned. But before that I planned to run the appealingly rocky UTWT race Transgrancanaria (TGC): 128 kilometres with 6,400 metres vert.

However, on Gran Canaria I suffered breathing problems early on. My lungs just felt restricted. I'd never had breathing issues before – although later I recalled similar sensations towards the end of UTMB (you're so wrecked, you hardly notice). I'd read somewhere that lungs are quite important. So I backed right off. I placed twenty-something, which felt a little embarrassing in the context of UTMB and a habit of top-ten finishes in UTWT races. I reasoned perhaps it was all the dust on the hot, dry, volcanic island, kicked up as we ran (even if others didn't seem affected), and I also had the mildest of lingering chest colds.

After a noisy race under a hot sun, getting back to familiar, quiet, cold and boggy British lumps in the dark felt like returning home to your mum after a raucous school trip to Butlins. Charlie Sproson and I had completed the other two big rounds in under twenty-four hours on sight, so we didn't expect the Paddy Buckley to be beyond our reach, even if we knew it'd be a bit hurty.

***

Of the Big Three rounds, the Bob Graham is the original, the one that gets all the attention. The Ramsay, those in the know whisper, is the special one. Eulogised in Jonny Muir's wondrous *The Mountains Are Calling*, it's more spectacular, more remote, and harder. 'The Paddy doesn't have the magnificence of the Ramsay, or get the attention of the BG,' says Nicky Spinks, who holds the double records and is also the previous women's record holder for all three.

Both the Ramsay and the Paddy are inspired by the Bob. Fascinated by the Lakeland round after a failed 1977 attempt with Chris Brasher – the same one Charlie Ramsay unwittingly gatecrashed – Paddy Buckley, although at the time more of a climber than a fell runner, hoped to create a Welsh alternative, initially to help train for the Lakes. He 'spent hours on the maps; measuring, calculating, trying variations, seeking shortcuts', and shared his idea with members of the Rucksack Club, including Mike Cudahy (who held the Pennine Way record before Mike Hartley), and Brasher, who suggested he take out the notorious knife-edge ridge of Crib Goch. They settled on a circuit of forty-seven summits and sixty-one miles with 28,000 feet of ascent. More summits and ascent than the Bob, and more distance than the Ramsay with the same ascent.

It wasn't until 1982 that anyone attempted to run it continuously. 'I remember it very clearly,' says irrepressible fell-running stalwart Wendy Dodds. '[With Paddy and Bob Roberts, I] set off from Capel, without pacers. At Aberglaslyn, Paddy had arranged a hot bath in the cottage of a local resident! He'd had problems on some attempts and thought the bath (and drinking milk) would be helpful. Bob and I had to wait for nearly forty-five minutes. Then we set off, with Paddy in long-sleeved top and long johns, even though it was very warm. After fifteen minutes, he retired. Bob and I continued, but he got the runs and eventually retired on Snowdon. I continued alone.'

There were some navigational mishaps in the dark above Llanberis, including climbing a 'moving slate mountain', which meant a sub-twenty-four-hour finish was impossible. But Dodds continued anyway. 'Paddy wanted me to give up, but I always think it's better to complete, regardless of the time, and then next time it's just a question of speeding up rather than wondering if you can get round.' Dodds completed it in twenty-five hours and thirty-eight minutes. Paddy Buckley, now in his nineties, still hasn't.

Technically, unlike the other two big rounds, there isn't a twenty-four-hour deadline for the Paddy; though most attempts aim to get under that time and you're not recognised as having completed the Big Three unless you do (only around sixty people have achieved that exclusive hat-trick). 'Paddy didn't focus on time,' Martin Stone told me for a *Runner's World* story. 'It's just not a big deal to him.'

Unlike the other two rounds, there's no website for it (though Paddy maintains a completion list offline) and it has no official start point, though traditionally it was Plas y Brenin in Capel Curig. That may sound helpful on the surface, but it throws up extra decisions, adding stress and confusion to the planning. Most people start from either Capel Curig or Llanberis. I wish Charlie and I had known that.

Which of the Big Three is toughest? That's one of those futile debates, because ultimately they're all different. But it isn't the Bob. 'As soon as I recced the Paddy I knew it was way harder than the BG,' says Nicky. 'If you fall off the path (or what is construed as a path), you end up in horrid rocks usually. For the Paddy I had to do quality training, put myself out of my comfort zone and scare myself silly – the descent off Tryfan, for example. The Paddy probably made me who I am.'

While the men's record for the Ramsay is 14:42 (Finlay Wild, 2020), the fastest ever time for the Paddy is nearly two hours slower at 16:37 (Matthew Roberts, 2020). You might argue it hasn't seen a record attempt by the same level of athlete yet, but fewer than 150 people have got round the Paddy within twenty-four hours – forty fewer than the Ramsay. 'The Paddy was definitely the hardest for me,' says Jasmin Paris, women's record holder for the Paddy and Ramsay (and previously the Bob). 'I ran it [in 2016], on the back of a huge season, so I was tired. But I suffered on the Paddy in a way I didn't on the BG or Ramsay.'

The Paddy has more rough terrain, more tricky nav and the weather seems more volatile. 'The Paddy is probably the one that catches most people out,' agrees Jim Mann, previously (sorry, mate) the winter record holder for all three. 'Underestimate it at your peril. The underfoot conditions are tough. If it's wet, it's slippery and the bog monsters come out to play. And there's a lot of rock too.'

Anecdotally it seems like more Paddy attempts are scuppered due to inclement weather than other rounds. 'The weather varies from valley to valley,' says Nicky. The Met Office estimates that Snowdonia and the Lake District get comparable amounts of rain – i.e. shedloads. However, 'Snowdonia is the first high ground that gets hit by the weather from the Irish Sea,' reasons Martin Stone, who's held records for doing all three rounds solo and unsupported. 'There are no hills to stop it. Whereas much of the BG is in the eastern Lakes, which are further from sea. At night-time, in bad weather, the Paddy can be extremely challenging.'

'The weather on the Paddy has cursed me,' says Jim. 'I had a perfect forecast (light wind and no precipitation) for my winter Paddy until forty-eight hours before. I ended up doing it in gales and white-out blizzard!'

'There is no easy section,' says Nicky. 'The Carnedds are generally regarded as the easiest, but the climb up Pen yr Ole Wen isn't exactly Dale Head, is it?! One huge difference between the Bob and the Paddy is the steepness and the pathless climbs the Paddy has.'

'It's a round you need to get to really know,' says Jim. 'You have to make friends with it.'

In places the Paddy is a little, um, idiosyncratic. 'I do get a little wound up by the nothing summits,' adds Jim. 'Some summits are less well defined,' agrees Martin, who refers to 'pimple peaks' and 'cheap summits'. Alex Copping refers to 'not sures' and 'not sees'. 'But the BG also has silly little Langdale tops, like Thunacar Knott and Sergeant Man,' counters Nicky.

Fatefully, I knew almost none of this when I met Charlie in March 2019 at Nantmor for a 7 p.m. start, going clockwise on a twenty-three-hour schedule.

It was already dark and claggy as we began the boggy climb up Bryn Banog. It was either hands-on-thighs power-hiking for thirty minutes or more, occasional jogging through long wet grass, or trying-not-to-kill-ourselves wet rock. Towards the end of the leg, we rose above the clouds to find a big moon lighting up silhouettes of dragon's-back ridges all around, and lights of distant Welsh mining towns. While reminding me of the appeal of a warm bed, it also made me feel sorry for those who never do these slightly loopy things.

At Llanberis we'd stashed a food bag and I devoured an eclair, chocolate milk and salty crisps. After a long and confusing climb through mines (our leg three), we ticked off a few more summits and the sky finally lightened. A huge moon hung in one direction, a pink sky in the other, mist in the valleys and huge lumps all around us. A little further on we stopped to ogle the sight of mist rolling into a steep valley below those endless zigzags. 'It's dragon's breath,' Charlie said.

After Glyder Fach we joined an avalanche of small rocks down to Tryfan, one of the most handsome yet daunting mountain sights in Britain. 'This is gruelling,' says Charlie, of the steep descent. My knees throbbed in agreement. 'This is harder than a BG or Ramsay,' he added, as we swapped kit and scoffed cold veggie curry at his van in the Ogwen valley. We were about fifteen minutes behind schedule. It seemed likely we'd still finish in the light, though, so I left my Petzl headtorch there. Oops.

It was a slow slog up Pen yr Ole Wen. But at the top views went on forever and out to sea. There were patches of snow, playful sunshine, good running along long gradual ridges. There was talk of what treats we'd buy in a Capel Curig cafe. But when we got there, there was no cafe any more. We were crestfallen.

After the attritional toil up Moel Siabod, from the Welsh for 'cairn of the bare, shapely hill' (though it should be named Hill with Seventy-Three False Summits), the clag curtailed our pace on a long, super-squelchy stretch following a fence. It was a floodplain. The bogs were deep, cold, hungry and full of frogspawn. Several times I sank to my waist. The damp climbed slyly up my shorts, up my baselayer, making me damp and cold.

This is the quintessential Paddy leg. There's no section on the other rounds quite like it. The terrain is confusing. The peaks are small, elusive and unsatisfying – the 'nothing summits' that wind up Jim Mann, though he also said, 'I kind of enjoy the humour in having to go out of your way to get something that really isn't a summit.' We weren't laughing. It was a treasure hunt without any actual treasure.

The clock was ticking faster than our legs were moving. From the mines, we had six summits left and two hours to get them. As we searched in the clag for the right lines, murky greyness turned to ominous darkness. Finally, we had just one summit and forty minutes left. Martin Stone calls the steep climb up Cnicht 'particularly savage'. There was still a vague chance of a sub-twenty-four-hour finish. However, due to my dim-witted complacency earlier, we were sharing one head torch. There was a half-decent path. But suddenly, in the limited light, it went AWOL, to be replaced by steep slabs of wet, slippery rock. We were topographically embarrassed. We wouldn't make sub-twenty-four hours. It was raining hard. We were cold, wet, tired, sore, grumpy. Why did we do this &*%@ again?

We reached my car in a disappointing twenty-five hours and forty minutes. The fact our time was so close to Wendy Dodds' first attempt was only a small consolation. The Paddy had beaten us.

At about 2 a.m., I awoke in my car, feeling stiff and confused, and started the long drive home. My phone pinged into life with missed calls from Charlie's wife Nicky and mutual good friend Paul Tierney. Neither Charlie or I had told anyone we were off the mountains and okay, causing some medium-level panic. I let them know. Amy shows comparatively little interest in what I'm doing, so at least she hadn't been worrying. In fact, regardless of how big the challenge is, she just assumes I'll do it. There's no anxiety or doubt on her part. Which is a compliment, I suppose.

The Paddy had proven harder than the other two rounds, the only one we couldn't complete on sight in under twenty-four hours. You can't just rock up and throw a few fancy moves on these distrusting, discerning Welsh mountains. You have to spend time getting to know the Paddy, win it over gradually. I respected it all the more for its unwillingness to bend to our advances.

'Maybe it's just me,' says Nicky, 'but I've always loved the low-key feel and the idiosyncrasies. I think it's way fiddlier than the other rounds, but in a way that's what makes it different. I would say it's on par with the Ramsay in being my favourite. And maybe even surpasses it.'

Ah, those idiosyncrasies. I asked Paddy Buckley about the common complaint that some of the summits are just bumps: 'I am not interested in other people's grumbles about the route,' he said. 'It was never intended to be an easy day out.'

Our disappointment soon faded. The stronger memory is of an adventure shared with a good friend – proper Type 2 fun. Our time didn't matter as much as those soggy memories.

* * *

Just six weeks later, I swapped wet Welsh mountains for sunny Californian canyons. Canyons 100k is an out-and-back race on the legendary Western States course. Foresthill, a former gold-mining town north-east of Sacramento, felt like a film set. Or maybe it felt so familiar because of the countless times I'd seen Western States films and followed *iRunFar.com*'s race coverage.

The journey over didn't go well. A flight delay of four-plus hours skewed my carefully planned itinerary and I reached my accommodation around 2 a.m. after a long drive. I hadn't really trained specifically for the race (I was just happier going up and down lumps in Snowdonia and the Beacons). Also, the idea it was top two or bust was hard to reconcile. Maybe I need to believe in myself more. But I have my best races when I feel relaxed and excited, and I didn't really feel that way in the US. It was the only time I'd turned down Lee's request to do a pre-race blog for the inov-8 website. I knew it'd be warmer than the UK, but I was checking the temperatures for Foresthill without knowing it'd be 10 °F hotter in the canyons.

I think I've got all my excuses in now. A little bit of that's bad luck. But most of it's on me. I had a wonderful time – they have a super-ace trail-running community. But I didn't have a great race. Here's me trotting out my excuses on social media (I'll spare you the hashtags):

☹ It was too toasty for me (30 °C-plus in the canyons). I was doing okay (not brilliantly, but okay). But when the heat hit I went backwards. I sat down at an aid station for the first time in years.

☹ To be honest, the prize at stake did make me race a little differently to how I normally would.

☹ It was also a course that highlighted my weaknesses.

☹ Sure, in an ideal world, I'd get out here a few weeks early, recce the course, and become fully heat and time-zone adapted. But I've got kids. And I don't want them to forget who I am.

☹ I told myself I wouldn't make excuses, but I just have.

☑ After all my excitement about rattlesnakes, bears and cougars, I got a tick.

☺ It's time to get back to races and challenges that play to my strengths, I think.

I couldn't have afforded the trip without inov-8's help, so I had that dreaded feeling of letting a team down again. After TGC and the Paddy, that was three relative failures in a row. My new life as an international elite athlete wasn't a roaring success so far.

On reflection, a regression to the mean after UTMB was probably inevitable. Heat, jetlag and tiredness from travel disruption were easy excuses. More likely, I'd simply been found out. I'm a limited athlete who tends to do better the longer and lumpier a challenge is (so I can do more hiking, but shush). I'm not talented or versatile enough to be internationally competitive at shorter, faster ultras, and the US scene is far more competitive than the UK. I'm okay with that. It was, after all, only a race. Or maybe I simply couldn't perform without a Summit Fever Media camera pointed at me? I was clearly also simply doing too many big things around then.

May was a good time to stop obsessing about myself and help others instead, namely Nicky Spinks and John Kelly on their Paddy Buckley efforts. The fact that they were both record attempts felt a little bit historic and added a sprinkling of extra excitement. It was in between following the notorious macaroon thief around with a bag of noodles and introducing the tea-dodging American to Tunnock's bars that my mind opened to the idea of my own record attempt on the Paddy.

The lightbulb moment happened on an easy six-miler at home. I had laced up my X-Talons that sunny morning feeling a bit glum, but once the Paddy hand grenade went off in my head, I returned home full of smiles. 'What's up with you?' asked Amy suspiciously.

I stuck Harvey Maps' *Paddy Buckley Round* up on the wall by my desk ...

13
GETTING IN A(NOTHER) PADDY

'If you have anything left at all, now is the moment to use it.'

I had a couple of records to my name, but they weren't Premier League standard. I hadn't considered myself capable of a credible fell-running record. Because I wasn't a fell runner. Fell runners live in ultra-lumpy places like the Lake District (highest summit 3,209 feet). I live in the manicured Cotswolds (highest summit 1,083 feet, but I live nowhere near it). And fell runners wear vests and bumbags and eat rusty nails for breakfast – and only eat breakfast after they've run up Scafell Pike twice in a biblical hailstorm.

The terrain is the key difference. I can run – or at least travel self-propelled (there may well be some power-hiking and shuffling involved) – a long way. But most of my races were on clear, firm trails, not rough fell terrain. That's usually little to no path, trail or trod; instead mud, bog, rock, long grass, heather and tussocks – often bundled together so your foot plays unlucky dip with each leg cycle. And it's often very steep too. Moving on fells rarely fits the description of running you'll read about in *Runner's World*. Don't get me wrong, I love all this stuff. But it didn't mean I was good at it. When I had run with bona fide fell runners, I'd felt inadequate.

But it suddenly occurred to me that my legs and my head had accidentally got to know the Paddy rather well recently, with four visits in the last few months. I'd run sixty miles three times that year, so my fitness shouldn't be far off. My nav was still bobbins, but in June I might get round without a head torch. I could be flexible and wait for a good weather window. I'd run out of excuses ...

Tim Higginbottom's record of 17:42 may have stood for ten years, but compared to Kilian Jornet's 12:52 for the Bob, there had to be a little bit of room in it. If I had a go in secret, there was nothing to lose. I visited Snowdonia one more time, to run a leg and a half at record pace; which felt encouraging. It'd be tough. But not impossible.

Of course, you'll run better if someone else carries your egg sangers. But going solo appealed too. I'd never run with pacers before – it seemed unnatural and mostly unnecessary. I'd also never tried to arrange a support team; it seemed like a huge headache and I didn't want the pressure of many people knowing. The flexibility of going at short notice in the best possible weather window could be key. I also felt really inspired by Martin Stone's and Dan Doherty's solo un/self-supported ethics (I'd been the sole supporter on a Paddy attempt by Dan in August 2018, my first taste of the seductive Snowdonia circuit). I wanted to be a lone warrior like them.

In the end I told four people, partly to nudge me towards actually doing it and partly because a little help might go a long way. Local speedster Michael Corrales, who I'd met when supporting John Kelly (see next chapter), was great company and knew parts of the Paddy well. He said he might be able to join me for the final leg. Other than that, I'd be solo. I didn't even tell inov-8's Lee Procter.

I figured starting from Llanberis meant getting rocky bits and bigger climbs done on fresher legs. After necking a banana and a stale pain aux raisins, I set off from the red Llanberis Lake Railway sign at 4 a.m. on Wednesday 18 June. Under a big moon and clear skies it was T-shirt temperatures. My head was giddy with adventure.

I didn't want to overcook that first big climb through the mines. But my first split could set the tone for the day. Would I be stressfully chasing my 17:40 schedule? Or ahead, feeling optimistic? I pushed a bit more than normal. I missed the optimal line, but hit the summit cairn two minutes up. Just forty-six more to go.

That first leg was glorious. Brilliant mellow light. A gentle breeze.

No one else about. I felt lucky and happy. It was just a cracking day out in the heady hills. I was thrilled but slightly alarmed to be twenty minutes ahead of record pace at the summit of Tryfan, nearly five hours in, but I felt perfectly comfortable. Inevitably I got caught daydreaming and missed the best line off the treacherous summit. And the second-best line, getting caught in a no man's land of boulders, heather and hidden potholes. I wasted time. But I didn't get annoyed. I was doing what I love.

It was a long slog up Pen yr Ole Wen at the start of leg two, but it always is. Then glorious plateau and ridge-line running. I tried not to look at my schedule, knowing I'd do better if I mostly ignored it. After dodging the optimal line again amongst the high heather descending Pen Llithrig y Wrach, I was still around fifteen minutes ahead at Capel Curig. There I eagerly grabbed my first stash of supplies, including brioche rolls crammed with nut butter, banana and chocolate spread. Yummo.

The day was warming up. I felt I was moving well, so was a little miffed to be only ten minutes up overall at the rocky summit of Moel Siabod. I ran the descent hard enough, but had gained back no time by the next peak. Nor the next. In fact, minutes were slowly seeping away. Then it got boggy. Not waist-deep, but not far off. Which slowed me more, as did identifying the exact summits of the byzantine bumps over the next couple of hours. I tagged a bonus one. D'oh! I was now behind schedule. *Don't panic. Don't let a scratch become a wound. Stay focused. Be efficient. Stay sustainable. Remember, this is what you love doing.*

As I climbed the brutish Cnicht I heard the rare sound of a cuckoo, just as I had done when here with Nicky. I ran hard on the stony trails and road that followed, not thinking of gaining back time, just trying not to lose more.

Scooping up more supplies from a bag in a bush at the National Trust car park, I left Nantmor twelve minutes behind record pace. I tried not to feel frustrated. This was all just an experiment, a fun day out, right? But I was starting to think the record was beyond my grasp.

I've never found a good line up through the boggy bracken to Bryn Banog. It was warm. I got dehydrated. The higher Moel Hebog was a monstrous climb. I was losing more precious time. My motivation dimmed. Sub-17:42 no longer felt possible. But the second-best time for the Paddy Buckley Round was 18:10, shared by Mark Hartell and Chris Near (on separate runs, remarkably). I could maybe still beat that? I sent a silly-face selfie to my wife and kids. I'd taken intermittent selfies too, as some kind of proof. By the end of leg four, Pont Cae'r Gors, I was nearly twenty-five minutes behind the record. But I had a secret weapon: Michael and his dog Dusty.

Michael nearly hadn't turned up. His car window had broken that day, replaced by a Sellotaped plastic bag for now. 'I really, truly think we can still break the record,' he said. I didn't believe him. But I was so grateful he'd made the effort to join me (I didn't even know about his car then) that I felt I owed him at least some huffing and puffing. He'd gradually see I wasn't really up to it, I figured, and we could just relax.

But Michael had different ideas. He encouraged, cajoled and politely bullied me on the long slog up Snowdon in the gloaming. For the first time ever, I saw all of Snowdonia bathed in golden light. We made up a few minutes at the first peak. A few more at the second. 'We really can do this,' he insisted. I grunted.

I left him in charge of my schedule. 'If we could get to the top of Snowdon for 20:01, it would make me very happy,' he said. I did that at least. On the summit a solitary fell runner wished us luck and really seemed to mean it. After Garnedd Ugain we hammered the descent like it was a one-peak fell race. I was trying to keep up with Michael – not just a proper fell runner, but one who wins downhill races. My legs protested loudly.

I hoped Michael would stop pestering me. But we kept on making up time. Drat. We had an hour left. 'Just four summits to go,' he said. He gave me all his water, though he was clearly thirsty himself. The Moels and Foels are grassy peaks, with good running. But they looked like tidal waves to me. The arms of my top were caked in sweat. Auditioning brilliantly for the role of super-coach in the next *Rocky* film, on the penultimate climb Michael said, 'If you have anything left at all, now is the moment to use it.' I did what I could.

'From the final summit, the schedule has thirty minutes to get to Llanberis!' said Michael, excitedly. There was a chance. Oh pants. I had to keep pushing. The final descent was the perfect gradient. Firm grass, runnable, the promised land of Llanberis below in the fading light.

We tumbled down the hills and hit the tarmac. Thankfully the main road was quiet, as I had no plans to stop for traffic. I grabbed the post of Llanberis Lake Railway, where I'd started, breathless, at 9.31 p.m. My total time was seventeen hours, thirty-one minutes and thirty-nine seconds, just eleven minutes under the previous record.

I couldn't quite believe what had happened. We took a few snaps. Having done four-fifths of the Paddy solo, I was a little anxious I might not be believed, so I quickly SMSed Martin Stone to let him know and tell him a gpx file would be forthcoming. He replied instantly with congratulations.

It was just an experiment, really, that went okay. The adventure/athletics pendulum had swung back towards athletics on this one. It sure took the edge off the parking ticket I found on my car windscreen. I felt huge gratitude towards Michael and wanted to invite him for a drink. But he needed to get home, so I celebrated with a drive back round to Pont Cae'r Gors, then to Capel Curig; then a mere whiff of ale on my own in my bunkhouse put me out cold.

In trying to get my gpx file to Martin the next morning I accidentally loaded it to Strava. Lee, otherwise rightly preoccupied with Paul Tierney's Wainwrights run, was in touch in a flash. 'What's this?!' he messaged. It felt good to casually mention I'd just broken a record on one of the Big Three rounds. Former record holder Tim Higginbottom sent me a lovely congratulatory email.

I wasn't expecting to hold the record for long. But I'd enjoyed the secrecy, the sense of mission, the emotional ups and downs, the drama towards the end (retrospectively anyway), and a success in a year of disappointments. The Paddy had helped me fall back in love with running again.

* * *

I won the Lakeland Trails 55k ten days later, but I knew it was unlikely I would do well at Eiger Ultra Trail, a UTWT race the following month.

It's a stunning course in the Swiss Alps, but breathing issues dogged me again (I just figured I was tired from the Paddy, coupled with the altitude), though I recovered to finish seventh. I was happy to sacrifice the race for the Paddy record and I'd had a fun day out in some incredible scenery, including running across the front of the Eiger.

I was really excited about Ultra Tour Monte Rosa (UTMR) in September, a 100-mile race in the Swiss Alps, created by five-time UTMB-winner Lizzy Hawker, a hero to me for both her incredible CV and her attitude to the world (I'd loved her book, *Runner*, an account of enjoying being in the mountains, communing with nature and, whoops, winning UTMB, again). On a three-day recce, joined at times by Lizzie Wraith and Beth Pascall, and meeting Lizzy (what is it with Elizabeths being amazing distance runners?) in a Grächen cafe, I found a route more rugged, beautiful and technical than UTMB, with more vert, bigger climbs, more wildlife (huge mountain goats), and a delicious remoteness and quietness.

There were some fellow UTMB top ten-ers there, including my Latvian buddy Roman Evarts, plus the 100k world champion, my roommate, Sweden's Jonas Buud. My training had been better than ever and it felt like I might have a chance of a first 100-mile win.

We knew when we started that the weather was going to deteriorate. I had no plans to push early on. I like playing the long game. But a Canadian runner kept trying to make a break for it and I just wasn't willing to let him. I stayed with him while it was comfortable, as we rose and fell on singletrack trails up and down the Zermatt valley with occasional views of huge menacing mountains through the clouds. We crossed the epic, swaying Charles Kuonen Suspension Bridge. And when he ran out of steam, I carried on.

I enjoyed the long climb up from Zermatt towards the Italian border, and attached micro-spikes to my Trailrocs for a glacier crossing in the clouds. I was starting to tire, but only in an expected way, as I reached the Gressoney checkpoint (eighty-two kilometres in) around twenty minutes ahead of the field. I was about to leave when a race official handed me a phone, saying it was Lizzy Hawker. 'I'm so sorry,' she said.

GETTING IN A(NOTHER) PADDY

'The weather is going to be really bad and we have to stop the race for safety reasons. I'm really sorry. But you've won.' What I heard was: 'You've won and you don't need to run through the night and a fuckton of biblical weather.' I was okay with that.

Sure, over time, the result has started to feel a little unsatisfactory. But I had a blast, eating pizza with Dan Lawson, Robbie Britton and Natalie White, and hanging out in Grächen pubs with Lizzie Wraith and other like-minded loons.

* * *

Aside from the Paddy, the other big thing that happened to me in 2019 was radicalisation by an extremist organisation. No, not the Bob Graham Club. Rather, that's how UK counterterrorism police laughably label strictly non-violent and actually ruddy lovely climate-emergency protest group Extinction Rebellion (XR). Look out, here comes the soap-boxy bit. (If you're only here for the boggy bimbles, lumpy loops and details of intimate chafing, skip to page 175.)

The science is unanimous. The planet is warming more rapidly than normal. And we're causing it. While, in the longer-term, UK runners may find heat-acclimating for MdS a little easier, there are other consequences. They're very likely to include rising seas putting hundreds of millions in coastal cities at risk, fresh water shortages, threats to food production, and increased deaths from floods, storms, heatwaves, droughts and wildfires (remember footage of Australia, Siberia, the Amazon and the US in 2020?).

A 'biological annihilation' of wildlife in recent decades means a sixth mass extinction in Earth's history is underway, with billions of populations already lost (according to peer-reviewed journal *Proceedings of the National Academy of Sciences* in 2017). More recently, dolphins have started dying from a painful skin disease linked to climate change. Bees, critical to our ecosystem, are being wiped out. A quarter of Britain's native mammals are 'at imminent risk of extinction', scientists announced in July 2020. I don't see hedgehogs any more in Wiltshire (every cloud ...), or badgers. Remember cuckoos?

Coral reefs are dying and two in five of the world's plant species are at risk of extinction as a result of the destruction of the natural world, often for farming (according to a report by the International Union for Conservation of Nature).

As well as record wildfires, 2020 saw the hottest year ever (according to NASA), the hottest ocean temperatures ever recorded (supercharging extreme weather), a record twenty-nine tropical storms in the Atlantic, and the hottest ever temperature recorded on Earth. Antarctica was warmer than ever, and the UK saw the wettest month and wettest day ever recorded. The six hottest years in human history have all occurred since 2014, and the 2010s was the hottest decade ever. Climate-heating gases have reached record levels in the atmosphere, despite global lockdowns in 2020, says the UN's World Meteorological Organization.

And then there's air pollution. In the UK there are 35,000 premature deaths a year due to air pollution, while current limits for particulate matter (the Air Quality Standard Regulations 2010) are two and a half times higher than the World Health Organization recommends. Runners are especially at risk, because they breathe deeply into their lungs.

We don't have long at all. The 2015 Paris Climate Agreement set a target of a 1.5 °C end-of-century rise in global temperature compared to pre-industrial levels. 2 °C is regarded as the outer limit of safety. It's estimated we'll hit 1.5 °C in twelve years. We're currently heading for 3.2 °C by 2100. Scientists calculate that global emissions need to fall by half by 2030 to give us any chance.

Some scientists link Covid-19 and an 'era of pandemics' (HIV, Ebola, bird flu, SARS and even mad cow disease) to climate change and our constant assault on the natural world.

And that's only the stuff we know about.

Yep, we've really fucked this place up. The apocalypse is coming? It's already on top of us.

This isn't alarmist propaganda shouted rabidly by someone with pink and green hair. It's all on the BBC and *Guardian* websites and most of it comes from the Intergovernmental Panel on Climate Change (IPCC), a United Nations body responsible for assessing the science related to climate change. Just like cigarette companies when links were established between smoking and cancer, fossil fuel giant ExxonMobil has spent millions of dollars funding climate-change denial since the 1970s (they were taken to court over it).

'Can anybody still deny that we are facing a dramatic emergency?' That's not some uncooperative crusty. That's the UN secretary-general, António Guterres, talking in December 2020. He urged global governments to declare a state of climate emergency until the world has reached net zero CO_2 emissions. 'Climate change is destroying lives across our planet ... Making peace with nature is the defining task of the twenty-first century ... for everyone, everywhere,' he added.

The planet is facing a 'ghastly future of mass extinction, declining health and climate-disruption upheavals' that threaten human survival because of ignorance and inaction, warned seventeen scientists from the US, Mexico and Australia in January 2020. 'The scale of the threats to the biosphere and all its lifeforms – including humanity – is in fact so great that it is difficult to grasp for even well-informed experts,' they warned in a report in *Frontiers in Conservation Science* which references more than 150 studies detailing the world's major environmental challenges.

'I find it hard to exaggerate the peril,' said much-loved wildlife documentary narrator David Attenborough in January 2021. 'This is the new extinction and we are halfway through it. We are in terrible, terrible trouble and the longer we wait to do something about it, the worse it is going to get.'

Of course, some politicians find it awkward to act because they'll be shafting their rich mates who put them in power (for example, the UK's business secretary Kwasi Kwarteng accepted substantial donations from fossil fuel investors and advisers as part of his 2019 general election campaign, revealed the *Guardian* in January 2020; Donald Trump may have been backed by fossil fuel giants by as much as $15 million). Plus why make such difficult and unpopular decisions when you can leave it to the next guys to sort out?

Like most outdoorsy types, I'd always *cared* about this stuff. But passively. My parents have voted Green for decades and have gone many years without flying because it's too much for their conscience. I knew the Arctic was melting and we had more storms named Derek and Daisy. But I had climate-change fatigue, a kind of environmental-news bonk. XR woke (pun intended) me up.

Here's what haunts me. If we do nothing, what will our children and their children think of their parents, grandparents and our generation as a whole? We had a chance to avert global catastrophe, we knew what was happening, and we were too busy liking strangers' posts on Instagram to do anything about it. They'll look back at us with disgust, shame and resentment. Selfish, greedy, lazy tossers. What did you do in the great climate and ecological emergency, Daddy? Well, I did call someone a crusty on Twitter. And anyway, I like hot summers.

In 2019 I took seven return flights. There, I've said it. The Swedish have a word, *flygskam*, meaning 'flight shaming', and I am very ashamed of mine. They just kind of happened. (One was a work trip that doubled as a family holiday, but that hardly vindicates me.) I told myself I was doing my job as an international ultrarunner. I had to fly for work, right?

A return flight from London to San Francisco emits around 5.5 tonnes of CO_2 equivalent (CO_2e) per person – more than twice the emissions produced by a family car in a year. A return flight from London to Berlin emits around 0.6 tonnes of CO_2e – three times the emissions saved from a year of recycling, according to 2018 figures from the International Council on Clean Transportation.

Extinction Rebellion (XR) burst into the national consciousness in November 2018 when some visually striking protests in London made headline news, and they were back in April 2019. Big pink boats blocked traffic. Women dressed all in red did choreographed mime. Banners said 'Tell the truth'. Their actions were highly photographic, with a clear message. Their hourglass symbol was profound, memorable and accessible. These 'uncooperative crusties', as Boris Johnson would call them, caused all sorts of disruption, blocking bridges to traffic, and sang joyous songs as they were led away by the police. I thought they were amazing. And their protests were very well thought-through and organised.

These classic civil disobedience tactics have worked effectively throughout history, from the suffrage movement to Gandhi and Martin Luther King, not forgetting our Mass Trespass friends on Kinder Scout back in 1932. XR have been openly backed by Stephen Fry, Emma Thompson, Benedict Cumberbatch, Jarvis Cocker, Thom Yorke, Massive Attack, Steve Coogan, Natalie Imbruglia (swoon), Ray Winstone, and many other authors, actors, scientists, journalists, doctors, and sportspeople (and the fact that came from a positive *Daily Mail* story shows how much influence XR have had). Oh and amazing Swedish teenager Greta Thunberg. XR brought our climate and ecological emergency back into the national consciousness at a critical time.

I felt a pang of pride when I learnt XR were formed in Stroud, where I went to school. And even more pride that my Bristolian sister had been involved with them for a while. I wanted to do *something*. But I didn't know what. And I feared being called a hypocrite. How could I get involved in XR, or even be vocal about our climate and ecological emergency, when I was flying around the world to indulge my midlife crisis?

'That doesn't matter,' said my sister. 'XR see our emergency as political, not personal. No one there will judge you. The onus isn't on individuals; instead we're urging governments and corporations to act, as they can make so much more difference.'

'When it comes to the climate crisis you are either a hypocrite or an arsehole,' says comedian Tom Walker in his Jonathan Pie persona. It kind of is that simple. From our food to our clothes to the energy in our homes and even sending an email, almost everything we do creates CO_2e emissions. So if we can't speak up till we're living off-grid in a hut in the woods eating only foraged mushrooms, well, no one will speak up till it's too late.

I started going to XR meetings in Bath. I joined protests in London. There was an infectious sense of community and determination, optimism and stoicism. It is all a bit hippie – they do like a good singsong – but then I'm a bit hippie. It felt good to be doing something, to care about something and act on it. It felt authentic and empowering to act according to strongly held values. Impressively Dan Lawson managed to get himself arrested, whereas disappointingly I only got told off by a copper for standing on a wall.

I was doing the political bit, but I wanted to make personal changes too, partly to lower my hypocrite rating, but more for my conscience. I felt bad about eating a burger or driving my car. Avoiding meat (especially lamb and beef – sorry, Spinksy) and dairy is the single biggest way to reduce our environmental impact (according to a 2018 study published in the journal *Science*).

I've made dietary changes gradually with Renee McGregor's guidance, hopefully without impacting my health or performances, and I'm effectively plant-based (I think that means the same as vegan but a bit less annoying?). But if my kids leave some cheese on their plate, I still fulfil my daddy dustbin role, because waste is worst of all. I'm probably ninety-five per cent vegan. Or, as author Jen Gale would have it, vegan(ish). I've gone from hating vegetables as a kid to mostly eating vegetables. It's surprisingly easy and fun being veganish. Another easy change is switching to a renewable energy supplier, such as Bulb or Ecotricity (owned by Forest Green owner Dale Vince), which takes just five minutes online.

I wanted qualified advice and independent verification on reducing my carbon footprint. Our Carbon, a carbon-auditing consultancy, analysed not just my but my family's CO_2e profile, estimated at 16.8 tonnes for 2019. That's comfortably below the average of thirteen tonnes per person in the UK (according to *How Bad Are Bananas?* author Mike Berners-Lee), but even then a huge chunk of it was my flights. We came up with a realistic (pre-Covid) plan to emit ten tonnes for 2020, comfortably inside Berners-Lee's idea of the five-tonne lifestyle (per person). Then we offset that by buying trees at Jim Mann's The Future Forest Company, making my family carbon negative for the year. Sure, offsetting is far from perfect, but it's the best option we have right now, and there is genuine reduction in emissions too. It's progress not perfection.

Amy also greatly reduced our plastic use, by shopping more smartly, using refills and companies such as Riverford and Abel & Cole who use minimal amounts of the evil stuff. You might argue plastic isn't a huge greenhouse gas emitter, but incineration of plastic waste is increasingly driving up emissions. A bottle can last for 450 years, and a study in the journal *Science* estimated that between 19 million and 23 million tonnes of plastic found its way into both rivers and oceans in 2016, killing animals across eighty different species (according to CSIRO, the Australian government's science agency). Microplastics are everywhere: in our food, at the deepest point on Earth (the Mariana Trench) and the highest point on Earth (the summit of Everest). The most comprehensive study to date found microplastics in ninety-six of ninety-seven seawater samples from Arctic seas (a huge proportion of which was polyester – 'the same width and colours as those used in clothes'). Our world is turning plastic. We're turning plastic. It's not fantastic.

Others have given up flying or been vegan for yonks. I could do more. Perfection, whether in ethics or anything else, will always be elusive. But we can make progress. I'm not telling anyone else how to live their lives. I still believe the way forward is primarily political more than personal. I will look like an idiot and a hypocrite at times. But I don't mind being an outspoken idiot if it helps keep the right things on the agenda. I won't always get it right. But I promise it comes from the right place.

I've been really inspired by fellow bimble-lovers Dan Lawson and Jim Mann. Jim is the co-founder of The Future Forest Company, which delivers large-scale reforestation projects in the UK; and Trees Not Tees (who Amy works for), which encourages runners and race organisers to plant trees instead of getting T-shirts they probably won't wear. The running industry has got into the unfortunate habit of creating millions of excess tees; it takes the same amount of water a person drinks in 2.5 years to make a cotton one, plus over two kilograms of CO_2e; while nylon and polyester can take up to 200 years to biodegrade. Aware of the terrible role the clothing and sportswear industries play in our climate and ecological emergency, Dan, his wife Charlotte and their two children formed ReRun Clothing, which does a brilliant job of extending the life of running clothes by recycling, reselling and redistributing unwanted shoes and T-shirts – as well as spreading awareness of a huge problem.

Being a sponsored athlete who says they care about our climate and ecological emergency is another contradiction. The fashion industry accounts for a whopping ten per cent of global emissions, more than aviation and shipping combined. Re-read that and let it soak in. As an ambassador for a clothing and footwear brand, I'm a cog in the machinery of planet-killing overconsumption. I have agonised over this. In all honesty, it's hard to give up something so hard-earnt. I try to rationalise it by telling myself it's better to be on the inside than the outside. And I'm careful about who I align myself with.

We're clearly over-consuming and I've been guilty of over-promoting new stuff in the past, helping create a desire for the newest and latest. The most sustainable kit is the stuff we already own. I've had to rethink what I'll promote. Luckily inov-8 are on the right side of history. They really care and really want to improve – and it isn't just words. Graphene, which lasts longer than conventional rubber, is an obvious step in the right direction, as is their recycled clothing, with more exciting ideas in the pipeline. Just like me, they might not get everything right (some of the issues they face are huge and complex, such as being sure of a sustainable supply chain when a shoe is made in China and can have 200 parts). But they care and they're trying.

I've politely pushed back on all my sponsors – and potential sponsors (it was agonising turning away a tea sponsor when I realised their product would arrive in non-recyclable plastic, while another brand seemed outraged when I said I'd only work with them if they have a sustainability policy) – to ask what they're doing to make themselves more sustainable, and have largely been encouraged by their responses. I'd thought I might get cold-shouldered, but I've had more companies approach me and more interest from the media; which shows that we all know this sea (pun not intended) change is needed.

I thought more ethically about my race schedule for 2020 and brought it down from four races abroad and five flights, to two races abroad and one flight. I've said no thanks to race invites in Mexico, Nepal, Oman and many more (I can hear those tiny violins). Not perfect. But progress. And then everyone copied me and stopped flying altogether (too soon?). I really like Jen Gale's approach (*asustainablelife. co.uk*), of being sustainable(ish), doing your best but being realistic, sometimes being #imperfectlygreen. I'm trying to be a sustainable(ish) athlete. Indeed the words *sustainability* and *efficiency* are key ones when it comes to both ultrarunning and our planet.

After I'd been banging on about stuff a bit, in interviews and on social media, Kilian Jornet got in touch to tell me about plans for his foundation (*kilianjornetfoundation.org*) and the Pledge (*outdoorfriendly.org*), encouraging brands, events, federations and athletes to be more sustainable. Like Dan and Jim, he's showing great leadership and it makes me optimistic about the global running community and how it might effect change. By definition ultrarunners like big challenges and we face the biggest one yet. One we can't run away from.

* * *

Anyway, I got a bit carried away there, trying to make you feel sorry for a middle-class white guy living the dream. You stole this book because you wanted to read about all the gloriously ouchy running, didn't you?

2019's unsatisfactory results made me question my training. I'd been self-coached for two years, one of which was my best ever and one of which felt a little flat (Paddy record aside). I'd been intrigued by US super-coach David Roche for a while. I'd read his book *The Happy Runner* and heard him on numerous podcasts telling everyone they were loved, cherished and amazing! I liked his relentless positivity but more so his science-based reasoning in an arena full of unqualified cowboys and crackpot ideas – and the fact that he's a former climate-change lawyer. Plus, almost everyone getting impressive results is coached by him, including Scott Hawker (third at UTMB in 2019), Clare Gallagher (Western States and CCC winner), Hayden Hawks (everything winner), and some bloke named John Kelly.

When I contacted David, I was happily bewildered by his signature hyper-optimism, calling me a 'freaking boss' and peppering our communications with 'amazing!' and 'fuckton'. He reduced my volume of training miles, but added endless hill strides and a strict weekly rest day, and told me I was amazing almost every day. I felt re-energised, both physiologically and psychologically. It's a good feeling when someone believes in you. He was making me a better coach too.

In October 2019 I emailed Martin Stone for information on Mike Hartley's record-breaking run on the Pennine Way. But David wasn't so enthused. 'I think that doing it in 2020 could risk undercutting your growth a bit,' he said. 'Plus the super-long FKT things can be done into your fifties physiologically! The top performance stuff has a bit more of a ticking clock.' I was okay with that. It was seriously daunting and another good excuse to put it off again. Yet I still found myself mentioning 'doing a UK FKT attempt that scares me' on Talk Ultra and at a talk at the Buxton Adventure Festival in February.

The Pennine Way was my Darth Vader: a looming threat that I was destined to one day face head-on (but hopefully without snogging my sister).

14

SKYWALKER OR SOLO? NOPE, A BEAR OF VERY LITTLE BRAIN

'There's another fool up here in the snow at 4.30 a.m!'

When Martin Stone, the custodian of long-distance records for the FRA and a super-enthusiastic authority on all such things in the UK, wrote some lovely words about my Paddy Buckley record run in *The Fellrunner*, I was struck by something he said. He suggested we were almost at the end of the era where overall records for the Big Three rounds could be broken with solo runs. Several people had congratulated me not just on the record, but for 'the style you did it in'. I presumed they weren't talking about my hair.

I was also finding out more about Martin, a link to the first golden age of UK long-distance running and a softly spoken but intense man. I first heard of him as the joint winner (with Helene Whitaker, nee Diamantides) of the inaugural 1992 Dragon's Back Race (then a pairs event). I phoned him to hear more.

Martin remembers reading a book about the first ascent of Everest 'and feeling very inspired by it' as a child. His parents weren't athletic but would do family jaunts to Plymouth and Falmouth to see yachts coming back from round-the-world trips. He saw Sir Francis Chichester (the first person to sail single-handed around the world by the clipper route) and Sir Robin Knox-Johnston (the first person to perform a single-handed non-stop circumnavigation of the globe) sail in. 'I was entranced by their stories.'

He was the year above Tim Laney at his Exeter school, though neither were runners. At university Martin was in the mountaineering club and did the Bob Graham at just twenty. 'I saw talks by the likes of Doug Scott and Chris Bonington about their ascents of Everest, but when Reinhold Messner and Peter Habeler climbed it without oxygen, their minimalist approach had a big impact on me. I just thought it was so beautiful how people were able to simplify things so much. Then Messner went back to solo Everest! I was really struck by that philosophy.'

In the 1980s Martin wasn't just a star of the scene, but a pioneer. In 1987 he became the first person to complete the Big Three rounds – also the second person to do a Ramsay, the first to do a Paddy within twenty-four hours. Until recently he was the only person to have completed all three solo-unsupported and had the only solo-unsupported Bob Graham and Paddy Buckley Rounds in midwinter. Oh and he set a new Scottish Munros 24-Hour Record, also solo-unsupported.

'I was an average racer, really,' he tells me. 'But doing these fell-running rounds solo and unsupported … No one else was doing these things, not setting records anyway. I could have done them with a team, but something made me want to do them on my own.

'When I set off on a solo-unsupported Ramsay Round there was definitely a sense of adventure, a sense of jeopardy. You've got to do it all yourself, there's no one to help you. Before winter rounds I would get incredibly nervous; I had an incredible sense of anticipation, almost a sense of dread. But you also can't bear not to do it either. It's so addictive, that feeling.

'I love being a team player sometimes. But it's a fantastic feeling knowing you did everything yourself. It's got to be more satisfying. I don't really believe people who say they don't care what other people think about them – I'll admit I like the reaction of people when they say things like, "You did what? How could you do that!?"'

I identify with what Martin says so much it almost feels like I'm listening to myself talking.

Few things in life are as satisfying as the afterglow from a long run in the mountains in winter. I love being wrapped up in my Stormshell and wrag (head scarf), being attacked by the wind and snow in the Beacons or Snowdonia, playing at being Skywalker on Hoth. You can't feel your fingers and toes, your cheeks are like embarrassed radishes, and there's snot across your face. You had a moment where the wind was so strong you seriously considered turning back, but you didn't. It's like being allowed into the lion's den at the zoo. How long will the ferocious big cat tolerate you? Will he pounce and tear you to bits, or just growl a couple of times and leave you alone? There's something about winter and the uncertainty of the weather that add extra drama, jeopardy and edginess to a bimble. And, of course, can make it incredibly beautiful too.

As winter approached I started to get a bad illness which made me itchy and restless. It's called Spine Fever and if left untreated it escalates. The only way to cure it is to commit to something else. So I started looking up winter records. The logical place to start was the places I knew well. The record for a winter Paddy Buckley Round was Jim Mann's 21:37. I'd run it four hours faster in the summer, so in certain conditions that should be beatable. But was I mining the pit to extinction by going back to North Wales for a third time? Was I trying to rekindle a holiday romance? I didn't care. I couldn't resist.

Winter records are more open to debate, because conditions can vary wildly. If you wait for the best possible weather it won't be very wintry, which is kind of against the spirit of it but within the rules. I wanted that perfect balance between it feeling (and, okay, looking) like winter, but without losing any extremities to frostbite.

Rather than my confused approach to the summer Paddy, I was sure of my 'style' this time: solo and unsupported. That felt more adventurous, but also in truth took the pressure off. If I couldn't match Jim's time, I'd have a worthwhile adventure anyway, possibly get the fastest solo time and still have the satisfaction of having done it all myself.

If I was trying to be a low-carbon athlete, I should get public transport to Snowdonia. Experimenting in fuelling without animal products was a fun challenge. Supporting on another round, I couldn't ignore just how much plastic waste was being created from the hill nosh. All those crisp packets, chocolate bars and bottles of sugary drinks. Only nine per cent of all plastic ever produced has been recycled, while seventy-nine per cent has accumulated in landfill, dumps and the natural environment, where it often ends up in rivers and the ocean (according to a 2017 study in *Science Advances*). Would it be possible to fuel adequately without creating any plastic waste? It was a puzzle I had fun unpicking.

In the end I carried two organic Riverford bananas, one sizeable slab of vegan brownies (made by Amy), a large helping of salty trail mix (from health-food shop dispensers), Outdoor Provisions bars (delicious vegan snacks in compostable wrappers) and a big paper bag of penny sweets from the local post office. I also carried an Extinction Rebellion flag my children had made me for my birthday. Unlike Martin I would have an Open Tracking tracker which doubled as a safety net. But I still felt very nervous. A severe windchill of -8 °C was forecast. What would it be like in the dark and the snow on my own? You both really want to find out and really don't want to. That sense of incredible anticipation was building. Eeeep!

The 3 a.m. start in Llanberis was exciting and nervy; a delicious sense of possibility hung in the air. Or was that a banana burp? Either way, the first leg, Llanberis to Ogwen, was special. That white crunchy-swooshy ground. The cold air in my lungs. The sinister wind jabbing at me.

I'd lost a little of that naive wonder when I found myself desperately hugging a big rock on Glyder Fach like a koala. I then spied fresh Mudclaw prints in the snow and thought, 'Oh wow, there's another fool up here in the snow at 4.30 a.m!' I followed them briefly. Then realised that, like Winnie-the-Pooh, they were, er, my footprints. And I was going the wrong way.

A bum-sledging descent from Glyder Fach to Tryfan was quicker and more fun than normal. It was a relief to get Tryfan out of the way and dawn broke on the long climb up Pen yr Ole Wen. Now I could see all that glorious rocky whiteness. The wind was grumpy, though, and soon made off with my map and my schedule (the third time that had happened).

I felt bad about littering. But I know the route well – in the daylight anyway – and had a gpx file on my Suunto. I loved crossing the icy rocks of the Carnedds, everything so white and new, but with the wind my constant companion I needed two pairs of gloves on and a wrag across my face. It was a bit edgy, really.

By Capel Curig, I was about thirty minutes behind my always-optimistic nineteen-hour schedule. But I had loads of time, right? At Plas y Brenin, the National Outdoor Centre, a handful of people popped out to cheer and clap, which was another wonderful surprise. Up amongst the white jagged towers I'd forgotten anyone knew what I was doing.

The climb up Moel Siabod was a slog, as ever. My breathing issues returned, making me slow, panty and frustrated. I soon forgot about that on the snow-covered summit as the furious wind tried to hoover me off.

Going solo felt thrilling. The extra vulnerability, doubt and jeopardy made me feel even more alive. There was no switching off and following the feet in front, no one to pick me up if I fell. The sense of concentration was huge.

The next leg is Bog Country par excellence, notorious for demoralising people. Even though I knew that, it still got me in a sulk. My ears echoed with squelching for hours. Just as I thought out loud how the bogs weren't as bad as anticipated, in I slid, up to my, er, groin region. Still, the cold water shock woke me up a bit. Soon afterwards it happened again. It is a helpful way to verify chafing levels.

I had sort of forgotten about the schedule and the record. I figured I could probably still finish before 11 p.m. (twenty hours). But everything was slower than in summer. Snow meant the ground was softer and familiar trods were hidden, making it easy to slip off the optimal line and into icy rocks or bog. My brownie-filled pack conspired against me too.

The Cnicht descent is one of the very few sections of the round where you can run for thirty minutes uninterrupted by anything other than the odd gate or antagonistic rock. Talking of gates, I couldn't believe my luck when I saw a Tunnock's bar enticingly placed on a wall, brand name facing me, right by the latch. Not long after a local man would confirm he'd left it for me, which was incredibly kind. But as I was unsupported (and it included dairy), I had to leave it. Nevertheless, the fact a stranger would make such a wonderful gesture filled my head with happy juice.

After Nantmor I sat by a stream for a minute or two in the dwindling light to get my breath back, slurp some cold mountain water, scoff brownies and adjust kit. I figured the next leg would take about three hours; the final leg, four. Which was lucky, because I had exactly seven hours left to break the record.

It got dark again on the summit of Bryn Banog. A trod I'd been on many times insisted on a mean game of hide and seek. Time haemorrhaged. The wind picked up. More bogs. More rocks. No views to sate the soul. Most intelligent people, including my family, would be tucking into lovely warm dinners in their lovely warm and well-lit houses before lovely warm baths and lovely warm beds.

A couple of wind-battered hours later I was on the rocky, uncivilised Nantlle Ridge. Then down, down, down the boggy long grass, into the woods on a hard trail with no excuse but to run hard. And hope.

At the start of the final leg, a long climb up Snowdon via cold squelchy fields and deceitful trods, I recalculated again. It'd be nice to finish by ... er, midnight? That'd be twenty-one hours. Hmmm, quite close to the record.

After Craig Wen (peak forty of forty-seven) there should be a decent trail to follow. But again, in the dark, it turned Machiavellian. The climb went on forever, if not longer. I forgot about keeping the crucial trickle of calories coming in. The higher I got, the windier and more blizzardy it got. My mitten blew away. I was losing more time and the record was very much in the balance. Then all of a sudden, I couldn't take another step. I had bonked. Like never before.

I rummaged and fumbled in my pack's side pouch for brownies. I finally found some and forced a handful into my reluctant gob. I ate snow for dessert, to try and stay alert. I rubbed it on my forehead too and the back of my neck. I nudged myself onwards. Lying down in the foetal position seemed appealing. So too did calling it a day and just getting into Llanberis as quickly as possible, via the Llanberis Path. No one need ever know I'd bailed out, right? Oh wait. That feckin tracker page on social media ...

I motivated myself with the meagre incentive of an extra layer at Snowdon's closed cafe just below the summit. There I knocked back more chunks of brownie and had a word with myself. Not such a hero now, are you? But wasn't this exactly the winter adventure you were daydreaming of?

Thankfully, after Snowdon it was downhill for a while and the remaining lumps were lower and less blizzardy. Faster running warmed me up. On Crib y Ddysgl (peak forty-three) I checked my Suunto. I had about an hour and forty minutes for the final four summits. It was still just about possible, dammit. I had terrible déjà vu from the summer's Paddy. I'd have to work effing hard for it. This record-breaking stuff can be unpleasant at times.

The final four summits, grassy and bulbous, are some of the best running on the round. As I moved with all the pace I could muster, I constantly checked my watch. I thought I'd reached the final peak. Yay! High five, me! Only to find it wasn't. Aaaaaagghhhhooooowwww! I'd love to tell you I howled at the moon. But it was more like I yelled at a bog.

There were going to be minutes in it. I felt desperate. It was so tempting to give in to the central governor telling me to stop. *Why are you punishing yourself like this? No one cares about this. You're no good at this. You're too old for records.*

Fuck off.

Finally, I was galloping off Moel Eilio, my hoofs thumping into the grassy slope. I arrived, breathless, at the red sign for the Llanberis Lake Railway where I'd started, exactly twenty-one hours and thirty minutes before. Just seven minutes inside Jim's time. I mainlined on a strong dose of relief.

Lee Procter had been waiting patiently (well, watching football in the pub). Though it's probable Jim's record was set in tougher conditions, he had pals to carry his pies. But he's a better runner than me. I later realised I'd also beaten Martin's solo-unsupported winter time of 23:40 from 1989, albeit his was in midwinter.

I barely slept that night. I was writhing with foot and leg pain (only remembering after a couple of hours that I could take some painkillers). I also cut my eye with my fingernail, desperately scratching to remove contact lenses after a shower had stuck them to my eyeballs. Quite the mountain slayer, eh?

Why do we do this stuff, Martin? 'I think folk are keen to go back and hurt themselves again and again because the delayed satisfaction and pleasure far outweigh the masochistic pain and suffering endured during the challenge. Also, when we look back at the journey I think we are able to detach all the pain and suffering and overlook it in favour of the fantastic sense of journey. I don't think we would do it otherwise.'

I fell asleep on the bus back to Bangor and missed my stop, enforcing a comically pathetic speed hobble through town. inov-8 put out a press release, including my pretensions towards sustainability, and I was surprised but secretly pleased at being called an activist in some write-ups. But it showed an appetite for positive climate stories. Even if all I'd done really was catch a bus and scoff some brownies.

The Paddy had bashed me up a bit, yet again. But it was just the adventure I'd wanted. It was never intended to be an easy day out.

It was nine months since I'd met John Kelly on the same Snowdonia circuit. I first heard of him after the 2017 Barkley Marathons, when the Tennessee man's win at his local race that often has no finishers (it's the toughest race there is) somehow got less attention than a runner who DNFed.

Incongruously, one Sunday evening late in 2018, John tweeted to ask about trail-running options near Bristol. I mentioned the Cotswold Way and the Brecon Beacons and he quickly direct-messaged me explaining he was moving to the area. I offered to take him to South Wales for a bimble when he arrived. As well as wanting to be hospitable, I'm always fascinated by the best ultrarunners (just ask Jez Bragg), trying to learn their secrets (usually via online research/stalking).

Before the Kellys arrived, John announced his audaciously madcap Grand Round idea: running the Big Three rounds consecutively, cycling between them (Mike Hartley did the same in 1990, but with car journeys). The ambition was jaw-dropping. I didn't think it was possible for someone so unfamiliar with our terrain. But it'd be fascinating to be a part of and I offered help on the Paddy.

The weather for May's Grand Round was what Tim Laney would call 'a tad moist' (i.e. pissing it down, with child-flattening winds) and most runners would have postponed an attempt. Waiting at Pont Cae'r Gors, a glorified lay-by, John's crew's car boot was full of pizzas and Krispy Kremes. When the American arrived, he and his two pacers looked bedraggled. They'd been running for nine hours in some pretty foul weather and John already had a dead-eyed stare. The pacer who was meant to continue with us said he'd had enough. The next leg was all on me. Gulp.

John was quick to thank me for coming out. 'Damian and I took off, moving well on the initial climbs and exchanging valuable information on the best snack foods the US and the UK have to offer,' he wrote on his blog (*randomforestrunner.com*). Much later, on the rocky Carnedds in the dark, I would thrust a first Tunnock's bar his way, which the snack connoisseur approved of. The leg was fairly uneventful, other than the grim weather.

Tom Hayward and Michael Corrales joined us in Llanberis. 'As we continued I realized why the weather is such a factor and why so many great fell runners schedule backup dates for their runs,' wrote John, who reminded me of Nicky Spinks with his quiet focus, not wasting excess energy on small talk. 'We hit the Glyders, and bogs were swapped out for boulder fields. I don't care who you are, what you're wearing, or what you're trying to do, you can't run on fields of smooth, wet rocks.'

John was cold and concerned about the wind. We summited Tryfan just as it got dark, and on its treacherous descent Tom estimated John fell or slipped twenty times, banging his knee quite badly.

The darkness, wind and rain continued on my next leg and John was slowing. Michael calculated we might not make sub-twenty-four hours and John upped the effort, though it looked uncomfortable. Finishing at Capel Curig after 4 a.m., he looked spent. But this was a man who had finished the farcically tough Barkley.

I went home, but was surprised to learn that after a snooze John cycled to the Lake District, and did the Bob Graham Round, in equally moist conditions. Then, understandably, that was enough. It was a truly inspiring effort.

John was very well organised, but in a different way to Nicky. He hardly knew the rounds at all, or what it was like to cycle on British roads, or what it was like to be in our (comparatively small) mountains in bobbins weather. But the data scientist loves a spreadsheet (his Grand Round 2.0 would comprise seven), and many hours and calculations must have gone into those and his long lists of instructions about exactly what calories and drink mixes he would need and when – even which pockets of his pack they should go in.

John was one of the first to congratulate me after my Paddy success a month later. Our sons are the same age and our families met up in August at the National Trust's Dyrham Park near Bath, where as a belated welcome to the UK gift we gave them some Yorkshire Tea and Tunnock's teacakes. Though John was adamant he only drank 'tea' that was iced (eh?), I secretly hoped to convert him. It is, after all, culturally obnoxious not to drink tea here. Over Christmas he sent me a huge selection of very sugary but not undelicious snacks from the US. I was always going to like John, because I find people who are uncommonly dedicated fascinating. But we're very different. He's coldly rational, a little bit Mr Spockish. Though he has a sandpaper-dry sense of humour too.

During a WhatsApp exchange in February, John told me he planned to attempt the Pennine Way record.

15
THE WAITING GAME

'Everyone has a plan till they get punched in the mouth.'

I wanted to kick myself. It felt like that girl you've fancied for ages, but have struggled to pluck up the courage to let her know, has just been asked out by your brazen mate, who's only just met her. And, to your horror, she's said yes. (In fairness, John's since told me he'd been pondering it for a while, the scamp!)

I replied to John: 'I must admit to have been eyeing PW for two or three years but I always chicken out of scheduling it in … I'll help if I can!'

And: 'When I started with [David Roche] I mentioned the same FKT and he talked me out of it! It didn't take much, tbh … I will one day. But not this year. All yours! I've always preferred the idea of north–south, partly for freshness on the eye … '

John replied: 'Haha, well I guess I'll have to put down quite the time for you to go for, then!'

I felt a little ashamed that this tea-dodging foreign interloper was confident enough to take on a thirty-one-year-old record, seemingly at the drop of a hat. He had the cojones to do it. Why hadn't I? I forwarded John the information Martin Stone had sent me.

My original schedule for 2020 included the 100-mile Ultra-Trail Mt. Fuji (UTMF) – a long-held agreement I now felt uncomfortable about because of the flights – in April and a fifth UTMB in August; I was eyeing a boggy Pennines bimble for 2021.

I finally took John to the Brecon Beacons on 12 March, the same day former Twitter addict and US President Donald Trump announced a travel ban from Europe because of some fast-spreading virus. There was a definite sense that this coronavirus was coming our way. This was back in those wonderfully innocent times when people still shook hands and the word *unprecedented* wasn't yet being used on an unprecedented scale.

On a beautifully snowy morning John and I jogged up Fan Fawr before splitting up for separate sessions. Some ultra races in Asia had been cancelled and I was expecting a decision on UTMF, so I checked my phone mid-run, discovering that it was indeed off for 2020.

It was a relief, in truth, with both the horrifying greenhouse gas emissions and, increasingly, this virus thing weighing on my mind. On the drive back we discussed possible permutations of our in-flux running calendars. My backup idea was more solo rounds, but I said if UTMB was cancelled I'd be very tempted to go for a bimble along the Pennines too.

John favoured starting from Edale and going south–north, like the Spine Race he'd just done (and won). I wanted to go north–south, partly because I'd gone the other way three times and didn't want to get bored of my beloved trail. I also knew Mike Hartley had done that. It made sense to me to get the Cheviots done first, where there are no practical crewing points for twenty-seven miles/five-plus hours and a good chunk of vert is in the bag. I suggested running from opposite ends at the same time, which we both thought sounded fun.

Soon after John messaged to clarify: 'If UTMB gets canceled and you decide to go for PW FKT, I wouldn't be opposed to doing it in tandem (with the understanding that if either started dragging they get dropped). Or racing in opposite directions.'

I wasn't so sure about tandem. It seemed full of potential compromises. It would effectively be a race and add another layer of stress. I love challenges partly because they're not a direct race and you get to design them all your way (weather aside). But we kept the idea open.

On 23 March, in a live televised address to the nation, Boris Johnson struggled to appear prime ministerial in announcing a full UK lockdown.

Thankfully we were allowed to leave our homes for daily exercise, but we weren't meant to travel anywhere for it (unless you were an unelected government adviser who needed to check his eyesight on his wife's birthday with a drive to Barnard Castle – just a few miles from the Pennine Way). On 27 March, having boasted about shaking people's hands against scientific advice, Boris Johnson announced he had been diagnosed with Covid-19.

I feared the worst. Not about Boris. That the lockdown might be as strict as in other countries. So I panic-bought a treadmill. John and I mourned together at the news that, due to the pandemic, Tunnock's Lanarkshire factory had temporarily halted production (though I no longer eat Tunnock's bars as they include dairy and palm oil, which is strongly linked with deforestation. Bit of a bummer).

Lockdown was unnerving at first. On one run I was suddenly hit by an incredible sense of sadness and fear: for my parents (had I seen them for the last time?) and my children (would this weird time leave them with some kind of PTSD?). But it was a time of great kindness too: neighbours looking out for one another; Clap for the NHS giving me sweaty eyes. In sharp contrast to my pathetic attempts to play at being a hero by running long distances in lumpy places, we were made acutely aware of who the real heroes are.

Once lockdown felt normal, I realised it was lovely, really (if you forgot about the huge existential threat of The Thing). With the kids at home, amazing weather and an empty diary, it felt like summer holidays, even if we couldn't go anywhere. Everything was cancelled: races, talks, courses, the endless children's parties. Squirming out of social occasions wasn't necessary, because there weren't any. Life slowed down. It was okay to have no plans, to be a bit lazy. We relaxed in our tiny sunny back garden, in between bunny-hopping to Joe Wicks and trying to get Grandad to unmute himself on Zoom. I felt more relaxed, was happier and was easier to be around, I was told.

With so much else going on in the world, running felt both irrelevant and paradoxically precious, an expression of liberation while we were imprisoned in our homes. I had some of my best ever runs, exploring new footpaths, taking new directions, getting lost. Maybe I was just less stressed? With seventy-five per cent fewer cars and fifty per cent fewer planes, we breathed cleaner air, heard more birdsong, saw more squirrels. All under skies that glowed brilliant blue.

UTMB was cancelled on 20 May, but it'd been expected for weeks. The Bob Graham Club had announced they wouldn't be verifying rounds for now, and we couldn't travel to Scotland, so those ideas were out. I had run out of excuses. On 17 April I messaged John with, 'I think I could be keen on some PW tomfoolery in June/whenever we're allowed back on it.'

Time to face my destiny with Darth Vader (forget the girl metaphor thing for now; we're back with Star Wars). I urge my coaching clients to sign up for things that scare them and this certainly intimidated me.

Now it was a real thing I was definitely going to attempt, the first thing to do was speak with Mike Hartley.

Mike set records on the 212-mile Southern Upland Way (55:55) and the 190-mile Wainwright's Coast to Coast (39:36), and in July 1989 ran the Pennine Way in two days, seventeen hours and twenty minutes (65:20), breaking Mike Cudahy's four-year-old record by more than four and a half hours. Oh, and the following year, because the Pennine Way hadn't tested him enough, he ran an unprecedented hat-trick of the Big Three fell-running rounds consecutively (in three days, fourteen hours and twenty minutes). But Mike wasn't just some super-stubborn fell-running warhorse. He was a world-class athlete. He represented Great Britain at the 1993 100k European Championships, finishing fourth with a time of six hours, thirty-seven minutes and forty-five seconds, still the fifth-best British time. At a forty-mile track race he covered the distance in a stunning four hours and twenty minutes. Yes, six-minute-mile pace, for four hours. I've run a marathon at that pace. But after 26.2 miles I was very much done.

That was what intimidated me most. Not the Pennine Way itself (though it always has many tricks up its sleeve) or the 261 miles (which would get a bit ouchy), but the calibre of the athlete and therefore the quality of the record. There was a reason it had stood for thirty-one years.

I knew of five attempts in the last three years, some by runners who'd won the Spine, and none had got close.

Mike was generous with his time and knowledge on the phone. Surprisingly, only one other contender had ever asked his advice. As a meter reader for the electricity board, Mike's job allowed him to get in 170 miles a week sometimes, and 90 miles over some weekends. 'I probably didn't need to do all those miles,' he said. I certainly wouldn't be doing that (if I wanted to keep my marriage intact).

He went north–south so the Cheviots were done early and emotionally he was 'running home', and mentioned the state of the terrain as a major reason for success – his run was in a heatwave that dried the Pennine Way out like perhaps never before or since (even Blenkinsopp, apparently). He designed a schedule that started at 5.5 miles per hour, reducing by 0.4 miles per hour every twenty-seven miles to allow for natural slowing. A 3 a.m. start was intended to get him to Edale without going into a third night. I knew he hadn't slept, but was awed to learn he 'didn't really suffer any sleep deprivation'. He fuelled mostly on rice pudding, fruit cake, pasta, cup-a-soup and milk of magnesia tablets.

'The key,' he thought, 'is being able to run fairly fast early on, without damaging yourself much.'

There was plenty to daunt me. But Mike was crewed at forty road support points, where he spent over three hours in total. There was some time to be had there. Also, his average speed was four miles an hour overall and most people can walk at three miles an hour at least. I'm not suggesting Mike was slow. The difficult bit is keeping going for two and a half days. But I clung to that four-miles-an-hour fact, which helped make it seem possible. I could also see that he slowed significantly towards the end, partly due to foot issues from the hard terrain. Which gave me a little more hope.

A lot has changed on the Pennine Way since 1989. Flagstones in the Peak District and Cheviots make navigation easier and conditions faster. We have better kit, nutrition and training knowledge, plus communication and navigation technology unrecognisable to a 1980s fell runner. But I doubted I'd get weather as good as Mike's.

John and I messaged regularly. We agreed on provisional dates, only to have to change them and change them again, due to the extended lockdown. My diary was entirely clear – all I cared about was this; whereas John needed to get it done ASAP, to fit in his Grand Round 2.0 too before the birth of his fourth child in September. I hadn't warmed to the tandem idea. Instinctively I just felt doing things my own way would be better. And sports psychologist Dr Josie Perry agreed.

Indeed, because John and I shared the same coach, the amazing David Roche, I figured our preparation might be similar, so logistics, tactics, having the right team and perhaps psychology might make the difference.

With no ultra DNFs, I must have been doing something right upstairs. But that didn't mean I couldn't improve. I suspected I suffered from a type of imposter syndrome or inferiority complex. I just didn't think I was in the same league as Mike and John. It had taken me four years to pluck up the courage to take on the Pennine Way. I'd had a handful of episodes in races where I'd sort of backed off when I was close to the prize. Not self-sabotage as such, but a weird apathy.

I was feeling some pressure too. I'd started recruiting a team, which had soon escalated to over twenty pacers. I didn't want to inconvenience them or let them down. Also I'd featured in a short video to promote inov-8's new shoe – the TERRAULTRA G 270, designed for long distances, with a cutting-edge graphene grip – where I'd implied that they could help me run all day long. So it would be quite comical, to everyone except me and inov-8, if I face-planted in the first few miles and had to call the whole thing off.

Lee had also lined up a photoshoot and interview with *Trail Running* magazine for the week afterwards; and my boggy bimble wasn't just going to be a film by Summit Fever Media, but a series of films. Gulp. Matt and Ellie are two of my very best friends (Matt's the guidefather to my son) and lockdown had been crap for adventure film-makers. When I mentioned my plans in passing to *Runner's World*, they asked if there was any chance of daily videos, like we'd done for the Cape Wrath run. Matt and Ellie loved the idea, as did inov-8. My every gurn, fart and tear would be seen by tens of thousands. Great if all went well; not so much if it didn't.

As usual Lee would be in the Pennines too, publishing video and images to social media as I went. Plus I'd just been made a book offer ...

I did have a say in this. I agreed to it all and it always gives me a boost to see Matt, Ellie and Lee out on the hill – they're my lucky charm. But there was suddenly a lot riding on me not stuffing it all up.

With so many people invested in me, I needed to prepare as thoroughly as possible, so there were at least two strong reasons to consult a sports psychologist, even if it felt a little bit taboo. After three chats with Josie Perry, and reading her excellent book *Performing Under Pressure*, I felt much calmer and she helped me make some key decisions. She thought success was more likely the more clear I was about my why and my outcome goal being wrapped in purpose. 'Be brave,' she said. 'Put everything into it. Own your decisions. Know your why and live by your values. Try to live authentically.'

I really liked that. It reminded me of something my dad, a psychotherapist, had said. I once asked him if he could boil down the overall reason why people are unhappy enough to seek out a therapist. He thought for a while and said, 'Too many people feel like their actions don't matter. They're not living authentically.'

With Josie, I worked on confidence, on doubt, on the difference between success and winning, on mental preparation and in-run strategies. She gave me homework, encouraged me to clarify my mantra and even name my chimp. We tried to maximise my motivation, my why. That was easy: it's always my kids. They don't care and they're not interested, but when things start to get difficult parents have an unfair advantage. Nothing is likely to stir you emotionally, to make you care, like thinking of your offspring. My biggest fear for them is the state of the world we're passing on to them. My main purpose was to spread awareness for our climate and ecological emergency. I had my why and a fuckton of purpose right there.

With the pressure thing, we simply reframed it as faith. All those people had faith in me. Several had already intimated that they wouldn't give up the time if they didn't think I would do it. That meant a lot.

For road crew I went to Mark Townsend first. He's experienced at this malarkey, an obsessive organiser and we each know what the other is like in demented, hedgehog-fearing, record-chasing scenarios. I wanted two people so one could sleep and they'd be safer overall, and Tim Laney gets on well with Mark. He'd done his own solo run down the Pennines a couple of decades back, and had even paced Mike Hartley's record run. In fact, Tim claims Mike, who was having foot problems, turned to him, asked his shoe size and proceeded to take Tim's dap, meaning the shoe-short pacer couldn't continue.

I'd never recruited a team of pacers before. I wrote a dream-team wish list, starting with people who'd done well at the Spine Race, plus the likes of Nicky Spinks, cos she's not afraid to give me a kick up the gluteus maximus. Some of them roped in others. Jasmin Paris, Marcus Scotney and Robbie Britton helped recruit well-qualified replacements. Every 'yes' made it feel more real, and I felt very flattered and grateful that so many people were willing to help, especially in a weird time where the threat of the virus still felt very tangible. Several commented that my team looked like a who's who of UK ultrarunning. Spinksy may rightly believe pedigree doesn't necessarily make a good pacer, but I figured I'd up my game around better runners and be less lazy. I'd have liked to have more women involved, but Carol Morgan, Sabrina Verjee (initially) and Beth Pascall all heartlessly snubbed me, albeit in favour of their own record attempts, which I suppose is forgivable. John and I clearly weren't the only ones scheming. Once lockdown eased, it was going to be quite the summer ...

The weather could be the most crucial aspect of the whole thing and I needed to be flexible. But I was still subediting six days a month for *Women's Running* magazine. I enjoyed the work, but it was likely to compromise when I could run, so nervously I served notice on my last regular bit of journalism. It would be a short-term financial loss, but for a bigger gain overall. Hopefully. As I'd also given up columns in *Trail Running* magazine and on *iRunFar.com*, it meant all my income was from running now (albeit mostly coaching), which felt like a big and scary moment. I'd gone all in.

It also made it easier to get in three recce runs. Lockdown was amazing for training. I was doing more strength work than ever, with Bath-based gym Strength For Endurance, founded by former Great Britain hockey player Kriss Hendy. I also bought a pull-up bar, which got plenty of use (when I could get my kids off it).

Something about David Roche's Jedi-esque coaching was working too: many weeks were only around seventy miles (an easy week in previous years), but there were endless hill strides, other artful tweaks and lots of 'You're amazing!!' He'd put a literal and metaphorical spring in my step.

As usual, I consulted friend and leading sports dietician Renee McGregor, who among other things reminded me to get protein in every six hours and suggested white bread instead of brown, less fibre making it easier to digest.

As with my winter Paddy, I was going to fuel without animal products and plastic waste. Research turned up amazing companies such as Delushious, 33Fuel, Outdoor Provisions, Lucho Dillitos, Two Farmers, Oatly, Oh My Gosh It's Vegan and Firepot. Plus the old classics: bananas, sandwiches, and banana sandwiches.

Regrettably, my run would create more car journeys than might have happened otherwise, which made me squirm, but it fitted into my carbon-negative budget for the year and the other option was not to do it.

As lockdown eased, I saw Shane Benzie to work on my perennially awful technique. He identified that my left and right feet were hitting the ground differently and gave me a six-point checklist to go through as I ran.

To finally nail cramp, I visited Precision Hydration for a bespoke sweat test, to see exactly how much sodium I should be replacing on the go. I'm a sweaty, salty bugger, so I would take on more electrolytes on the Pennine Way.

VW lent me a Transporter van, which meant plenty of room for food, kit and a lie down (someone who witnessed both my and John's runs up close saw the van as an example of superior organisation).

In an unprecedented move, despite being suspicious of Excel's dark magic, I created a spreadsheet from scratch. I was rightly mocked for its glaring inadequacies by the likes of Spinksy and Martin Stone, who couldn't resist jumping in and tweaking it. It mostly made sense in the end. I used Mike's timings as a starting point, but dialled back the fast start a tad (although as, unlike him, I'd be on flagstones in the Cheviots I might accidentally match him anyway). And I didn't allow for as much slowing down towards the end, or as many rest stops. I thought the second night would be the critical time, when sleep deprivation would hit hardest. I didn't plan any sleep stops, but was aiming to build a buffer – by going with the flow when I felt good – which I could dip into for power naps and any other microdramas.

The fact that my timings were designed to deliver me to the Nags Head in Edale comfortably before last orders was no happy coincidence. I hadn't had alcohol in four months. Just another mini incentive. A side bet with John that whoever ran slower had to drink the tea of choice of the faster runner, was a much bigger one.

The trail officer warned there was a diversion in place at Torside Reservoir, which would add 2.5 miles to the route. I shared the news with John and we debated various vessels and even swimming (no thanks). Thankfully, via a shout-out on Facebook, we were able to contact the team there, who kindly said they would let us through.

Copying all I'd learnt from the big Spinksy book of record-breaking preparation, I hadn't planned for my wedding as thoroughly as this. The Pennine Way was my holy grail. Everything else in my life was on hold.

But the cage door was about to break open. Frustrated runner-tigers were being released onto the hills, breaking records that had stood for decades. There was definitely something in the air that heady summer. Whether it was months of training uninterrupted by damaging races, extra time to dream and plan big or the sense of throwing caution to the wind – or all those factors – people were about to do extraordinary things. The pandemic was a sobering reminder that life is short. It was time to get on and live it.

On Monday 6 July at 3 a.m. Sabrina Verjee set off for a second attempt on the Wainwrights. Her first effort a month earlier had been stopped because technically she was breaking lockdown rules (we weren't allowed to stay away from home overnight). But now lockdown was over. I assumed I would no longer see Sabrina in the Pennines. Ditto my former GB teammate, smiley assassin Kim Collison, who was attempting the Lakes 24-Hour Fell Record. Incredibly, he broke Mark Hartell's twenty-three-year-old best of seventy-seven summits on 12 July. With my boggy bimble scheduled for 22 July, I figured he wouldn't be keen on, or possibly capable of, a twenty-mile run so soon after such a huge effort. 'You have not got me on your schedule!!' said the email. I was very happy to amend it.

John and I were still debating dates. Tim Laney couldn't make the week John wanted to run, and having the right team was more important to me than going at the same time as another record attempt. I was going for 22 July; John had selected the 13th. The day before, I messaged: 'Good luck tomorrow, man! I'll be genuinely thrilled if you break the record (but not by much, please).'

For the next three days I was glued to his Open Tracking webpage and social media, exchanging messages with his crew Nicki Lygo plus Matt and Ellie. I thought he would start aggressively, but was still surprised by his pace. After sixty miles he was a whopping six hours ahead of Mike's time. John's told his story on his blog (*randomforestrunner.com*) and Summit Fever Media do an amazing job in the film/gurning contest, *Totally FKT*. The short version is that his stomach 'wasn't behaving as expected'; he started slowing and having regular power naps to try and reboot. By day three he looked down and out. But despite persistent tummy issues (later suspected to be intestinal bleeding) and a huge calorie deficit, in a typically gutsy (pun unintended, honest) performance, the tea-dodger prevailed where most would have quit, and got to Kirk Yetholm after two days, sixteen hours and forty-six minutes. Some thirty-four minutes ahead of Mike Hartley's record.

I was pleased for John that he'd rescued victory from the jaws of defeat. It was the perfect result as far as I was concerned. He'd shown me it was possible, but without knocking it out of the park – leaving the door open.

'Congratulations, man,' I messaged. 'And thanks for semi-honouring our agreement (4 mins would have been more gentlemanly). I imagine you're celebrating with a huge cuppa tea.'

'Thanks, man! I thought anything under an hour was fair. 😊 I'll be cheering for you next week. Hope you can get out there and take it down (or is it up? 😏) another peg. No one would deserve it more.'

He encouraged me to phone as he was being driven home. I did, but primarily to congratulate him. It didn't feel right to pepper him with questions for my attempt.

Other than tweaking my schedule by thirty-four minutes, John's run didn't make me alter my approach. We're different people and had different strategies. As well as the opposite direction, I planned to start at 6 a.m. rather than his 10 a.m., making it unlikely I'd go into a third night without sleep. My schedule had the bare minimum splits to get me to Edale a little inside the (new) record. I wanted to feel relaxed and enjoy it as much as possible; forcing the pace towards an overambitious goal would stress me out and likely be counterproductive. If I'm ahead of schedule, I'm happy. If I'm running happy, I'm (probably) running better. Joy, or as much as you can have when you run 261 miles, would bring the best result, I felt.

It's all very well having a plan. But as the coach of a famous boxer once said (and as John had demonstrated), 'Everyone has a plan till they get punched in the mouth.'

Talking of boxers, I felt like one, waiting in the curtains for the PA announcer to call me into the ring, fizzing with fear and excitement ...

16

#PWFKTEA

'Let's see if my sofa fits in his bumbag.'

There's always something. Tim, Mark and I got to Kirk Yetholm a day early, to relax and allow time for Summit Fever Media to poke cameras up my nose and any last-minute dramas. And indeed one pacer dropped out, but Nicki Lygo rescued the situation in a flash, kidnapping not one but three runners from John's WhatsApp group. In fact, around half the pacers did both Pennine Way runs, which says plenty about our wonderful running community.

After talking to Amy and the kids (who as usual wished me 'Bad luck, Daddy!'), I joined Matt, Ellie, photographer/film-makers Dave MacFarlane and Steve Ashworth, Lee, Mark and Tim for my Last Supper in the Border Hotel, the jovial banter helping me relax (I'd been tetchy with Mark and Tim the night before). The wonderful staff also prepared vegan curry takeaways for the next morning.

Before reading a book (a non-running one, to try and take my mind off my imminent boggy challenge) and falling asleep, I messaged John: 'I do feel a bit conflicted about all this. There are many reasons why I may not succeed. But just so you know, you are a bit of hero to me. And your bimble was incredible. Thanks for all your help, man.'

'Back atcha, man,' he replied. 'You're doing great things. Nearly anything worth doing (and certainly everything exciting!) carries many risks for failure. But there are many measures of success and no matter your time on this you'll have nailed the ones that matter most. But if you can, let me know your favorite, even your favourite, tea. I need to be sure I'm prepared. ☺'

I was nervous, but somehow calm too (I slept surprisingly well). The weather forecast was mixed but not awful (I'd take drizzle over heat any day). I couldn't think of anything I could have done to prepare better. Above all, I felt a serene sense of gratitude that so many people were so willing to help me on my madcap quest. I kept reminding myself that if I could maintain four miles per hour it was possible.

At breakfast at 5.30 a.m., I was surprised to see Nicki Lygo, who'd just driven up from Leicestershire. The Pennine Way fanatic (who has trekked it five times, including two doubles, and is the life and soul of the Spine Race) crewed John and had offered help. I didn't need any more, but said she was welcome to tag along, expecting to see her around the Peak District perhaps (she's great company and her medical nous might not go amiss). I was thrilled to see her, although a tiny bit concerned about the dynamic in my crew, as she hadn't met Mark and Tim before. (In fact they got on like a peat moorland on fire.) I knocked back some jam on toast and two gallons of tea.

To the amusement of all, I wrote 'F F F' on my forearm with a Sharpie. It felt right there and then that it represented a repeated swearword. But it was meant to be key reminders of Food, Fluid, Form; and also the motivational factors, Family, Friends, Future (Friends being primarily all the people out there helping me). It sounds naff now, but that was my why. The plan was to also collect litter as we went and I hoped to raise money for Greenpeace (XR, I thought, might be divisive). If I was able to give my best possible performance on the Pennine Way, while acting according to these values, it would be a success. A record was just a bonus (I tried to tell myself).

'I fly-tipped a load of old furniture and poo bags near Cross Fell for him,' wrote Paul Tierney in the WhatsApp group. 'Be a shame not to give him a proper challenge. Let's see if my sofa fits in his bumbag.'

The weather was perfect: overcast, temperature around 10–12 °C. Andrew Higgins and Mark Clarkson arrived in good time. My Suunto said 5.59. Deep breath. 6.00. Gulp. 'Oh bugger,' I said and pressed my watch ...

The three of us bounced across the village green to the backdrop of a few claps and cheers. It's a huge relief when something you've been intensely anticipating for months finally starts. No more faffing, tweaking and worrying. Life had suddenly become profoundly simple. Just run, and scoff my face.

But less than a minute in I glanced at my watch and, to my horror, it wasn't working. Massive fail! I pressed it again and hoped the record wouldn't come down to seconds. Being so well prepared had clearly lulled me into a false sense of security, as I also forgot my kit bag, which was still in the hotel (thankfully spotted by my crew).

I divide marathons into thirds: the final six miles feels like ten and will be a battle whether you're doing badly or well; the middle ten miles is where you can make the real difference (can you move well as it starts to get difficult?); and the first ten miles is where you can stuff it up (don't get carried away). At 261 miles, the Pennine Way was just like a marathon timesed by ten. The aim of the first 100 miles was not to stuff things up.

I'd promised Andrew and Mark I'd go no faster than scheduled. But I felt once-in-a-year amazing. I reached the first timing point, the Cheviot summit (not strictly on the route any more, but Mike had included it), twenty minutes up and with a Strava KOM (not many people live around there).

Talking as you run is a great way to test you're not overdoing it, and a good way to get to know people. I felt really grateful to Andrew and Mark, who'd had an early start, a long drive and a day off work. Even if Mark had a comical knack of breaking most gates he opened.

I was obsessed with efficiency. As well as Mike's three hours at crew points and John's two hours of sleep, which I hoped to take advantage of, there are 287 gates on the Pennine Way. Even if this sounds horribly like a fairytale about an ill-fated king, if a pacer could open every gate for me and I saved ten seconds each time, that would be forty-seven minutes (though Mike and John presumably had the same assistance).

I do love the Cheviots. There's a sadness to those landscapes denuded of trees; but there's a surprising and refreshing remoteness to the big, green, windswept domes. And for the first time, I saw gangs of the mythical wild Cheviot goats.

'Can I offer you something wet and warm from inside my shorts?' said Tim as he met us at the former Roman camp of Chew Green, nearly five hours in, plunging his hand into the aforementioned area and locating a soft flask of tea.

Oh man, those first few hours were blissful. It would never feel as good again.

I'd scheduled five and a half hours for the twenty-seven miles of big boggy hills. It'd taken less than five (some twenty minutes quicker than Mike). But everything felt comfortable. At Byrness I grabbed half a banana and a nut butter sanger from Mark and slurped half a cup of hot chocolate. And in less than a minute was gone. It was sad to say goodbye to Andrew and Mark, but they'd been superb (and even half-laughed at one of my dad jokes).

Poor Jason Millward. Every other leg had at least two names next to it on the schedule, but Byrness to Twice Brewed had none. So when he kindly volunteered for another leg, I bent his arm into this one. As my sole supporter, he was carrying everything as we surged along fast Redesdale Forest trails. The nav was on me, however, and there was a moment of slight confusion on Lord's Shaw. But Jason would prove his worth several times over, not least when he threw himself between me and a big black dog, then, in the next farm, an overly enthusiastic horse. I had wondered whether John might have scattered litter behind him to slow me up, but it seemed he'd sent trained animals instead.

We lost a minute to a missed turning in Bellingham. But my ace crew bought me chips, which mixed well with a brownie. I was almost an hour up when Jayson Cavill replaced Jason at Ladyhill, some fifty miles in. Jayson had kicked my butt at the inaugural Peaks Skyrace in 2014 and I'd watched his progress ever since as he'd turned into one of the best fifty-mile racers in the UK.

I was still quite chatty and more bad/dad jokes were shared as we battled with the relentless short sharp rises and falls of Hadrian's Wall. If you can ignore whinging calves, the wall always exudes a special, stirring drama, a throwback to when Romans and Scots glowered at each other across a border. Damn, the woods were boggy, though, and I was concerned about how firm the terrain would be ahead.

At Greenhead, Pennine Way hiker Kathy Faulks kindly donated some Kendal Mint Cake and said I was a 'slackpacker' for not carrying a pack. Which was fair enough. I'd run sixty-seven miles in twelve hours when I said goodbye and thanks to Jayson, who'd been textbook, and hello to John Knapp and Kim Collison.

With barely a word, John, a three-time top-four Spine finisher, went ahead, making it clear he was the navigator. Kim, just ten days since running up seventy-eight fells in record time, was my mule. It was like having Roger Federer as my ball boy. My plan to round up everyone who'd beaten me in a race and make them run through bogs carrying a heavy bag was working well. I had so many questions about Kim's recent record run, but I was starting to feel less chatty. Plus there were the singular delights of Blenkinsopp Common to be enjoyed, one of the two most notorious boggy sections on the Way. It was fittingly squelchy.

A bleak and fiddly section followed, with John impeccable with nav. My old inov-8 buddy James Rogers, who'd helped crew me at UTMB in 2017, joined us briefly on a road with his bike. I was flabbergasted to learn he'd cycled four hours from Carlisle to come and say hello.

A small crowd had gathered in Slaggyford. 'Are they here for me?' I asked Kim, puzzled. I guess not much happens there. But I felt very flattered. They clapped, cheered and yelled 'Don't forget Slaggyford!' (and I haven't).

I needn't have worried about my newly acquainted crew all getting along. Some innuendos about a muscle gun seemed to have provided the necessary social glue. But despite the new toy, they had tea, hot chocolate, banana and a sandwich all ready. I was some seventy-eight miles in and somehow two hours and twenty minutes ahead of schedule. It wasn't meant to go this smoothly.

The section to Alston is most people's least favourite of the entire route. It's not awful, just tedious, fiddly and unspectacular fields and roads. But all passed smoothly. I felt like royalty: every gate was opened for me, all my items were carried, treats and drinks were proffered regularly. I could get used to this.

It was dark at Alston at 9.30 p.m. and the crew point was under siege by midges. Which helped make it a quick transition, necking some tea and something warm and sloppy from a bowl. Unbeknownst to me Mark had banged his head on the van boot, a nasty, bloody cut; while Nicki had a punctured tyre.

In Garrigill I said goodbye to John and Kim, who'd been gold standard, and hooked up with Paul Tierney, plus the three late replacements, Elaine Bisson, Max Wilkinson and Martin Wilson, who I'd not met before. Again, they snapped into their roles and led off without a second wasted. It was great to catch up with Wainwright record holder and sweary Irish ex-copper Paul, which took my mind off the long slog up Cross Fell, the highest point in England outside the Lake District and notorious for foul weather. The climb was interrupted by occasional rain, toads and fierce hedgehogs (did John send you too?).

I'd saved a Gregg's vegan sausage roll to eat outside Greg's Hut, ninety-two miles and seventeen hours and twenty minutes in. A hideously squelchy bogginess was exchanged for a blowy summit and a long section with faces into the wind and rain, and a downhill to Dufton, where at 2 a.m. I had my first sit-down in Nicki's collapsible chair. Mark strongly disapproves of chairs and I wouldn't see it again.

My feet had been wet for twenty hours, so a change into an identical pair of TERRAULTRA Gs and socks seemed smart. I didn't twig till later, but the stranger who helped get my muddy shoes off was the legendary Martin Stone.

I had passed 100 miles. The first 'third' was done. And I was nearly three hours ahead of schedule. It was going better than my wildest daydreams. It was starting to feel more difficult, but there were no signs of any real issues. It was here that I made my first real mistake. Retrospectively, this would have been a good time to pause and get a proper meal in. But I was so obsessed with efficiency that instead I left with a bag of rehydrated baked beans. However, I soon went off them on the long steep climb up High Cup Nick, and didn't eat many at all. Or anything else, really.

Across the squelchy moors we continued, with Elaine, Max and Martin acting with military-level efficiency in intermittent rain. They did an epic stint with me, some thirty-six miles, total strangers happy to give up sleep for a night-long run in the rain, in return for some grunts and guffs. Down the slippery snarling rocks by always-angry Cauldron Snout as the sky slowly turned battleship grey; then the equally treacherous rocks along Falcon Clints. Mentally I was starting to slide. After an unusually flat section by the rumbling River Tees and its waterfalls that felt so much longer going the wrong way, we finally arrived at Middleton-in-Teesdale at 7 a.m., almost four hours up on schedule.

Four hours! It was the furthest ahead I would ever get. I was greeted by a small cheering crowd (possibly just my crew and pacers on reflection). It sounds so ungrateful now, but I wasn't in the mood for attention. I felt raw and a bit fragile. I wanted a huge breakfast and to curl up in the foetal position in a warm bed. But I wasn't quite halfway and people were looking at me expectantly. Especially my three new pacers, who were ready to go. So I grabbed a curry sandwich, had a big swig of tea and left.

I had reached the stage where my rate of progress was unsustainable. Again at Middleton I should have taken an extra few minutes and got a good dump of calories in. I normally see fuelling as one of my strengths, though it never goes perfectly, but both my mouth and my mind were bored of putting things in.

My replacement team of three-time Spine finisher Gwynn Stokes, his very tall mate Alastair Black and inov-8 employee Chris Davies led me into a stretch of classic Pennine Way. No real moments worthy of photography, but plenty of unspectacular and undulating boggy terrain. Things started out social, but they gradually realised I was getting morose. We made okay progress. Except for when I kicked a rock and totally stacked it. But I didn't feel so good. I started to think a power nap might be what I needed. It seemed smart to act decisively rather than plod along at a decreasing speed. But I hadn't expected to have a sleep till the second night, and it troubled me that Mike had run the whole thing without sleep.

In an insalubrious lay-by on the busy A66, an inflatable mat was placed on top of my kit bags and I lay on it for fifteen minutes under a sleeping bag.

I slept for perhaps ten.

That, and more tea, seemed to reboot me, for a bit.

We continued over boggy, mostly featureless terrain. The moors were squelchy, the views grey, brown and dull green. It rained again and the wind tried to casually flick us aside. Sleightholme Moor rivals Blenkinsopp as the Pennine Way's most notorious bog, but I've seen it worse. At one point Alastair held out an arm to help me across an especially squelchy bit. I accepted the physical assistance without thinking what a controversial topic that had become of late.

The Tan Hill Inn, Britain's highest pub, is always a very welcome sight, a mirage in a desert of desolate moorland. I was looking forward to having crew support there. It wasn't so much the food and drink (which felt like a chore by then); more the supportive faces, Tim telling me to get a move on and another micro-milestone reached. I tried not to think about the strong temptations of the pub, with its roaring fire and comfy sofas.

Mike Hartley was waiting in the rain. Though I knew he'd turned out to see John and was half hoping he would for me, I blushed at the thought this fell-running deity had made the effort for a midlife-crisis bog-botherer. I had retreated into my Stormshell but hoped I didn't look too pathetic, too undeserving of the Pennine Way record. We forearm-bumped and he told me I was looking good, the kind fibber. The presence of Tim (I never did check whether he asked Mike for his trainer back) and Martin Stone, who helped me into an extra layer, made it quite the old boys' reunion. It was a Spine Class of 2015 reunion too, with Matt Neale joining us and only Beth Pascall missing from that memorable day in that biblical Cheviots blizzard (she was busy preparing for something or other in the Lakes...).

I say Tim was there. He was in the pub. Super-sub Jess Palmer took over crewing duties. It was refreshing to see a different, smiley face and to sample a bowl of vegan rice pudding with a sharp tang of raspberries, exactly what my beleaguered palate needed.

Don't tell Spinksy, but Matt Neale was the first name on my pacer wish list. As well as being a multi-time Spine-finisher, Yorkshire Dales ranger and Continental biscuit connoisseur, he'd been helpful in the build-up, advising on terrain and pacer guidelines, as well as locals' attitudes towards visitors during the pandemic. Plus anyone who considers being out in weather that blows grown men over to be one of their 'best ever holidays' is someone you want on your side. His emails would often sign off with things like 'Got a nice under-the-radar 75-miler planned for Tuesday'.

Semi-pro road-crew manager Jess would later compliment my pacers. 'For record attempts, you need top-class runners. But they're a different breed, not as well organised. They turn up with just a bumbag, you come out with a big bag of food and they'll look at you blankly. A lot of people pacing you were from the Spine family and their attitude was different. They were very well versed. They knew their roles: carry a load, drip-feed you, keep running.'

Indeed Chris had enjoyed the bogs and rain so much he volunteered for another leg, while Gwynn (who later that year would become one of only five people to run a Double Bob Graham) and Alastair had to get back to the real world. Thanks, fellas.

I felt slightly reenergised as I headed out across the moors in the afternoon rain with Matt and Chris, and Martin Stone soon joined us. I'm not sure when I started whinging at Matt about the pace being uncomfortable. But despite my power nap and a decent feed, something about my internal engine wasn't firing on all cylinders. My legs were fine. Lungs again?

We trundled across the plain but somehow pleasing Stonesdale Moor, happy to be going mostly downhill towards little Keld, where the trail crosses the Coast to Coast, the spot where I'd first seen a wooden Pennine Way waymarker, oblivious to the huge impact it would have on my life.

I had felt conflicted about using pacers on the Pennine Way. But I was enjoying the community element, seeing old friends after much of the year not being able to see any, making new ones and sharing running experiences.

I felt a bit wobbly going round the fiddly undulating paths towards

Thwaite and needed some sugar. There seemed to be a pacer I didn't recognise waiting for me at Jess's van. I thought Andy Berry, who runs very fast winter Bob Grahams and works for Jim Mann's Future Forest Company, was joining me soon, but I couldn't remember when. In retrospect, I'd given no thought to how being almost four hours ahead of schedule might affect the people coming out to help me. It could mean getting up at 2 a.m. rather than 6 a.m. A lot of these amazing folk had already taken a day off work. Martin hadn't been able to resist jumping in to tweak my spreadsheet with more accurate estimated times.

In was a new Low. Or rather, the mysterious new guy was Martin Low (sorry), replacing Chris and Martin Stone. You can never have too many Martins on your Pennine Way record attempt (another mistake by John, who on reflection I'm sure would acknowledge he had too many Jameses). It transpired New Martin was on holiday here, from Stroud of all places. We had a mutual friend, also called Martin (seriously?!). When he heard about my boggy bimble he got in touch offering help. It was fortunate timing, because my shifting schedule had an Andy-Berry-sized hole to fill.

I was feeling increasingly weary and wasn't looking forward to the huge climb up the beastly Great Shunner Fell (716 metres), the second-highest point on the Pennine Way, where I'd had several kickings administered by the weather in the past.

If New Martin was unhappy to be battered by the wind and rain on the endless climb he didn't show it. He maintained a smiley, chatty demeanour and I felt grateful to have him along. It took yonks, though. I felt kind of stodgy. Somewhere near the top, a friend of Matt's was waiting in the rain with some nuts, which were yummo (thanks, man!). I decided on another power nap at the bottom, at Hardraw in Jess's van, which I reached at 3 p.m. I'd done 146 miles in thirty-two hours and was about three hours and twenty minutes ahead of schedule.

But I was a bit stressed, unsettled because I felt a bit off and couldn't pinpoint it. I mean, you should feel a bit below par after 146 miles. But I wanted to fix it. I wanted to run like I imagined Mike Hartley had. He hadn't slept. Why was I failing?

I even failed to sleep. After fifteen unproductive minutes of face in pillow, I rose with bags under my eyes, increased fogginess and uncooperative legs. Andy finally joined us. I'd been looking forward to his joshing, but instead felt compelled to apologise for my sulky state. He tried heroically to make me laugh and include me in conversation. But he and Matt soon wisely gave up trying and moved ahead, yabbering contentedly away, leaving me to sulk behind them.

The weather was clearing as we plunged further into the Dales. There are good trails once you're up high. But I was finding eight-minute miles a struggle. I had no real physical issues. It was something internal holding me back. I whinged again, because they were going 'too fast'. But really it was a howl of frustration. A surprise crew stop by Jess at Kidhow Gate perked me up – more tea! – but didn't get me moving any quicker.

In fact, I was losing time. We reached Horton-in-Ribblesdale, 170 miles in, at around 7 p.m., less than three hours ahead of schedule. There was a double surprise of a crowd of strangers and some unexpected friends, and the return of Tim, Mark and Nicki. I knocked back some tea and mango (a genius Nicki idea) and something wet and not disgusting from a bowl. Simon Franklin, husband of Carol Morgan (did I see her somewhere? And Father Christmas doppelgänger John Bamber from the Spine?), was scheduled to join me here. He's one of those people you meet frequently but fleetingly at races and feel confident would be a really good chum if you ever actually spent time together. Dan Bye too, a theatre director and playwright I'd connected with on Twitter (and friend of seriously good fell runner, *Wild Running*-author and former Chumbawamba guitarist Boff Whalley, who nearly came along too; whose first band, Chimp Eats Banana, had a member called Michael Hartley).

Surprisingly Sabrina Verjee turned up too, just eleven days after her second controversial Wainwrights run. Seven weeks later, Sabrina would also start out from Kirk Yetholm to run the Pennine Way, trying to beat her own women's record of eighty-two hours, set during the Summer Spine Race. She succeeded, arriving in Edale on a glorious morning, in seventy-four hours and twenty-eight minutes. But she had received some physical assistance again. This time from me: on Wessenden Moor, as she lay groaning on the ground at around midnight, I massaged her glute with my elbow.

A more excellent support cast I couldn't have wished for. But though I tried to make small talk, I felt anything but social. I was feeling kinda seasick on the long steep climb up Pen-y-ghent (but the crowd called out for more). I was telling pacers I felt 'fine … really'. But Sabrina wasn't having it.

'How do you really feel?' she said, like a psychotherapist.

'Well … um … I'm a bit goosed, to be honest.'

She asked what sleep I'd had. 'Here's what you need to do,' she said with typical directness. 'You've got enough time to have a proper rest, a full forty-five minutes, and still be around three hours ahead. Do that.'

It was hard to give up some of the precious time in my buffer. But otherwise my pace would probably continue to spiral downwards imperceptibly. Even if it'd mean giving up some daylight, it sounded like a decent idea.

At the rocky summit I was greatly cheered to see my old pal James Harris and the equally smiley and encouraging Tory Miller. I tumbled down the haphazard natural rock-steps in an eerie orange-grey dusk, straight into Jess's waiting van at Dale Head.

'I'll cover you up,' said Jess. 'But I'm not giving you a kiss.' The meanie.

Ah sleep, how I've missed you.

I'd lost more time. I was now around two and half hours ahead of schedule. My hard-built buffer was slipping away …

17

EDALE

'Fucking eighty!'

I awoke after perhaps thirty minutes to a forebodingly grey and misty late-dusk, feeling relatively refreshed. My new team of pacers waited patiently as I treated myself to fresh socks (whoop!). Or rather, I treated myself to Jason Millward's fresh socks (my kit was in the other crew van).

I was excited to finally meet GB fell-running ace and fellow tea aficionado Ben Mounsey. When I emailed him about my Pennine bimble idea, he phoned straight away, pumped with enthusiasm. But I couldn't shake the feeling he would be disappointed in my lack of witty patter, sullen face and dead eyes. His excellently surnamed partner Kirsty Hall was joining in the palaver, while Jason was recklessly back for another stint and the diligent Simon Franklin continued. Someone told me the forecast was good. We were soon in drizzle.

Fountains Fell can easily be underestimated and there was a spot of confusion up in the misty darkness. I was even more confused when a pot of Halva (a pistachio-nut-based snack I love, but which isn't particularly common on the hills) was sitting on a stile. Eh? I would later learn that an amazing man I'd never met had run up to meet me, but couldn't wait around long enough. Thank you, kind person!

But it was dark, I was still tired (maybe it was something to do with all the running?) and everything was soggy. I was now only two hours and ten minutes ahead of schedule. What had happened to my almost four-hour buffer? I felt frustrated. And concerned. If I'd been offered breaking the record by over two hours beforehand, I'd have taken it. But I was not only disappointed at the time I'd wasted, but worried that if the trend continued it'd soon be squeaky-bum time.

Spinksy joined us at Arncliffe Road, 180 miles in, at around 11 p.m. Amy would later tell me that watching Summit Fever Media's videos it's clear that seeing Nicky gave me a lift. Her presence was a huge shot of reassurance into my arm. I honestly felt, 'It'll be okay now. Nicky's here.' She's my Obi-Wan Kenobi.

I was into the dreaded second night, which I always knew would be the toughest, perhaps the pivotal, time. Nicky wanted to know what I'd been eating and I admitted not much. She handed me a few sweets. She'd brought some coffee beans, pretty much the only thing I don't like (it feels like a betrayal of tea for starters), and persuaded me they didn't actually taste much like, er, coffee. You'd have to be pretty gullible to believe that. Or just have gone two nights without sleep ...

The devil's droppings were soon being spat out across the field. At least it gave us all a cheap chuckle.

Jason offered me a hummus and avocado sandwich. It glided down. Game changer! It covered the three macronutrients, with an easy-to-suck-down texture and a delicious fresh flavour. When I next saw my crew I told them that's what I needed from then on, please. Not an easy request to facilitate at 2 a.m. But the amazing Nicki Lygo would spend most of the rest of my run making me these specific posh sangers.

We tumbled on around Malham Tarn, then slowed to a hike on Malham Cove's stunning limestone pavements, which are a deathtrap to run on. Kirsty, presumably trying to perk me up with some feel-good conversation, asked me what pets I had. I was so surprised by the excellent if left-field question, I struggled to expand on 'Er, two cats'. A re-up in the village was very welcome. More tea.

After midnight I started to fantasise about sleep. My pacers offered an array of snacks, most of which were met with a sulky silence. Nicky stayed by my side, encouraging me to get a few sweets in and drink a bit of cola (not something I go near in normal life, but it's great for this stuff). But the benefits were short-lived. I wasn't in any pain or much discomfort, just the inevitable muscle fatigue which made my legs feel heavy. I just really, really wanted to sleep. Anywhere would do. I hinted to Nicky maybe a fourth power nap would be a good idea. She didn't think it was.

My crew would later tell me that Airton at 3 a.m. was the first time they felt concerned about me, the only time I got crotchety with them. Not about the lack of organic avocados; rather I wanted to clean my teeth. But I hadn't told anyone where my toothbrush was and when I was asked I simply grunted 'bag' at Tim. There were a lot of bags. But he obligingly went to look. I sat, for only the second time, on the van floor, to brush my teeth, on the pretence of freshening my taste buds. But really I was hoping to sneakily lie down when no one was watching. Just for a few minutes. Even a minute ...

Neither Nicky or Mark ever said I couldn't sleep. We were all adults and it would be my decision. But I'd gone into this weird childish state where they represented strict parents who wouldn't let me do the thing I wanted to do most in the world. I fantasised about just letting myself fall sideways on to the kit bags in the back of the VW. But I felt them watching me disapprovingly.

With slightly less foul-smelling breath, I shuffled on.

It turns out cleaning your teeth doesn't make you less sleepy. Every time I mentioned feeling sleepy Spinksy shoved a sweet in my face. Just a quick power nap, down there in the lovely wet grass, or a soft squelchy bog. Oh beautiful, squelchy bog! But I could feel her passive-aggressive, oppressive disapproval (even if it was only in my head).

Meanwhile, Jason, Ben and Kirsty ... wait, Ben and Kirsty have gone? And been replaced by Sam Green, who I didn't even know was coming? I was confused. But I knew one thing. I wanted some sleep. Nicky knew what I was up to and like a prison guard wouldn't leave my side. Though I was slow and self-pitying, the three of them kept me trundling along through endless flat wet fields, where I should have been making up time, but was somehow haemorrhaging it instead.

'You were quiet and expressionless,' says Nicki of when I met my crew in Gargrave at 4 a.m. 'You were sat on a wall and just staring ahead. I looked at you and thought, "You know, he needs some sunshine, or just *something*." I'd not seen you like it before. It was a stark contrast from Dufton [the night before], where I could hear you for quite a long time beforehand. You were normally relaxed and chatting. Not in Gargrave. I asked how you were doing. "I've got eighty miles left to do," you said. "Fucking eighty!"

'You weren't moving any differently, you weren't poorly. You just looked like ... ugh. Like when you think you're on the home straight but you realise the home straight is eighty miles.' I lost seventeen minutes on that leg.

Remember, it never always gets worse.

I was amazed when, at around 5 a.m., headlamps ahead turned out to be coaching client Amanda Sterling. I felt so grateful she'd come out at this ungodly hour that I wanted to stop and chat. Spinksy was having none of it. We had to keep moving. She could see I was getting distracted, losing focus, losing time, letting a record slip away ... I needed someone to fire a pistol next to my ear.

A strip of orange light was expanding on the horizon, as two more head torches approached. My next two pacers had turned up early, Mark Rochester and Galen Reynolds. I was a bit in awe of meeting Galen – the Canadian's won the Dragon's Back and twice placed second at the megahurty Tor des Géants. We stopped to talk. Again, Spinksy shot straight over and broke us up, giving Mark strict instructions to go ahead and nav. There was no mistaking who was in charge. 'I thought I was too bossy!' she remembers. 'I snapped at Mark and Galen within minutes of them joining. But they framed themselves into a really good team.'

'A record attempt isn't the time to be taking photos and sharing jokes,' Nicky told me some weeks later. 'You owe it to the people who've given up their time to support you, to put in your best effort. If you're away from your loved ones for the weekend, make it count for them. When you're feeling rubbish it's not fair on your loved ones to just give up or slack off.'

I should be more focused. Like Nicky. Like John. But I get distracted easily. I'm often guilty of enjoying it (apparently you're not meant to). Nicky had kept me on the straight and narrow. She played a key role (twice).

When dawn broke, everything changed.

Thanks to Galen's fine patter, muling skills and surprising knowledge of naval idioms, and Mark's very sharp nav, we were bombing up and down dales like we had a train to catch. Galen told me I had looked pretty tired in yesterday's video update. I'd forgotten about those. It felt like other people knew more than me. I was tempted to ask what else had happened to me. 'By the time you got to Cowling, the sun was up and you were chatting away again,' remembers Nicki. 'I heard you coming!'

Going past the Top Withens hut, the alleged influence for the Earnshaw family house in Emily Brontë's *Wuthering Heights*, the sun came out for the very first time. It felt like an omen. Things seemed rosy and optimistic, buoyed further by a surprise aid station and bonus tea, Tim yelling 'Hey Damo, where ya been?'

That was so kind of them. I was surprised my sullen ingratitude hadn't turned them off me. I still bonked a couple of times and had to be hand-fed grapes. My nutrition was on a knife edge and we didn't have time for a pub lunch.

Another coaching client, Cass Chisholm, popped out to see me above Hebden Bridge. 'Don't be shit!' she yelled after me, making me smile for a while. And my crew had arranged another unofficial aid station at the bottom, the ruddy legends. More tea, vicar? Ahhhh.

A handful of people turned out by the Stoodley Pike monument at the top of Calderdale and I was starting to hear congratulatory sentiments shouted my way, by friends and strangers alike.

From Pinhaw Beacon to the White House pub at around 11 a.m., Mark and Galen had rebuilt that precious three-hour buffer plus change.

Friend and coaching client David Riley and his mate Paul Clough took over at the White House. They know the Peak intimately and had recced this leg. Martin Stone joined us again for a bit, with an update on Beth Pascall, who was flying at Wasdale, three-fifths of the way around, some forty minutes up. Wow! Though Beth's world-class at the long and lumpy stuff, she doesn't have so much fell-running pedigree. This was exciting and gave me a huge lift. My pal Adrian Hope from inov-8 popped along too. It was beginning to feel celebratory, like a done deal. Even though there were still some thirty-two miles to go.

I relaxed, too much. It got warm. I forgot about the schedule. I forgot to eat and drink. I was faffing, stopping to adjust kit. I had no headwear and my shiny head was getting sunburnt. Wessenden Moor sapped the life out of me. I bonked. Amazingly, a pacer told me that John had been tweeting about our climate and ecological emergency on my behalf.

Jamie Rutherford joined us. I heard people discussing the diversion at Torside Reservoir. I was confused, because I thought that was all sorted. Jen Scotney jumped in to provide a pop-up bonus aid station. (The universe – à la Dan Lawson's quote – was providing.) But at the A635 my advantage had slipped to two hours and twenty-four minutes. The record was slipping through my hands like sand.

Black Hill felt like a Himalayan mountain. My beardy old mucker and coach Marcus Scotney met us at the top, with much-appreciated watermelon. I bonked again along Laddow Rocks and had to have a sit-down to try and get some cold tinned spaghetti in. I'd been careless, complacent. If I had a major setback now, an injury, a nav mishap, then everyone's hard work would be for nothing. I was angry with myself. I'd lost more than thirty minutes on the last leg.

Torside Reservoir had worried me. But my amazing team had got it sorted. Indeed Tim, Mark and Nicki had been a brilliant combination. Mark is staunchly fact-based and claims because of Asperger's he can only say what he honestly thinks. So he won't tell me I'm looking great if I'm not (and he didn't). But he will say, 'Get to Dale Head by 9.45 p.m. and you're still bang on target.' And you trust him. Nicki fusses like the wonderful mother she is, but offers warmth, kindness and those all-important muscle-gun innuendos (and knows the Pennine Way even better than some guidebook authors). Tim, the old warhorse, has seen and done it all, and his laidback aura makes you think everything will turn out okay. Between the Three Muskateamakers there were years of military, medical and logistical experience, not to mention long-distance-running and Pennine-Way-yomping nous. I had this generic sense of reassurance that, as long as I wasn't too rude to them, all bases were covered. I wanted to break the record for them. They'd worked harder than me, with a good deal less complaining.

At Torside, the workmen not only let me through their locked gate, but had made banners cheering me home. It was an incredible gesture. But I was too stressed by the wasted time to really take it in. In my head it was a failure if I broke the record by anything less than three hours. At the VW van on the south side of the reservoir, with fifteen miles left to go, I asked Martin Stone, who loves schedules like no one else, if he thought I could still break the record by that much. He ummed and aahed a bit. 'It's possible,' he said. 'Just about.'

Everyone had placed a brick in that three-hour wall we'd built together, starting over two days ago with Andrew and Mark in Scotland. But it was starting to come tumbling down. I honestly cared about nothing else in the world right then but those three hours. I owed it to my Friends and Family and the Future to rebuild that wall. Not for the first or last time, I imagined explaining over breakfast with my kids the next day how I didn't quite break the record. 'Did you try your hardest, Daddy?' they would ask. I needed to be able to tell them I did. I thought of social media headlines: 'Balding bimbler breaks Pennine Way record by three hours'. It sounded so much better than 'Balding bimbler breaks Pennine Way record by two hours and a bit' (which on reflection still sounds okay). But three hours was everything. Like those crucial three minutes back at the Highland Fling that kind of turned my life around.

I had three and a half hours available for those last fifteen miles, which sounds like plenty of time perhaps, till you factor in a 1,200-foot climb, the rocky undulating terrain and the 246 miles in my legs. But I had a secret weapon: Spinksy was back.

I made the mistake of telling her that three hours was still just about possible. 'Can I see your schedule?' she asked. She took it, tucked it in her pack and never gave it back. She later explained she didn't want me looking at it, that she didn't want me to get distracted, to have any regrets. She rightly felt that I'd want to be sure I'd given everything.

In my daydreams, that final leg was going to be a happy procession with friends, laughing and joking and celebrating together; a moving party, as Jasmin Paris had called the final stretch of one of her record-breaking rounds. It was nothing like that. It was the hardest part of the whole thing. And it was all That Farmer's fault.

Nicky may be in her early fifties, but she can sure shift up a hill. She shot up the long climb up Bleaklow (where she used to train for UTMB) and I had my lungs in my mouth trying to keep up. It went on and on and on. She fed me sweets and cola, while Jamie Rutherford remained on my shoulder, saying just the right things. 'You're doing great, man.' 'You've got this.' 'Keep it up.'

But my breathing issue was back. I couldn't power up the climb as well as my legs wanted to. 'If you're hurt, take a painkiller!' Nicky yelled back at me at one point, clearly disappointed in my pace. I didn't, because I wasn't. I just couldn't breathe properly. I promised myself I'd get it properly looked at this time. There's a chance running for two and a half days and two nights isn't all that good for you.

After Bleaklow, the head-high trenches of the Devil's Dike were a torturous labyrinth, with Nicky constantly disappearing around the corner ahead. Jamie pretty much saved my life at Snake Pass, holding me back as I almost stumbled into fast traffic (my second piece of unwitting physical assistance, though several experienced fell runners have assured me it's not enough to face a disqualification tribunal).

We went straight over the last support point, pacers collecting more cola, tea and sweets from my crew. I was constantly confused about whether the sugary fuelling options were Nicky's or mine, and didn't want to share her bottle, what with the virus and all, or steal all her sweets.

Twenty minutes on flattish flagstones to Mill Hill felt like a tempo run (but in reality was probably barely troubling eight-minute miles). My breathing was constantly heavy and desperate, just trying to keep up.

'Nicky!' I yelled. 'I don't care about the three hours any more! 2:50 is fine! You're killing me!'

She pretended not to hear. I sort of hated her. I frequently asked Jamie if that three-hour prize was still possible and even sometimes what the next bit was like, a little self-conscious that as the official guide-book author I should probably know (though everything seemed back to front).

Three runners I didn't recognise tagged on to us on the Kinder plateau. I tried to drop them, seeing them as hangers-on. One of them tried to speak to me, but I was feeling less than social. To my great embarrassment it would later transpire they were multiple-record-breaking fell-running deities Mark Hartell and Mark McDermott, and Geoff Pettengell, who'd paced Mike Hartley all those years ago. Names I've seen so many times on lists of record-breakers (and again, if you're called Martin or Mark you're definitely very good at running long distances in lumpy places). I feel incredibly flattered by that now (sorry, guys).

Nicky kept punishing me. It felt personal. Was it because I kept calling her Spinksy? Or because I'd given up beef? Or because I didn't have any macaroons this time? Jumping from rock to rock, my hamstring twanged alarmingly and I had to pause for a few seconds and give it a rub.

Finally we were tumbling down Jacob's Ladder and I could smell the Valhalla named Edale. Fellow Hartley-record-botherer Jack Scott joined in the jamboree. But I felt frustrated at how easily everyone else seemed to be running. Matt Green was filming. I thought, 'I'll show how unbroken I am', and imagined I was dancing down that stony staircase like Kilian Jornet. Whereas in *Totally FKT* I'm moving like an arthritic eighty-year-old.

There were still some roads, some fields, some stiff little climbs, repeated looking at my watch. Jamie assured me, for the fifth time, that three hours was possible. We were acting like it was make or break. Three hours or failure.

Martin Stone joined me for a third time, but caught a toe on a rock and hit the deck. It looked really painful. I stopped to help him, but someone told me to get a shift on. I did, but I felt bad.

There was a group of about seven or eight with me now, some shouting 'Come on, Damo!'

'Remember UTMB,' said Matt. I asked him, in a slightly aggressive tone, if the three hours thing really mattered to his film. He didn't answer. I felt like everyone was forcing me to go sub-three, and I didn't care any more. I just wanted it to be over.

Finally, I was through the last gate, the others dropped back, allowing me to go first down a narrow shaded path, round a corner and ...

Wow, why are there so many people here? Are they waiting for the pub to open? Is Edale resident Jarvis Cocker giving an impromptu gig?

I touched the wall of the Old Nags Head at 7.35 p.m. on Friday 24 July and stopped my Suunto. Then turned to see the crowd.

I did a massive, emotional, goofy grin. Followed by a tea-drinking celebration (not a dig at John – I've done it at several finish lines, copied from US women's footballer Alex Morgan, cos I like tea) and attempted to unfurl my children's XR flag, but I was confused and had it sideways.

I'd thought it'd just be my crew, but there were maybe fifty people. I wanted to ask what exciting event was happening. And why they were all looking at me. Was I meant to do something?

Even a magnanimous John Kelly was there, Mike again, plus the Marks (soz, fellas!), Otto Copping, several more friends and people from the Spine Race. Mike and John joined me, the latter joking he had the record for having the Pennine Way record for the shortest time (eight days). I felt bad for him. But he was incredibly gracious, even fulfilling his bet by drinking a cup of PG Tips from the Nags Head. He wasn't won over, but he did finish the (small) cup. I tried his ice tea too, which had come all the way from Tennessee. It was disgusting.

David Carr, who'd run that crucial part of my first Spine Race with me and Bez Berry back in 2014, was there. In fact I still owed him a pint, though he insisted on getting me one. If I'd quit back then, I probably wouldn't have ended up here now. A chair was pushed towards me and soon a magnificent pint of ale was in my unsteady hands.

I felt drunk on the sense of occasion and gratitude; so very, very grateful to my road crew, my pacers, the wonderful people who were there, all the people who'd turned out en route, both runners and non-runners. I felt hugely relieved and satisfied. I wanted to hug everyone. But that wasn't allowed. And I also felt really bloody tired.

James Thurlow from Open Tracking would later verify my time (after my watch fail at the start) as 61:35:15, or two days, thirteen hours and thirty-five minutes – three hours and eleven minutes quicker than John. We'd collected around eight kilograms of rubbish (no sofas spotted, thankfully), and raised £4,500 for Greenpeace. To top off everything, I was told Beth had broken the Bob Graham record, running a stunning fourteen hours and thirty-four minutes, bettering Jasmin's record by fifty minutes (though I felt a bit for Jasmin too).

Mark had thoughtfully bought me two pizzas. Mostly I wanted to lie down and finally get some precious sleep. But I also didn't want that magical day to ever end.

18

THE AFTERMATH

'You just trust the universe, yeah.'

It's 2 a.m. on Sunday 26 July 2020. I'm sitting at my kitchen table, wide awake. My big toe throbs. The nail is broken, black, partially raised and wants to get away. The skin around the nail is radioactive red. And dirty. Not 'I just stood in some mud' dirty; more 'this specimen has been buried for 300 years' dirty. There's a small yellow blister between that toe and the next one (brought on by the application of a plaster over that big toenail, which has been trying to go AWOL for yonks). My feet and ankles look like they've been stolen from the Elephant Man. I have ouchy tendonitis on the lower calf of my right leg, and cuts on the top and back of my lower calf. My legs are swollen and just generically ache. My knees are making sure I know they've not been left out. One hamstring is bigger than the other. One Achilles is smaller than the other. My tummy's bloated. There's skin missing from the palm of my hand, which is yellow and throbbing. My mouth is sore – anything with sugar or salt hurts to eat. My lips hurt. I have a mysterious large bruise on my backside and chafing between my butt cheeks (yes, ha bloody ha). And I need to get my breathing issue looked at properly. I feel kind of hungover-drunk, blurry-headed (or should that be bleary? I think it's both. I can't think straight ...). I wore my boxer shorts the wrong way around all day yesterday. I've been stumbling everywhere. I squeal when I accidentally kick things with my big toe. Which makes my children laugh at least ('I did it all for you!' I want to shout at them, only forty per cent in jest, and only twenty per cent in truth).

Running's good for us, right? I'm sure I read that somewhere.

I'm happy as hell, I'll remember later, after more sleep and cheesecake. But right now I'm a little bit FKTed.

I'd had so much help on my boggy bimble and I wasn't used to that. I felt wracked with a weird sense of guilt mixed with gratitude. They'd done so much for me, but what had I done for them? I was caught in a paradox between feeling odd about having so much help, which had made it feel less of an adventure than, say, Cape Wrath and eradicated any sense of self-sufficiency; but also being very happily surprised by how much sharing the adventure meant – especially in the unprecedented circumstances of 2020.

It took my muddled head hours to negotiate what I thought were the right words to send to my incredible supporters:

> I think it'll be a while before I can approach a gate again without expecting an arm to magically reach out of the darkness ahead and open it for me. The fact that demanding "Coke!", "Tea!" or "You couldn't reach down there with a bit of Vas, could ya?" is no longer a legitimate way to behave is proving a harsh, cruel reality.
>
> This is my weird way of saying I'm still struggling to find the words to thank you all appropriately. That's partly because I'm all fucked up. And partly because each of you did such amazing things Out There. Some of those things are really obvious to me. But there are still doubtless so many things I don't even know about (though I would love to know).
>
> My memories are blurry. But didn't a bonus pacer appear out of nowhere? (Martin, was it, for Great Shunner Fell?) Who arranged that? And how? And how can I contact Martin, please, to thank him? Er, was he called Martin? Or have I got him confused with Martin Stone? Who also acted as a bonus pacer. And also did many key things to help, not least with the 'spreadsheet' (the standard of which we can debate another time, ahead of next time 😉). There were bonus surprise road support points! And bonus support road points manned by people I didn't even

realise were involved! And treats left for me at the top of mountains! Vegan, plastic-waste-free ones! I believe there was an incident with a tyre. And a head injury. And someone drove a long way to return a USB charger I'd randomly dumped on them. And something about a muscle gun in Slaggyford.

It's incredible what you all did. For me. For us. To support some other ideas too.

THANK YOU so much. I look forward to returning the favour.

I feel guilty about not being better company. In fact, for some of you, I was pathetic, miserable and sulky company. I know I whinged at at least two of you. I'm sure I didn't thank you all in person. Not all of you got a thank-you ale (partly Paul Tierney's fault). Doubtless many teas and avocado and hummus (who gave me the first one of those? They were amazing!) sandwiches were made, only for me to ask for something entirely different. Thank you all for your forgiveness.

As you'll have probably guessed, my hormones are a little out of whack.

In reply John Knapp wrote:

While it's nice getting thanked for whatever little I did, Damo, please don't forget how much pleasure you've given us too. It's fun and fulfilling to be part of your chosen crew. There's a wonderful cohesive spirit to being a cog in a successful endeavour. The last couple of weeks it's been a blast getting to meet and run with the very best in the country, not something we get to do in normal life. While there's no races for people to get together, you and John, and those taking on other records and rounds, help provide that bit of community that I for one have missed. Thanks goes both ways.

Which I thought was really lovely and helped me feel okay about it all.

I had thirty-two people help me directly on the Pennine Way. The sense of team, of shared experience, of community, was so powerful I felt uncomfortable being the centre for it. I felt undeserving of the praise and attention I was getting. 'My pacers and crew did all the real work!' I wanted to scream, and often did say in the many interviews that followed.

I had fled from team sports to an individual sport, to try and find myself a little bit, seeking some authenticity. But it felt good to belong to a group again too. I was no longer my ten-year-old self, an outsider desperate to be accepted. I could be on my own. But belonging to something, a one-off collection of brilliant like-minded loons, felt good.

Those two July 2020 Pennine Way runs seemed to transcend our little niche corner of the world and go very briefly mainstream. As I endured night sweats and scoffed cheesecake for second breakfast (the moment when your waistline tells you third breakfast is no longer a valid option is a particularly devastating one), I went live on *BBC Breakfast* with John and an audience of several million, spoke to the *Guardian* and even the *Daily Mail*, and did roughly 703 podcasts. Barbra Streisand didn't tweet about me, though. In the absence of professional sport, stories of record-breaking running were presented as an antidote to lockdown, rare good news in a strange and stressful time.

I wanted to pay back some karma and was soon back on the hills, running a couple of legs of the Paddy with some guy called John Kelly, who was already getting his rebound shag in, with some epic fell-bothering on his Grand Round 2.0. The weather was better this time and he was happy for us to carry his kit and nosh (thanks for the Krispy Kreme, man). John continued to be really gracious about the Pennine Way run. And hinted he'll go back for more (north–south this time).

In September I paced Tim Laney on his 'sixty-one peaks at age sixty-one' Lake District challenge, which was pretty special. Then two days later found myself back on the Pennine Way, balancing a plate of cream tea for Sabrina as she broke her own women's record. It was fun to be a supporter this time and to give her advice about eating and sleeping.

I couldn't resist going to see my fellow XR terrorist pal Dan Lawson (my man crush) on his record-breaking LEJOG jog. His whole approach is the polar opposite of Nicky and John. He had no list of pacers, no schedule, barely even a plan, other than a destination each day. 'You just trust the universe, yeah. And it works! The right people constantly came out at exactly the right time. That random element really works beautifully. The right person with the right energy seems to come along. It's such a nice energy, a beautiful thing, a collective there to help you achieve your egotistical dream. It's changed my mindset. I prefer these now.' We could all be more Dan.

In October 2020 I popped to the Brecon Beacons to apologetically steal another record off a friend (in my defence, most of the records worth having in the UK are owned by friends): the seventy-three-mile, thirty-one-summit South Wales Traverse from Dan Doherty, by a mere five minutes, in fourteen hours and thirteen minutes. It was a stunning day out, which completed a hat-trick of records for the year.

The problem with the Year of FKTs was that although I gained three records, I lost two. I never expected to hold the Paddy record for more than a few weeks, so was chuffed I had it for a year. Till local runner Matthew Roberts smartly used a full team of pacers to help him better my time by around fifty minutes. Of course it's a slight dent to the ego, but having your record bettered is one of the best worst feelings you can have. Because ultimately, you held a record.

Watching Kristian Morgan chase down my South West Coast Path record was a stranger experience. He phoned me up, was very polite about it all, we exchanged messages throughout and I genuinely wished him well. But watching his tracker for nearly eleven days was like watching powerless as someone burgles your house in slow motion. He'd correctly identified that if he could do a little more on the two days where Mark's knee had slowed us, he might do it. He went without sleep on the final night to beat my 2016 time by three hours. After previous, dubious, proof-free claimants, I was also pleased it was done transparently. I was asked if I'd go back, but the urge isn't there at the moment. I'm still scared of that hedgehog.

I also tracked two people going for my winter Paddy record, both falling short. I guess it's a bit like a footballer watching his team from the substitute bench. In a way you want your replacement to do well, because ultimately we're all kind of part of the same big team. But honestly, you'd rather they didn't do as well as you. Because, well, we're all human too. And a few of our primal survival instincts still remain.

It was an unprecedented year of course, but 4,409 FKTs were registered with *fastestknowntime.com* in 2020, a 434 per cent increase on 2019. We also saw the rise of the OKT (only known time): a fun term for creating your own route or spotting one no one has claimed yet. The concept showed again how brilliant running is for DIY adventures. And we needed that more than ever in 2020. Whether it's a record, an FKT or an OKT, this is a wonderfully egalitarian sport. *Sport* never feels like the right word for it; it's much more than that. It's a chance for anyone to have a record. If you can't find one to attempt to break, just create one yourself. Even if it's your nan's back garden. But it's not about the record. Not really ...

19

YEAH BUT WHY?

'We're ruthlessly exposing our own shortcomings, to see what's left when we're alone on the heath like King Lear howling at the wind.'

In the absence of races in 2020, I ran three challenges: a winter Paddy Buckley Round, a 261-mile bog-bothering Pennine bimble, and a South Wales Traverse (finally locating those elusive two summits). And, apologies in advance, it made me think about stuff.

Yep, this is the horribly tortured bit of the book where I try to get all profound and make sense of it all by clumsily shoehorning running into some psychobabbled theory about life, the universe and everything. But rather than simply take my word for it all, I asked a bunch of runners the same questions. Essentially, why do we do this long hurty stuff anyway? And, do you get anything from a personal challenge that you don't get from an organised event? Some answers may surprise you …

This is part of our biological nature, existing in a small percentage of each population. All plants and animals do it. Life grows and expands, which fosters survival of each species. Humans settled in the Arctic and the equator, then explored the highest and lowest places on Earth, then space. We also run/hike/bike/swim/paddle/ etc. as far/fast/high as we can – all part of the same biologic urge!

Races are great; it's natural to compare oneself to others. They also cost money, require one to do a certain thing at a certain time, at a certain place and using a certain method, and they have very limited parameters to solve: do this exact thing, the same as everyone else.

On the other hand, FKTs are unlimited! They require a much broader skillset. You can choose your own meaning, and must create your own situation. Experienced people want to engage more of who they are and what they can do – organised events are quite limited in scope …

I enjoy everything I do. If someone doesn't enjoy what they do, maybe they should do something different. Indeed, I personally suspect lack of personal self-worth drives many of the best athletic (and other) achievements, which I personally question as appropriate motivation.

Buzz Burell

Races come and go, but there's a sense that rounds or FKTs endure, offering a greater sense of permanence to the achievement and comparison (albeit imperfect) across generations of runners.

Chris Dowling

It's the beauty of our sport that you can go off and do something brilliant all on your own if you want to. I have just gone for soft or new records. It's just more enjoyable. That's partly down to the fact my body has let me down a bit over the last few years, as there is nothing I love more than driving myself to the edge of my own limitations to chase a historic mark on a trail or route. It's more about self-discovery and experimenting with what actually happens when you're sleep-deprived or physically and emotionally empty. For me, part of the super-long stuff is about digging the biggest hole I can, skirting around the edge of it and then, if I fall in, find out how I can get out. Sometimes you just end up crying on the side of the road. Other times you push through. So discovering what makes the difference between those two is fascinating to me.

Robbie Britton

Races and FKTs/personal challenges aren't necessarily binary opposites. Whether it's a race or a challenge, I think there's a set of common themes underlying the attraction to trail and ultrarunning. Escape, wilderness, freedom, communion with nature, for example. Also camaraderie, competition and community. We instinctively associate some of these more with races, and some more with FKTs. But you can get them all regardless, in whatever combination you like, depending on the event.

We might imagine races that have fully-flagged courses, regular support, and aid stations piled high with hummus and avocado sandwiches; while on the other hand imagining personal challenges as nothing but us, a compass and the howling dark. But actually, some are much wilder and less supported, while some personal challenges are much more hospitable or communal efforts … I think a lot of the stuff people say about what distinguishes one from the other doesn't necessarily hold up under the light …

When racing, you can get into a ding-dong with someone, and it turns out competition actually does bring something out of you. But in these personal challenges, it really is just you against the clock. It's you against you: you the athlete against you the self-saboteur, you the brave against you the coward, you the tough against you the lover of stopping when it hurts.

In this sport we're fascinated by ruthlessly exposing our own shortcomings, to see what's left of us when we're alone on the heath like King Lear howling at the wind. That's obviously true in racing as well as in personal challenges, but in a personal challenge that exposure is all the greater for not having anyone else to deflect it on to. You've put yourself out there and however many supporters you have, you're still alone. Maybe having loads of supporters around even makes this worse: it's only you can deliver on their investment; it's only you can let them down.

Dan Bye

For me it's a combination of reasons why I like to run long distances in the mountains. I enjoy being outdoors and if you're out for a long time you get to see a lot of the outdoors. I also like to see how far I can possibly go, be it physically or mentally, to see how far I can push myself … I have a competitive nature as well, whether it's racing or a personal challenge or adventure. The appeal of an adventure is the sense of freedom. It opens up so much more potential.

Donnie Campbell

The reason I do these long challenges is for the brief moment when you finish and you have achieved something on the edge of your limits, creating the biggest smile. I do these challenges as it's a great way to explore, journey through and be part of nature.

Kim Collison

A challenge, record or FKT is testing oneself. The runner actually may not set a fastest time, but they will know what their fastest time was for a given distance at a certain time of year. That provides a benchmark. There is also the isolation, the mental challenge, the need to plan in a more meticulous way.

Ultimately, personal challenges are more rewarding, at least for me. It's so different to plan everything and action that plan, in contrast to having all the planning done for you. But I must clarify, we need both!

Anything I do is personal and I am not going for FKTs. Just adventures where I set my own timeframe and challenge. I test myself, but looking for a balance of enjoyment and hardship.

Ian Corless

I always achieved more satisfaction from multi-day runs. It was always more about the journey than the arrival. A fast time would be a bonus, really ... I've always preferred independent runs to races. Okay, I've won a few races, but to be honest I'm not that competitive. It was much more important to get the best out of myself. I placed second on two of my very best runs. I had nothing but admiration for the winners. I can't deny there is a certain amount of kudos in winning or recording a fast time. Of course, often those two things occur at the same time. But I feel sure the achievement of that fast time, or the perfect run, is more important than the win.

Mike Hartley

It's important to try things you don't "know" you can do. It builds future capacity to face difficult things in all spheres in life. And it makes life colourful and interesting.

A challenge is personal. It is yours; it is on your terms. There is something significant about being somewhere incredibly beautiful, alone with your thoughts, and alone without thoughts ...

Lastly, you can use a journey, a challenge, to tell a story about something that matters to you, whether that be mental health, climate change, or the plight of a species. Something that is, in all other ways, self-indulgent, can be used to, at least, try and do good.

Emma Hazeldine

I don't know what I'd do if it weren't for time outdoors. I often feel like I don't belong when in the confines of inside life. And I do feel like I fit in when I am in a wild place, even if it's kicking my butt with its weather or terrain. The feeling goes all the way to my bones; it's instinctual. I just know I am supposed to be outside.

Long efforts are uncomfortable, no ifs, ands, or buts. For me and most of the time, the positives of the experience far outweigh the negatives. I don't think we know for sure if there's a disproportionate growth of FKTing and personal challenging, but it feels like it to me. If that's in fact happening, there's a super-easy explanation: it's stinking fun! ... That's why I keep going out! I come back a little different each time – with a new skill or piece of information or my memory bank loaded up with the experience of that wild place.

Meghan Hicks

It gives me strength to know I can do stuff myself. That I have the mental strength to keep going and that I have the skills and knowledge about myself to solve problems as they arise along the way. That I am not depending on others. I believe that exploring my own abilities and developing skills to solve and overcome challenges, makes me into a better version of myself.

Kirsten Isak

Long solo challenges (including long ultras) are hugely enjoyable when they go well. It's a way of being so fully attuned to what you're doing that you don't notice the miles ... When it goes badly, though, there's nothing worse. You become very focused on yourself, whether it's discomfort, lack of energy, dehydration or whatever, and it can quickly become a downward spiral that just eats away your self-confidence and belief. Good moments can turn to bad moments so quickly ... At its best, the sense of achievement is just amazing. At its worst, the dark moments are just crushing. The good times outnumber the bad (fortunately!). Otherwise why would we do it?!?

Tim Laney

I think it's incredibly important for us to all do challenging things that test our limits and force us to grow and improve. Most of us are blessed to live lives where we don't have any sort of *real* danger or make or break situations: we're not getting chased by lions; we're not at war; we have food, shelter, life's basic necessities. But it's those extreme type of situations that magnify our strengths and weaknesses and allow us to see who we really are, and to in turn improve who we are and apply those lessons to aspects of life that matter a lot more than running really far …

Both races and challenges are important. To me it's about personal growth and doing challenges that I'm passionate about, but sometimes it's useful and even necessary to be able to benchmark myself against others … Competition is also an incredible motivator, and that's something that I personally have a difficult time with in FKTs. I tend to do just good enough and then subconsciously back off. In an FKT that's a constant measure. Whereas in a direct competition situation, multiple people are trying to do just good enough all at the same time and continually pushing each other's goalposts further.

To me competition is a tool, something to push me further and measure how far I've come. The real outcome and prize, though, is being able to apply that improvement to accomplish personal goals that are meaningful, rewarding, and that otherwise would have been impossible. Things like FKTs give me the creative license to apply my abilities to the things that mean the most to me and in the ways that give me the most joy and satisfaction. They also allow me to control more variables, increasing the complexity of the challenge and giving me even more of an opportunity to optimise things to my strengths – the very strengths I've learnt I have by doing these things in the first place.

John Kelly

A record attempt feels more like a journey, more like an adventure. You feel like you've got more time to take in the surroundings ... When you're in a race with a few hundred others it's not quite the same as when it's just you. All those people who come out to help you ... it's such a nice energy, a collective there to help you achieve your egotistical dream ... There's less pressure and it's more natural. You're just going out for a run. Instead of racing other people, everyone's pushing in the same direction; they all want you to achieve your goal. It's changed my mindset. I prefer these now.

Dan Lawson

At the end of the day, it's all just one big game: we do it because it's fun ... I like having a focus to my running and am competitive by my nature, but I also really like the social aspect of running, especially with a small group ... I love it when there are team races – mountain marathons, the High Peak Marathon, the PTL – because you are genuinely a team. You help the person who is suffering, carry their bag, feed them and so on. It becomes a shared experience where you win or lose together. It's a special camaraderie. Rounds are much the same.

Don't get me wrong. I love to race too, but that is very different ... Even friends become enemies when racing. In fact, some of the people I'm most competitive with are my best friends and I don't mean that in a bad way – I still want to see them do well (just not as well as me 😉). There is something special about racing really hard against someone and then having a joke or beer with them at the end, knowing those bragging rights belong to one of you until you meet again and perhaps there is a different outcome.

Jim Mann

With long hurty things, the greater the challenge, the greater the personal reward/satisfaction seems to be afterwards. By pushing the limits of what you attempt, you discover that you can actually do an awful lot more than you'd assumed, which is a powerful thing. It leaves you wanting to try it again, once the immediate memory of the suffering has passed, and gives you confidence which extends beyond running into general life. These FKTs/rounds are the days that leave you feeling most alive (ironically, given that they simultaneously leave you feeling pretty broken), the ones that stand out in the general blur of the passing year/work/everyday life.

In contrast with races, FKTs/rounds are more focused, there is less distraction, and it's more about the personal challenge. I enjoy the planning, knowing that things are down to me rather than chance – one can change the day and time of an attempt to catch a weather window, suit daylight hours and so on. When FKTs/rounds are supported, I very much enjoy running with friends (or making new ones, on the rare occasions when I don't already know my supporters well). It always feels like a great shared adventure and team effort. On the other hand, when FKTs/rounds are unsupported … there is the sense of satisfaction that comes with being self-sufficient and navigating for oneself. It sort of magnifies the FKT/round experience. Also, since I don't advertise my FKTs/rounds etc. beforehand, I don't feel the same pressure that I sometimes get when racing, which is nice too.

I think FKTs offer a chance to challenge yourself in new ways, wherever you are, without having to travel the world to seek out exciting adventures. When climate change is such a pressing concern, this is a real advantage over racing.

Jasmin Paris

I think it's the extremes of emotion that we experience doing longer challenges that are addictive. Those massive highs and massive lows are difficult to experience in other aspects of life.

Doing my Bob Graham made me realise how easy racing is. When racing you just have to show up, maybe with one other person to hand you some gels, and run. A round or FKT is much more of a long-term project. Learning the route, meticulously putting together a schedule, organising a big support team. Much more time and energy goes into pulling off something like that (at least for me it did). I wonder if that is why the reward can be greater when things go right …

If [the Bob Graham] had been sandwiched between races in an ordinary year it probably wouldn't have meant so much. With everything else that had gone wrong in 2020 (cancelled racing, cancelled wedding, cancelled sabbatical, crappy time at work) it felt like something had finally gone right. The overwhelming feeling was relief when I set the record.

But I'll probably always prefer racing. I love the competition. But if another round or FKT catches my attention then maybe I'll go for it.

Beth Pascall

For the Big Three rounds, it's about the routes for me: they're rougher, often without paths, they go up and down fells. I like that challenge of rough terrain. I like to have some control. There's a lot more to organise. Some people are perfectly capable of turning up to a race, but organising people is different. I enjoy the recces, trying to work out how I can cut time out.

A round is harder than a race. There's more pressure on you: you've organised it, if the weather comes in people will ask if you should have gone in. You've not got the competitors to keep you going, just the time element. You haven't got people coming past you, people to run with who are feeling the same. My main motivation for finishing a race is the other competitors. When you finish a challenge it's all you – you've got your supporters, but you organised them. I think it is more satisfying in the end. You've taken it on and organised it yourself and made all the key decisions.

Supporting on a successful round is just special. Like helping you get to Edale – just helping you achieve something I knew you'd be proud of.

Nicky Spinks

I gave a talk to my students after UTMB and summed it up with this message: 'Practising things being uncomfortable, finding those moments of raw reality, is like a vaccination for life. This vaccination boosts willpower, appreciation of when times are good, and immunises you with self-knowledge – that when things are bad, you can get through them.' I think this applies even more to personal challenges than events.

Most trail or ultra races are a little bit sanitised in terms of adventure. A personal challenge brings a whole new level of route-planning (a rewarding and fun task in itself if you're a maps geek like me!), logistical planning, and ultimately risk. Sometimes you need to cut away security and back yourself against a wall to get closer to the truth of who you are and what you can do.

Steven Saunders

When I heard about the Lakeland 100 I wanted to do it straight away. It was a massive, massive personal challenge, not being sure you could do it. You got the huge sense of accomplishment from just getting to the finish line. People want to hang round the watercooler and tell people what they did at the weekend. There's definitely a little bit of ego involved. But my reasons have changed. I have more of an appreciation now for running in nice places. It's time without constant noise in the background. It's your relaxation as well as your training. It often doesn't feel like training.

YEAH BUT WHY?

Mike Cudahy's book *Wild Trails to Far Horizons* put ideas in my head that you could go and do a route whenever you liked. The possibility of breaking Steve Birkinshaw's Wainwrights record was more achievable than winning certain races. I would love to do well at Tor des Géants, but I'm not sure I'll ever be winning it … Because so many people were involved it felt like a team effort and maybe I do miss that side of sport (from my hurling days) … It's a bit clichéd, but there is a good community of people out here and being an outsider it was nice to get so much backing from my peers, from people I look up to.

I got more out of it than a race. The Wainwrights was a totally different feeling of accomplishment. Because it gathered legs and we were raising money for Mind, there were all these other factors that made it special … If I could get into the top ten at TdG I'd be massively happy, but it still wouldn't have the same significance and invoke the same feelings in me as the Wainwrights. A race is going to go ahead without you, but with a challenge, if you weren't doing it, it wouldn't happen. It's more personal. The satisfaction of executing something well is huge.

Paul Tierney

Challenges/FKTs to me are adventures with a small group of friends that can become a very tight-knit team. One is running against the clock rather than against others. Whatever role one plays is rewarding. Obviously being the runner is the most satisfying, but supporting a friend and helping them succeed is almost as good. Races are also great fun, but one is solely concerned with beating other runners. Also, there isn't the feeling of being part of a team.

Both activities and the training required to do them is very good for me as it helps me cope with Asperger's, depression and battling demons caused by the things I suffered as a child.

Mark Townsend

I was struck by how varied the responses are, what different things people get from their distance running, whether a race or an independent challenge. Or are they all in fact alluding to the same thing?

I felt like I was staring naked and forlornly into a mirror when Buzz Burrell linked athletic achievements to a lack of self-worth. Dan Bye made me realise I'd fallen into a trap of framing challenges as wilder, more independent adventures than races, which isn't necessarily true. And indeed there was a fair bit of love for the competitive environment of events, which some still prefer if forced to choose. In 2020 I felt I preferred the opposite (but then I can barely remember what a conventional race is like); my three experiences felt as profound and satisfying as any race experience, perhaps more so. Above all, they were adventures (safe ones, but adventures). Jim, Kim and Meghan mention smiles and fun. Has the modern world taken away too much of the simple joy we found in childhood, and is running a way to get unrecognisably muddy and have a good giggle about it again? (That's definitely part of it for me.)

Most answers touch on the themes of pushing boundaries/testing limits, adventure (a big one for me), exploration and self-discovery. They mention nature, freedom, independence and defining your own challenge, turning it into a story and making it more meaningful. Some reference the solitary nature of such things; others the shared experiences and higher intimacy level, the versatility, the purity, the removal of the safety net, and the greater satisfaction to be had. Realistically, for some, a running challenge is a way to 'win' when we might not be able to win certain races. (Nowt wrong with that.)

The answer, for me, is fairly simple: running makes me feel alive. And that's vital. On a daily basis, the simple act of moving that way alludes back to our primal ancestry. But when we take on a challenge that really tests us, that has us howling at the wind/power-sobbing into a puddle of our own urine, it's a test of our character, of who we really are, and a chance to act authentically. And eat alarming amounts of custard.

Running makes us feel alive through survival role-plays that push us to experience primal emotions – of fear or triumph, of desperation or hope, of 'Why do we have to go so fast – are we being hunted by a sabre-toothed tiger, Spinksy?' These experiences remind us what it is to be human.

It's easy to slip into a safe and predictable life, to go through the motions, not really feeling much, not really living. But when you wake yourself up, make yourself vulnerable, attempt to do things you may not be capable of, struggle (with or without yielding), come up short, hurt (both physically and emotionally), ask for and receive help, cry a bit, try to run 261 miles through bogs, pretend you're Luke Skywalker ... That, to me at least, is living.

Similarly, watching someone trying really, really hard to reach for a goal that may be beyond them, however pointless and indulgent it may seem, is one of the best things you can witness. It's not pointless. It matters. I've heard it said that a person's real character comes to the fore in a crisis, and while these ultra-distance challenges are self-created, voluntary crises, they can feel pretty real and intense at the time.

Contemporary life has made things too anaesthetised and detached, and running is a return to that primal base. Running allows us to put our backs against the wall, to howl at the moon on that heath, to receive a punch in the face (yep, like *Fight Club*), to try and see who we really are. We're hurting ourselves to feel alive, to be authentically us.

When we do this long hurty stuff, we almost inevitably peel off our layers of subconsciously learned social pretension, like we're an onion, leaving us vulnerable, raw, and quite possibly teary. Our true personality can be exposed (even it's not always pretty, my Pennine Way crew can confirm). There are fewer pretensions, pleases and 'Would you mind if I possibly ... ?'s. Instead it's 'I need a fookin' hummus and avo sandwich or I'll cry!'

Authenticity is 'behaviour that we have freely chosen and which allows us to express who we are ... authentic people act in ways that reflect their values and identity ... authenticity involves feeling like "yourself" and not feeling like you're wearing a "mask" that prevents others from seeing who you are', writes American psychologist Elizabeth Hopper on *healthypsych.com* (presumably unaware of how topical masks would become).

When I run, I feel like I'm me.

* * *

It's ten years since that life-changing half marathon on the honey-hued streets of Bath. 'Discovering' running has been life-changing. It's now my job, my passion, my identity, my life. Running long distances in lumpy places has given me real happiness and a powerful sense of purpose. Running's also given me a sense of self-worth I can see now was lacking. It's given me a sense of being good at something that was absent. And it's given me, I think, a sense of being more alive and feeling more authentic. And some very strange but brilliant friends and fewer toenails.

I've never found anything that can make me feel so very broken, physically and mentally, and yet paradoxically so very happy at the same time. Afterwards, it allows a deep sense of peace, euphoria, finality. Like you could just lie down and die, the happiest person in the world.

Running adventures can push us to feel alive, to feel more fundamentally human in a primal sense, and can be incredibly meaningful.

I'd go so far as to state that, outside of parenthood, the most meaningful experiences of my life have happened in a pair of muddy daps.

Talking of which, I'm off out for a run ...

ACKNOWLEDGEMENTS

It takes a village? Nah. It takes a flippin' city.

For crucial help on The Bimble, thank you Pennine Way Queen Nicki Lygo, Tim Laney, Mark Townsend, Jess Palmer, Jen Scotney, all my wonderful support runners, everyone who turned up in Edale and en route, or followed online, sent messages and contributed to the fundraising; to James Thurlow and Open Tracking, Caroline McCann and the wonderful staff at the Border Hotel. For critical preparation, thank you Shane Benzie, Renee McGregor, David Roche, Paul King, Matt Holmes, Kriss Hendy and Dr Josie Perry.

For key support at other times, thank you Tom Jones, Beth Pascall, Michael Corrales, Mark Macintosh, Dan Summers, Gary Tompsett, Kerry Sutton, Ian Sharman, Marcus Scotney, Elisabet Barnes, Ian Corless and Ruth Pickvance.

For tolerating my uncleaned teeth, not always stealing my contact lenses, and capturing some of the best moments of my life on film, Matt and Ellie Green from Summit Fever Media.

For important contributions to this book, thank you Martin Stone (he could be thanked in most categories, tbh, not least for inspiration), Nicky Spinks (I guess I owe you some macaroons), Charmian Heaton, Paweł Cymbalista, Victoria 'Tory' Miller, Jim Mann, Mike Hartley, Jasmin Paris, Sophie Power, Paddy Buckley, Alex Hutchinson, Wendy Dodds, Neil Talbott, John Knapp, Bob Wightman, Ally Beaven, Sabrina

Verjee and all the ace people who gave their cherished thoughts in chapter 19. And Bevo, for feedback, as well as those formative adventures.

To significant running pals Alex and Otto Copping, Dan Doherty, Allan Cox, Lizzie Wraith, all the Bath Bats, Charlie Sproson, Jo Meek, Nathan Montague, Robbie Britton, Dan Lawson, Rob Lewis, Ben Hart and tea-dodger John Kelly, for buns and doughnuts and for breaking the ice.

To my coaching clients, who keep me honest and in ample supplies of teabags and nut butter.

Big gratitude to my primary sponsors inov-8, and especially Lee Procter, who've made a genuine difference in all of this. Thanks also to James Bridgeman, Søren Sørensen and Tomax Technology, Precision Hydration, 33Fuel, Outdoor Provisions, Delushious, Lucho Dillitos, Petzl, Suunto, SunGod, Leki, VW, PHD Designs, Supernatural Fuel and Our Carbon.

For the word stuff, thank you Mario Cacciottolo, Alyssa White, Paul Simpson, Paul Hansford, Andy Westbrook, Jonathan Manning, John Shepherd, Graham Coster, Tobias Muse, Patrick Kinsella, Nick Van Mead, Lucy Warburton, and everyone at *Women's Running*, *Runner's World* and *Trail Running* magazines, plus *iRunFar.com* and *fastestknowntime.com*.

Thanks to Kirsty Reade for the idea, guidance and encouragement. Thanks also to Vertebrate Publishing's Jon Barton, John Coefield, Jane Beagley, Cameron Bonser, the amazing Emma Lockley, Jess McElhattan, Becky Wales, Lorna Hargreaves, Julie Atkins, Sophie Fletcher and Col Perkins; and to Moira Hunter for proofreading.

Thanks to ace snappers Graeme Hewitson, Mikkel Beisner, Mick Kenyon, Andy Jackson, Matt Brown, Dave MacFarlane, Lee Procter, Tom Jones, and Summit Fever Media.

And lastly, to Amy, Indy and Leif. Sorry about all the muddy daps and being such a 'stinky Daddy'.